INVESTMENT

A Student-centred Approach

Other books by Joseph Chilver

Introducing Business Studies: a case-study and assignment approach
  (Macmillan)
An Introduction to Business Calculations through Assignments
(Macmillan)
*The Organisation in its Environment; assignments for BEC courses
  (with J. Harvey)* **(Macmillan)**

The Human Aspects of Management: a case-study approach **(Pergamon
  Press)**

INVESTMENT

A Student-centred Approach

Joseph Chilver

B.Sc. Econ. Hons (Lond.), A.I.B. (and Trustee Dip.)
A.I.P.M., A.M.B.I.M.

Dorset Institute of Higher Education

First published 1982 by
THE MACMILLAN PRESS LTD
London and Basingstoke
Companies and representatives throughout the world

ISBN 0 333 29415 7 (hard cover)
ISBN 0 333 29416 5 (paper cover)

To my wife, Joan

Contents

Preface

A few years ago I took twenty-seven young bankers through a course
on Investment. They were a pilot group from one of the major banks,
sent by their Head Office on a full-time HND (Banking) course. We
decided to take the Optional Investment paper of the Institute of
Bankers *en route*. The results were pleasing but we were handicapped
by a dearth of textbooks suitable for young students without any
practical experience of the subject. Subsequently I found myself
dealing with a group of overseas students on a similar course, and
the problems were magnified.

  This book is my attempt to provide material geared to the needs
of students who have little or no previous knowledge of investment
matters. It is designed with the Institute of Bankers' examination
and the new BEC courses in mind though it should be of interest to
all students of business. Bearing in mind the eventual need of
students to be able to *discuss* investment matters with their clients,
a number of assignments have been included to stimulate group
discussion where this is possible. At other times the students are
invited to tackle a series of multiple-choice questions to test their
understanding of the preceding narrative. Guidelines and solutions
for the assignments are given at the end of the book.

  The case studies which are included are intended to be as realistic
as possible but the companies, individuals and situations described
are wholly fictional.

  Finally, I take the opportunity to acknowledge the assistance I
have received from the following friends and associates, who have
kindly read the typescript for me and contributed their expertise:

Mr J H Nield, partner in Joliffe, Flint & Cross, Stockbrokers,
  Bournemouth.
Mr Nigel Edwards, District Services Manager, Barclays Unicorn Group,
  Surrey and Sussex Districts.
Mr Ron Ellis, Senior Lecturer in Management Studies, Dorset Institute
  of Higher Education.

Joseph Chilver

Acknowledgements

The author and publishers wish to thank the undermentioned for permission to include various extracts as acknowledged in the text:

Financial Times
Investors Chronicle
Daily Telegraph
The Times
Industrial and Commercial Finance Corporation Ltd
Guest Keen & Nettlefolds Ltd

Questions in Chapter 23, where specified, are reproduced by kind permission of the Institute of Bankers and the Chartered Insurance Institute.

Students may like to take advantage of the arrangement available to them whereby regular copies of the *Financial Times* can be obtained at half price. Details can be obtained from the *Financial Times*, Bracken House, 10 Cannon Street, London EC4P 4BY.

1 An Overview

A simple definition of Investment would be a 'laying out of money with a view to gaining some future advantage or profit'. This definition would cover the case of an employee who saves a small sum from his wages each week, placing the money on deposit in a Trustee Savings Bank. He is saving for his summer holidays, knowing his money will be earning interest (or appreciating) in the meanwhile. The definition would also cover the case of the great multinational corporation which has decided to spend a vast sum of money exploring a distant continent for new sources of energy. Nor are the two happenings disconnected. The deposit by the working man will be added to similar deposits throughout the vast banking network and will form part of the financial reservoir which is used to provide funds for the multinational's operations. The finance might come by means of a direct loan from one of the major banks or an inter- national banking consortium. But it is just as likely to reach the corporation through a succession of investors. For example, the Trustee Savings Bank in question might carry a balance with one of the commercial banks and this bank might be approached for a loan by one of its customers. The purpose of the loan? To purchase shares in the multinational corporation which have been previously acquired by an Issuing House. The corporation sold the shares to the issuing house in the first place to raise funds for the present programme of exploration. In such ways is the decision by the person to save for his summer holidays linked with the decision by the industrial company to search for new sources of energy.

The 'laying out of money' (or investment) is vital to our economic well-being. It is the means by which we marshal our resources and direct our efforts in a highly complex technologically advanced society.

Where there is a scarce commodity (in this case savings), for which there is an effective demand and a limited supply, a market can be expected to appear. We have already glimpsed some of its basic features:

1. It is international in nature and capital will flow across national boundaries wherever it is allowed to do so. Constraints such as exchange controls, tariffs and embargoes might be im- posed, however.
2. It is a system for collecting, collating and transferring re- sources through the intermediary of money. The resources include people, and people are central to the system in that they are the means by which the system functions and the purpose for which it functions. People remain indispensable to the provision of goods and services and are also the providers of the financial input in the form of savings. The system is effective only so long as it serves the needs of people.

1

3. The market is diffused. In the words of K. Midgley and
   R. G. Burns: 'It is in progress all over the land, wherever
   suppliers and users of capital get together to do business. Much
   business is transacted over the telephone, so that there need be
   no geographical site at all for certain activities. However,
   parts of the market are concentrated in well-known centres, the
   most renowned of these being the Stock Exchange, which deals in
   company securities and those issued by governments and local
   authorities.' (*The Capital Market: its nature and significance*
   (Macmillan, 1977).)
4. It is a system which involves the circulation of funds (see Figure
   1). Funds are utilised in projects which produce wages, dividends
   and interest as well as goods and services, and the part of these
   earnings which is saved generates the next cycle of investment.

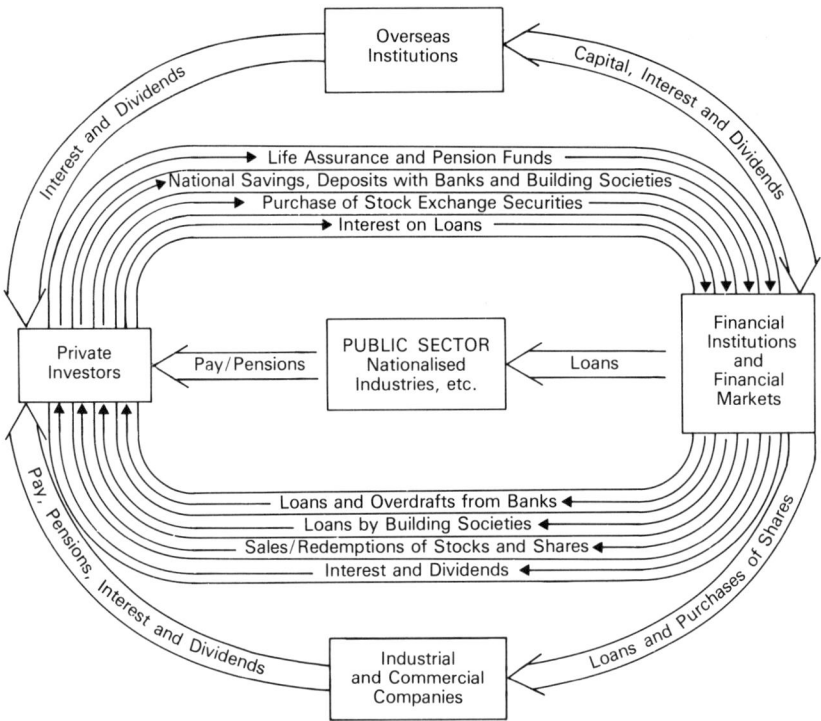

Figure 1 *The main investment flows*

The need for such a system arose out of the original Industrial
Revolution. Goods and services were required to be produced on a
larger and larger scale. The resources of a single individual were
not enough to provide the capital required for operations of such a
magnitude and even those with great wealth were unwilling to stake
the whole or part of it on a single project which might be drastic-
ally unsuccessful. It was in order to escape from this impasse that
the concepts of limited liability and the joint-stock company were

developed. To this day it remains a central feature of the system
that small sums are brought together to provide the large sums
required to promote major technological progress.

SAVINGS
It is apparent that savings play a central role in the system. As
a first step we might distinguish savings from consumption. Savings
are represented by the gap, if any, between what one earns and what
one spends, though one might spend money on goods which last for a
period of time, in which case they can be viewed as an investment.
In other words, the consumption of these goods is delayed or spread
over time. Thinking along the same lines, we would include in
savings contributions to pension funds and premiums paid on insurance
policies which would similarly have the effect of delaying consumption.

   However, we also need to consider another type of saving which
might be termed 'involuntary saving'. This would happen where, for
example, the government reduced our earnings by taxing them and used
our money to invest in motorways, hospitals, schools and improved
railway services. In a mixed economy such as ours there is both a
private and public sector. The private sector contains the myriad
of sole traders, partners and joint-stock companies, while the
public sector consists of the various state enterprises such as the
National Coal Board and the Post Office. The point is that much of
our savings are diverted into the public sector where they are
virtually invested for us by our representatives in Parliament or
the Town Hall (i.e. the local authority).

TAXATION v. PROFIT
One of the taxes levied by the central government is Corporation Tax
and through this tax on company profits we might observe how the flow
of investment funds is divided between the public and private sectors.
By levying this tax the government is, in effect, removing decision-
making powers from the companies subject to the tax. Instead of the
companies selecting investment projects it is the government which
does so, though the government can decide to distribute funds for
immediate consumption rather than investment if it so wishes. The
effect of distributing funds rather than investing them is to pass
on the investment or consumption choice to those who receive the
distributions.

   To the extent that company profits are left intact by the
government, the investment or consumption decision rests with the
company. It will be free to choose how much profit is to be distributed to the shareholders and how much is to be retained for investment within the company. The object of 'ploughing back' profits
is to ensure that future profits are enhanced. It is a form of
self-finance which is common in the business world, but it has to be
remembered that the profits of a company are eroded by inflation.
The real value of paper profits may be much less than they appear.

   While the example of corporation tax has been used, other taxes
such as Value Added Tax and Income Tax will also siphon profits away
from companies and thereby transfer investment decisions into the
public sector. The only difference is that the effect of these
other taxes will be less obvious.

   Who is better suited to make investment decisions, the government
or businessmen? It is a subject for political debate, but it can be

said that in Britain we have made our decision. By choosing a mixed economy we have decided that the decision-making powers should be shared, though there will inevitably be some who think the government have too much power, while others would like to see Parliament's control over the economy increased. Without taking sides in the debate we can note that businessmen will be guided mainly by motives of profit. When we see profit as simply an essential gap between economic inputs and outputs - a measure of efficiency - it seems logical that decisions should be made with profitability in mind. There are two justifications for this attitude towards profit:

(1) Our economic well-being depends on the profitability of our business enterprises, and
(2) A welfare state presupposes economic surpluses (or profits) having been generated somewhere in the economic system.

On the other hand, a contribution from our political representatives is equally essential to ensure that:

(1) Wider social implications are brought into account from time to time and in certain key areas, and
(2) The economic surpluses achieved within the system are distributed among the members of society in an acceptably fair manner.

THE ECONOMIST'S ROLE

The economist has a vital role to play in two distinct areas of the decision-making process. First, he has a contribution to make in evaluating prospects in the economy generally and in particular industries. The data he collects and the forecasts he makes will determine to a large extent which options are taken and which directions the investment flows take within the overall system. It is logical that the economist who is concerned with the allocation of scarce resources should have a role to play in discussing both the range of options and the pros and cons of such options.

The second area of interest for the economist is related to the economy's growth, which is tied up with savings and investment. Consider the machinations of the industrial company with regards to the distribution of profits to its shareholders. We have seen that profits retained by the company become available for investment and are thus used to generate higher profits and dividends in the future. This operation can be viewed as a microcosm of what is happening in the economy at large. When individuals forgo immediate consumption their savings become available for investment. And the present scale of investment determines the future limits of consumption. Such factors are obviously related to economic growth and are therefore of concern to the economist. One of the facets of the problem is that the poorest people in society have the least opportunity to forgo immediate consumption. While this may be a truism it also represents a dilemma for a society which is seeking both a high level of investment and a fairer spread of wealth. The two goals are not always compatible.

Economists are also concerned with investment because investment is closely associated with unemployment. Investment creates employment in the manner previously explained and since unemployment statistics are an indication of the state of health of the economy,

the concern of economists is understandable. Tied in with the overall problem of unemployment is the debate on the extent to which
central government should provide incentives for industrial and
commercial firms so that work is created in areas of high unemployment.

THE CONTINUUM
Man is a decision-making animal. He is constantly called upon to
choose one course of action rather than another. The mechanism for
decision-making is the same whether he is choosing a girl-friend or
an investment. He looks at the range of alternatives, weighs up the
pros and cons, and then chooses the option which seems to offer him
most profit, though some benefits are non-monetary. The methodology
is always the same and the advent of the computer was no more than
an extension to man's own thinking patterns. The microprocessor
simply adds a further degree of sophistication to an unchanged
decision-making process. Figure 1 (p. 2) might be looked at again
with these latest notions in mind. The diagram represents a flow of
funds. But it also represents the results of a myriad of decisions
made by a mass of divergent investors over a continuum of time.
    The vast majority of people are employed by organisations of one
sort or another, either in the public or private sectors. They
receive pay, but this is depleted by (a) taxation, (b) national
insurance (for old-age pensions and the health service) and (c)
contributions to occupational pension funds. The first two of these
are used to transfer spending power from one section of society to
another. The less privileged benefit at the expense of the more
privileged. The sick benefit at the expense of the more healthy.
At the same time be it noted that in these cases the investment/
consumption decisions are transferred from the individuals to the
government. By contrast the contributions to pension funds might be
described as quasi-voluntary.
    Apart from the constraints mentioned, the individual is able to
select his own spending patterns. He can indulge in immediate consumption such as food or entertainment, or he can delay consumption
either by purchasing consumer durables such as refrigerators or
motor-cars or by entrusting his savings to others such as banks and
insurance companies. In either case chains of interlinked investments develop. The individual invests his savings in a life assurance policy. Others do the same. The insurance company invests the
funds in the purchase of shares on the Stock Exchange. As a result
the persons or companies selling the shares acquire funds and the
need for a decision on how those funds are to be invested.
    The role of the financial institutions is to lubricate the transfer
of funds from those with surpluses to those who are prepared to pay
for the use of them. The distinction between the Stock Exchange and
the other major financial institutions is that it organises investment for others without providing funds directly, while institutions
such as banks and insurance companies are closely involved in borrowing and lending operations. The Stock Exchange, for its part, offers
a market for existing securities and a mechanism by which new capital
can be raised by companies which have been approved by the Stock
Exchange Council. It is reassuring for investors in Stock Exchange
securities to know that their investments can be converted back into
cash without undue delay.

Through the medium of the financial institutions the accumulation of funds is passed on as loans or in the purchase of shares to:

(i) Overseas governments and companies
(ii) Industrial and commercial companies in the United Kingdom
(iii) National and local governments and public corporations in the United Kingdom.

The various institutions employing the funds in the promulgation of their own projects will generate a return flow of interest and dividends as well as payment of wages to workforces and a return of the capital invested in due course.

Among the overseas institutions involved in the investment process are the international banking organisations such as the European Investment Bank, which offers funds to industrial companies operating in the European Economic Community (EEC). Another institution is the World Bank, which consists of three separate institutions catering respectively for:

(i) National governments (the International Bank for Reconstruction and Development),
(ii) Underdeveloped countries (the International Development Association),

and

(iii) Industrial and commercial companies (the International Finance Corporation).

For the larger companies access is also available to the Euro-dollar market.

RISK AND RETURNS
An investor is concerned essentially with the degree of risk and the volume of returns likely to be associated with his investment. Risk has two particular dimensions. First, there is the danger that the whole or part of the capital sum might be lost. And, second, there is the uncertainty about payment of interest and dividends. The objective of all investors is to minimise risk and maximise returns, but price can be seen to act as a regulator in that investments which are regarded as riskless and give high returns are compara-tively expensive while high-risk/low-return investments are compara-tively cheap. In other words the price mechanism tends to compensate for the varying degrees of risk and the likely level of returns, introducing an equilibrium in much the same way as it does for the demand and supply of any commodity.

There are a number of ways of avoiding or eliminating risk, but it usually involves some expense. One way is to pool a large number of similar risks. For example, it would be very risky for an individual to agree to meet any losses sustained during the course of a year by a motorist friend in return for a single and compara-tively small payment. Yet the insurance companies are able to eliminate risk both for themselves and their policyholders by combining a large number of similar risks.

Another way of avoiding risk is to hedge against loss, and this necessitates choosing two eventualities which will cancel each other out. It is like betting that both teams in the Football Cup Final will win. As F. W. Paish and R. J. Briston explain:

Not infrequently the loss to one man means a gain to another, and
if the two can get together, they can exchange risks in such a
way that neither of them runs a chance either of an exceptional
gain or of an exceptional loss. Thus a producer can protect himself against the risk of being unable to sell his product when it
is made if he can find a buyer who is willing to enter into a
firm contract for its purchase at a future date. If the price to
be paid is also fixed, the seller is protected against a fall in
price (though not against a rise in costs of production) and the
buyer against a rise in price (though not against a fall in the
price at which he can resell). (*Business Finance*, 5th ed· (Pitman,
1978).)

A third way of at least reducing risk is to be well-informed about
both the options and the dangers when assessing projects for investment. Thus a company which is marketing a new product will normally
engage in market research, and the investor contemplating the
purchase of shares in a particular company will study the company's
past records and, as far as possible, its future prospects.

THE TIME FACTOR
While the flow diagram shows a spatial movement of funds, there are
other dimensions to the flow. The movement of funds obviously takes
place over time and there is, for example, a time-lag between people
making deposits in a building society account and other people
receiving mortgages to enable them to buy houses. In the same way
there is a period of time between the purchase of shares in a company and the receipt of dividends.
  Interest has been described as the reward for waiting, but the
rewards are often completely eroded in a time of high inflation.
An investor is now obliged to allow for a depreciating currency in
his reckonings, but this shows again that the time factor is not
peripheral to the subject of investment. Time is of the essence.

AN EXPLANATION OF WHAT FOLLOWS
A study of the system is essential for business students since they
will be able to function more effectively - and profitably - if they
know as much as possible about business operations including the
various financial aspects. From a broad point of view everyone
living in a mixed economy such as ours should understand how it works
so that the system can be evaluated, criticised and improved where
possible, through the democratic machinery which is available to us.
The Stock Exchange in particular is a vital component in our economic
system and merits study on these grounds alone.
  Furthermore, the majority of people employed in banks, insurance
companies and other financial institutions will find themselves discussing with clients at some time in the future the various channels
of investment open to them. They will be expected to display a
reasonable grasp of the subject and their views will be treated as
those of experts. What follows is aimed at giving students a grasp
of the basic principles and an appetite for further study. Investment is a technical subject, but that is only part of the story. It
is an ongoing subject and all serious students will need to read the
financial press regularly if they are to keep abreast of developments.
  An overview of the text? In the early chapters we look at various

types of investment media which are available, considering their
merits and demerits from a variety of angles. We follow up with a
study of some of the detailed mechanisms by means of which the system
functions. At that stage we are able to contemplate some simple
exercises in portfolio planning.

In the final chapters the attempt is made to remind the students
of other dimensions and different perspectives. One has only to
note the infinite range of factors which affect the prices of securities on the Stock Exchange to appreciate that there is nothing narrow
or parochial about a study of investment. Vision and perspective
are essential. This is particularly true now that exchange controls
have been suspended. A new vista of markets have been opened up for
the UK investor providing a wealth of opportunities and no doubt a
mass of pitfalls.

The volume as well as the composition of the various flows of
investment are important to an understanding of the processes involved and this explains the statistical diagrams which have been
included at strategic points in the text.

A final section is devoted to the subject of examinations, which
remains for the great majority of students the vital target. A
technique for helping students to pass examinations is offered, together with an assortment of questions and model answers.

2 Ordinary and Preference Stocks

Before we commence our analysis of the various investment media it
will be necessary to clarify the way it is intended to use the basic
terms of *Stocks* and *Shares*. The following definitions will indicate
the range of interpretations possible:

> '*Stocks*: In the U.K. the term is usually used in reference to a
> fixed-interest security issued and quoted in units of £100.
> However, the term is sometimes used synonymously with ordinary
> shares (or with ordinary shares and fixed-interest securities
> collectively), as in the term *growth stocks*. In the U.S.A.,
> however, where ordinary shares are called *common stock*, the term
> is used quite generally in reference to ordinary shares.' - *A
> Dictionary of Economics and Commerce*, edited by S. E. Stiegeler
> and Glyn Thomas (Pan Books, 1976).

> '*Stocks and Shares*: Terms which tend to be used interchangeably,
> the distinction becoming blurred. Stocks, however, denote money
> lent to a government, local council or company and involving a
> fixed rate of interest; shares denote part-ownership of a company's
> capital, issued in a variety of terms and yielding variable
> returns.' - Alan Gilpin, *A Dictionary of Economic Terms*, 4th ed.
> (Butterworth, 1977).

For the purpose of this study the terms *stocks* and *shares* will be
regarded as interchangeable in so far as they relate to the securities of limited companies, while the term *stock(s)* will be used to
describe the fixed-interest securities discussed in subsequent
chapters.

So an investor who wishes to acquire a stake in an industrial or
commercial concern can do so by buying stocks or shares in a limited
company. The ordinary capital of a company is usually stated in £s
of stock (or shares) which is divided into units of, say, £1 or 25p
(or shares of £1 or 25p), or whatever nominal value is chosen by the
company for its units of capital. The use of the term 'stock'
indicates that the units have been fully paid, while the use of the
term 'shares' indicates that the units are either wholly or partly
paid for. In the vast majority of cases the shares will be fully
paid, which is why it is suggested we should regard the terms as
synonymous here.

A variety of stocks are available which give an investor both a
stake in, and membership of, a company. For example:

ORDINARY STOCKS (OR SHARES)
These are commonly described as 'equities', indicating that the
holders are entitled to what is left of the assets and profits, after
certain prior claims have been met.

The stock is broken down into units of, say, 50p each, which is then described as the nominal value. This is the value used for the calculation of dividends. So, if a dividend of 10 per cent is paid on a 50p stock unit, the dividend will amount to 10 per cent of 50p, i.e. 5p.

The dividends on ordinary stock will be related to the profits made by the company. Thus, if the profits are good the ordinary stock-holder can expect to receive an attractive dividend. However, before the dividend is paid the directors of the company may wish to recommend part of the profits being ploughed back into the business.

The fact that dividends normally vary in line with profits gives the person who holds ordinary stock some possible protection against the falling value of money - another description for inflation. This hedge against inflation operates in the following manner. In the case of a typical manufacturing company, where there is a rise in the cost of raw materials and wages, the company can usually com-pensate for this by raising the price of its finished goods. In this way its profits can be increased, wholly or partially, in line with the general rate of inflation.

Ordinary stocks normally, but not invariably, carry voting power. Some stock units are even issued which give more than one vote per stock unit, but multiple voting stock, as it is called, is not common. Details of voting rights will be found in the terms of issue or in the Memorandum and Articles of Association.

Some investors are willing to accept non-voting ordinary stock (usually designated 'A' stock) on the grounds that they do not wish to exercise voting power in any case. However, when there is a takeover in the offing the voting stocks could become more valuable and for this reason the market price of the voting stocks would be expected to stand at a premium over the price of the non-voting stocks. It is Stock Exchange policy to discourage new companies from issuing non-voting stocks and they are pleased when a company arranges to grant voting rights to hitherto non-voting stock. In this case the existing voting stockholders often receive a small scrip bonus (additional stock units) by way of compensation.

Whoever owns over 50 per cent of the voting stock is sure of con-trolling the elections to the Board of Directors. Yet many boards own much less than this proportion of voting stock between them. They are able to select their own replacements for any directors who die or retire, but at each Annual General Meeting a proportion of the directors have to be re-elected under a rota system. The directors remain in effective control so long as the company's performance satisfies the majority of the voting stockholders. But if the company falters there could be a stockholders' revolt leading to the replacement of the existing board - or at least elements of it.

A typical equity certificate is shown in Figure 2.

PREFERENCE STOCKS
Dividend rates on Preference Stocks are fixed at the time of issue and when payment is due to the stockholder this is calculated by using the rate in conjunction with the nominal value of the stock. So, if you hold £1000 6½ per cent preference stock you can expect to receive a dividend of £65 less tax per annum. Since the introduction of corporation tax and tax credits, however, Preference Dividends are stated at a net rate i.e. the rate payable after tax has been deducted.

CERTIFICATE No.   TRANSFER No.   DATE   NUMBER OF SHARES
  12996   C 343824   13th August 1981   **384**

ELC

EURO LEISURE CRAFT LIMITED
Harbour House, Baiter's Reach,
Poole, Dorset.

This is to Certify that the undermentioned is/are the Registered Holder(s) of fully paid Ordinary Shares of One Pound each in EURO LEISURE CRAFT LIMITED as shown herein subject to the Memorandum and Articles of Association of the Company.

NAME(S) OF MEMBER(S)   NUMBER OF ORDINARY SHARES OF £1 EACH
    John Brody Esq.,   **Three Hundred and Eighty Four Shares**
    12, High Street,
    Linacre, Essex.

Given under the Common Seal of
EURO LEISURE CRAFT LIMITED

Paul S Stone -
Director

Seal

Figure 2 *A typical share certificate*

The preference dividend has to be paid before any profits are allocated to the ordinary stockholders. A common misconception is that the preference stockholders necessarily have a prior right to the repayment of capital in the event of a winding-up of the company. They usually do have priority, but in some cases the preference stocks rank equally with the ordinary stocks *(pari passu)*. It is essential to refer to the terms of issue or the Memorandum and Articles of Association in order to ascertain the respective rights of the ordinary and preference stockholders.

If the preference stock is described as non-cumulative it means that when the directors decide to pass a dividend (i.e. they decide not to pay it) the dividend is lost permanently by the stockholder. By contrast, a cumulative preference stock will rank for payment of all unpaid dividends before the ordinaries receive further payments. The stockholder is entitled to assume the stock is cumulative unless it is described as non-cumulative.

A worked example
A Ltd makes a distributable profit of £312,000 on the year's trading. The directors decide to recommend a transfer of £112,000 to Reserve, which leaves £200,000 to be distributed. The capital structure is:

	£
Ordinary Stock (units of £1 each)	1,000,000
8% Preference Stock (units of £1 each)	500,000

11

The profit will be distributed thus:

	£
Profit available for distribution	200,000
Preference Dividend (8% on £500,000)	40,000
Remaining for Ordinary Dividends	£160,000

Ordinary Dividend will be

$$\frac{160,000}{1,000,000} \times 100 = 16\% \text{ or 16p per unit less tax.}$$

An example for you to work
B Ltd makes a distributable profit of £840,000, 50 per cent of which the directors decide to retain. The company has issued the following stocks:

	£
Ordinary Stock (units of £1 each)	1,000,000
7½% Preference Stock (units of £1 each)	400,000

Complete the details below:

Profit available for distribution =

Preference Dividend   =

Remaining for Ordinary Dividend   =

Ordinary Dividend expressed as a   =
percentage

Another worked example
C Ltd has the following capital structure:

	£
3,000,000 Ordinary Shares of 10p each	300,000
150,000 8½% First Non-cumulative Preference Shares of £1 each	150,000
120,000 10½% Second Preference Shares of £1 each	120,000

The distributable profits over the last three years have been:

	Year 1	*last year*	*this year*
Profits	£105,372	£15,086	£47,696
Transfer to Reserve	32,022	2,336	3,746
∴ First Preference Dividend	12,750	12,750	12,750
Second Preference Dividend	12,600	nil	25,200
Ordinary Dividend	48,000	nil	6,000
" "	16%	nil	2%
" "	or 1.6p per share	nil	0.2p per share

A final example for you to work
D Ltd has the following capital structure:

	£
Ordinary Stock units of £1 each	200,000
8½% First Preference Stock units of £1 each	50,000
6½% Second Non-cumulative Preference Stock units of £1 each	40,000

	Year 1	*last year*	*this year*
Profit for distribution (transfers to Reserve having been made)	£18,850	£4250	£16,850
Payment to First Preference stockholders	=		
Payment to Second Preference stockholders	=		
Payment to Ordinary stockholders	=		
Ordinary Dividend (%)	=		
Ordinary Dividend per unit	=		

REDEEMABLE PREFERENCE STOCK

Occasionally preference stocks are issued which have a redemption date. When they are due, the redemption monies have to come out of either profits or a new issue of stocks. Otherwise the law would regard it as an illegal repayment of capital jeopardising the security of creditors.

Even if preference stocks do not have specific redemption provisions the company may repay the capital if they have funds available.

PARTICIPATING PREFERENCE STOCK

This is a particular type of preference stock which allows the holder to participate to an extent in profits above a certain level. For example, the stock might give the holder a fixed 5 per cent non-cumulative preference dividend after which ordinary and preference stocks rank *pari passu* for dividend up to a maximum of 8 per cent.

Assume a distributable profit of £124,000 and a capital structure of

    600,000 Ordinary Shares of £1 each
    200,000 5% Participating Preference Shares of £1 each

Calculation of dividends

	£
Profit to be distributed	124,000
5% Preference Dividend (5% on £200,000)	10,000
Remainder	114,000
8% on 600,000 Ordinary and 200,000 Preference Shares jointly (8% on £800,000)	64,000
Remainder	£50,000

$$\text{Ordinary Dividend} = \pounds \frac{50{,}000}{600{,}000} \times 100 + 8\% = 16\tfrac{1}{3}\%$$

$$\text{Participating Preference Dividend} = 5\% + 8\% = 13\%$$

SHARES OF NO PAR VALUE

These are common in the United States and the distinguishing feature is that the shares do not have a nominal value. The principal effect is that dividends are expressed as a money payment per share (e.g. $1.25 per share) rather than the percentage declared in the United Kingdom.

PRICES

Prices of ordinary stocks will vary according to the expectations of the investors. Prices will rise when the company's prospects are seen to be good, and they will fall when prospects are seen to be unfavourable. It is the expectation of profit which is the determining factor. To a considerable extent profits will be affected by external events such as a reflationary budget (pumping more money into the economy) or a world recession. But prices will also be related to what investors can earn on alternative securities. So, if a return of, say, 12 per cent per annum can be expected from stock in a similar risk class and the stock in question is giving a return of 18 per cent per annum, the price which can be expected will be

$$\frac{\text{actual return}}{\text{expected return}} \times \text{nominal value}$$

$$= \frac{18\%}{12\%} \times 100\text{p} = \pounds 1.50$$

The prices of preference stocks can be calculated in a similar fashion once one knows the rate of return which is expected. However, the price of preference stocks will be related to interest rates generally rather than to the expectation of profits. So, if investors are looking for a rate of return of about 10 per cent per annum, an 8 per cent preference stock unit of £1 would be worth

$$\frac{\text{actual return}}{\text{expected return}} \times \text{nominal value}$$

$$= \frac{8\%}{10\%} \times 100\text{p} = 80\text{p}$$

Assignment

Make a weekly plot of prices of the following equities on a graph over the next three months. The prices should prove sufficiently different to allow you to draw them on a single diagram. At the end

REQUEST FOR PAYMENT OF DIVIDENDS

A SEPARATE FORM MUST BE USED FOR EACH ACCOUNT

Please use BLOCK CAPITALS

TO THE CHIEF ACCOUNTANT, BANK OF ENGLAND, NEW CHANGE, LONDON, E.C.4.

Name of Stock   3% Redemption Stock 1986 - 96
(Title in full)

Amount of Stock £   1000.00

standing in the name(s) of—

STOCK ACCOUNT No.
(Please quote if known)
689 - 03 - 084

For Sole Account:– FULL NAME AND ADDRESS (any change of address may be notified by quoting former and present address).

Mr. John Brody of 12, High Street,

Linacre, Essex.

For Joint account:– FULL NAMES ONLY required: addresses need not be given

Please forward all Dividend Warrants due, † and to become due, and payable on the sum of Stock mentioned above, or on the amount for the time being so standing, to—
★ *(See footnote)*

Full name of the Bank, Firm or Person to whom Dividends are to be sent.

Barchester Bank Ltd.,

Station Approach,

Linacre, Essex.

This form must be signed by all the Stockholders, Executors or Administrators, as the case may be.

Signatures(s)   *John Brady.*

Date   3rd September   19 81
(8822)

★ If a Bank is nominated to receive the dividends—
  (a) details of the banking account to be credited must be given to the branch concerned and must not be included in this form.
  (b) this form should be sent to the branch concerned who will insert, where necessary, their reference number(s) in the box below.
† If instructions are received less than one month before a dividend date it may not be possible to apply the instructions to that dividend.

FOR USE BY BANK NOMINATED TO RECEIVE DIVIDENDS.

Reference Numbers:–

(1) Sorting Code No. ....

(2) Account No. (if any) ....

Stamp of Bank Branch

Figure 4 *A dividend mandate*

1. John Brody is acknowledged as having loaned £1000 to the British Government. However, the date shown on the certificate indicates that Brody was not the original purchaser of the stock since 3 per cent Redemption Stock was issued by the government many years previously. He has obviously had the stock transferred to him either

17

as the result of a purchase from another stockholder, or as an inheritance.

2. The Bank of England will pay 3 per cent per annum interest on the stock. Thus John Brody will receive £15 (less tax) twice a year on this particular holding. If he completes a dividend mandate (see Figure 4) and sends this to the Bank of England the interest payments will be credited directly to his bank account.

3. The loan will be repaid (or redeemed) at some time between 1986 and 1996. The government will choose the date which suits it best. 3 per cent is a very low rate of interest and it is most unlikely that the government will redeem these particular stocks before 1996. However, if interest rates fell significantly below 3 per cent by 1986, a development which seems highly unlikely at the time of writing, the government would find it beneficial to redeem the 3 per cent redeemable stock at the earliest possible moment - replacing it with stock offering an even lower rate of interest.

Prices are quoted in terms of the price per £100 of nominal stock, but purchases of stock can be made to the nearest penny. Thus, if you invested a round £100 in $3\frac{1}{2}$ per cent War Loan you might find yourself holding £312.13 of the stock. How much interest would you expect to receive? This stock pays interest on 1 June and 1 December, so you would receive an interest warrant from the Bank of England for £5.46 (less tax) on each of these dates. The calculation is as follows:

$$\frac{3.5}{100} \times \frac{£312.13}{2} = £5.46$$

Some government stocks have redemption dates, such as the 3 per cent Redemption Stock referred to in the stock certificate shown in Figure 3. Other stocks are 'undated', which means there is no formal date for repayment. Undated gilts such as $2\frac{1}{2}$ per cent Consols (Consolidated Stock) or $3\frac{1}{2}$ per cent War Loan are unlikely to be repaid by the government because they represent such a cheap form of borrowing.

The non-redemption feature is seen as unattractive to many investors, yet profits can be made as prices change, for example in response to changes in general interest rates. The following simple example shows how this might happen.

Case Study
Interest rates are in the region of 10 per cent per annum when Robert Gange decides to invest a small sum in gilts. The price of $2\frac{1}{2}$ per cent Consols is standing at 25, which means Robert can buy £100 of the stock for about £25. He decides to buy £400 $2\frac{1}{2}$ per cent Consols at 25 and has to pay £100 plus expenses for a holding of this amount. The gross return on his investment (the sum he receives *before* deduction of tax) will be 4 × £2.50, i.e. £10, which is what an investor would expect to receive on £100 when the rate of interest is 10 per cent per annum.

After a while Robert hears that interest rates have fallen to $7\frac{1}{2}$ per cent per annum. From the point of view of his investment in the Consols this is good news. The price of the stock should now rise from 25 (the price at the date of purchase) to about 33. Why 33? Because an investor who bought, say, £300 stock at this price would pay about £100 for this holding, which would bring him interest of £7.50 per annum, i.e. a return or yield of $7\frac{1}{2}$ per cent per annum on his investment.

The rise of 8 points in the value of the Consols (from 25 to 33) represents an increase in the capital value of about one-third. Should Robert now sell his $2\frac{1}{2}$ per cent Consols in order to take his profit, bearing in mind that prices could fall again at some time in the future?

Solution

There are three factors to consider:

1. What is going to happen to interest rates in the future? If they fall further the price of Consols will rise again. If interest rates rise at some future date then the price of Consols will fall. They may even fall below the price originally paid by Robert Gange, involving him in a potential loss of capital.

2. What would Robert do with the cash if he sold his $2\frac{1}{2}$ per cent Consols? What are the available options? Until you knew what these were it would be impossible to advise Robert.

3. Gilts do not attract Capital Gains Tax when they are sold at a profit so long as they have been held for a minimum of one year. Taxes are dealt with in Chapter 16, but this is certainly a matter which would need to be considered in the situation outlined here.

* * *

Robert Gange invested in an undated gilt but the prices of dated gilts will also be affected by changes in interest rates. However, in this case another factor has to be brought into account, namely the redemption date. Thus, even though interest rates are high, and one would expect the price of a gilt-edged security to be correspondingly low, the fact that the redemption date was close at hand would keep the price of the stock close to par (parity = 100). If the redemption date was a long way off, however, the tendency for the price to keep close to par would be lessened.

Occasionally one will find the price of a gilt-edged stock going over par. This will occur when the government are obliged to borrow funds at a time of high interest rates. One can look at a stock such as $12\frac{1}{2}$ per cent Exchequer 1994 and whenever interest rates are significantly below $12\frac{1}{2}$ per cent the price of the stock will tend to drift over par. Thus, if interest rates are around 10 per cent, the price of $12\frac{1}{2}$ per cent Exchequer Stock will move towards 125, but it has to be remembered that the government will only repay the amount they originally borrowed. Investors will be reluctant to accept such a large loss on redemption so it is unlikely for the price to go as high as 125 and, indeed, as the redemption date draws closer the price will move towards par whatever the current rate of interest might be.

For purposes of comparison with other dated stocks the percentage gain or loss on redemption is annualised and added or deducted from the (flat) yield which then becomes the redemption yield.

Dated gilts are usually classified according to the time remaining before redemption. 'Shorts' are those with up to five years remaining to redemption. Medium-dated stocks are those with between five and fifteen years to run. Long-dated stocks have fifteen years or more to run before the government are due to repay the loan.

One type of short-dated gilt on offer is the so-called *variable gilt*, for which interest rates are fixed at 0.5 per cent above the average Treasury bill discount rate for the preceding six months. The interest is calculated on a daily basis.

Many people from overseas invest in British Government stocks and in order to make such investments attractive the Treasury has issued a selection of stocks for which interest is paid over without deduction of tax to a resident abroad. Because they have this attrac-

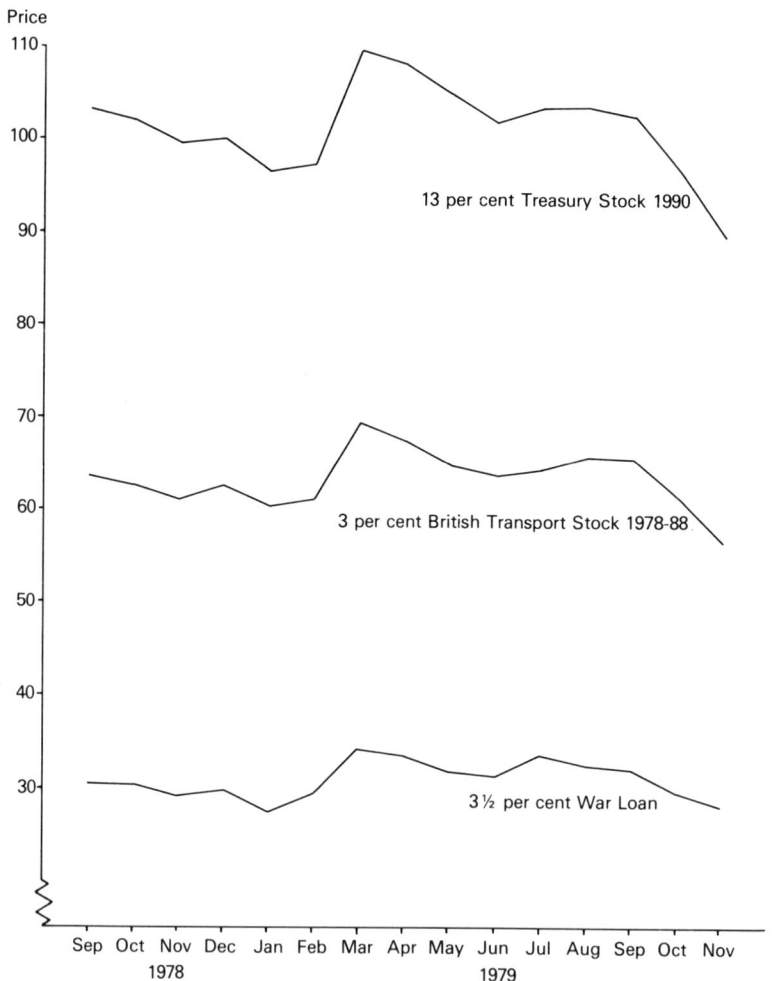

Figure 5 *A comparison of price trends for a selection of gilts*
Source: Central Statistical Office, *Financial Statistics*
(Dec 1979)

20

tive feature the stocks in question will normally be marginally more expensive to purchase.

In Figure 5 the price-changes for three typical stocks are shown over a period of fifteen months. The graphs show the tendency for gilt prices to move broadly in sympathy with each other.

Government Stock on the National Savings Register
Whereas gilts are normally purchased through a broker on the Stock Exchange, it is possible to buy certain government securities through the Department for National Savings. In this case purchases are made by application to the Bonds and Stock Office at Blackpool. Purchases and sales are made for the Bonds and Stock Office by the National Debt Commissioners on the London Stock Exchange at the price ruling at the time the transaction takes place. There are some fifty government securities listed on this register, ranging from the un-dated 4 per cent Consols to the long-dated 7 per cent Treasury Stock 2012-2015.

Interest on the stocks on this register is paid without deduction of tax, which is a benefit to non-tax-payers, though details of in-terest have to be declared on any returns of income made to the Inland Revenue.

Quotations
If you look for the prices of British Funds (another name for govern-ment stocks) in the columns of the *Financial Times* you will find the following sorts of entries:

1980

High	Low	Stock	Price	+ or −
$85\frac{3}{8}$	$74\frac{5}{8}$	Treasury $14\frac{1}{2}$% 1994	$80\frac{7}{8}$	$+ \frac{1}{2}$

This particular stock is 'free of tax to residents abroad' and will be noted accordingly. In the first column you will see the highest price which has been quoted so far in the year. In the second column is the lowest price so far this year. The price column shows the middle price at the close of business the previous day. The middle price is the mid-point of the dealing price which in the price given would normally be $80\frac{3}{4}$ to 81 (the selling and buying price respec-tively of £100 stock).

For the above stock the quotation might be $80\frac{3}{4}$-81, which means that you can sell this stock for £80.75 for every £100 stock you possess. While if you wish to buy Treasury $14\frac{1}{2}$ per cent 1994 Stock you will have to pay £81 for every £100 stock.

The fifth column shows the change of price since the previous day. It should be pointed out that we would expect to find more + signs than − signs since each day's price includes an additional element of accrued interest. However, this does not apply in the case of short-dated stocks (with a life of up to five years) for which the purchaser pays the market price plus the gross accrued interest since the last date of payment.

The merits of gilts as a medium for investment
1. The stocks are easy to sell and the proceeds can be obtained quickly.
2. The dealing costs are low.
3. The yield (or return) on gilts is normally high compared to that obtainable on other securities.
4. A redemption gain is available on dated gilts purchased at a price below par.
5. It is possible to avoid capital gains tax.

The basic flaw in gilts as an investment
The interest on gilts is fixed, so £10,000 invested in 3½ per cent War Loan in 1973 when the price was standing at 40 would have pro-vided about £875 gross interest every year since. In 1973 it would have been possible to buy a new car with £875. How far would £875 go towards buying a new car today?

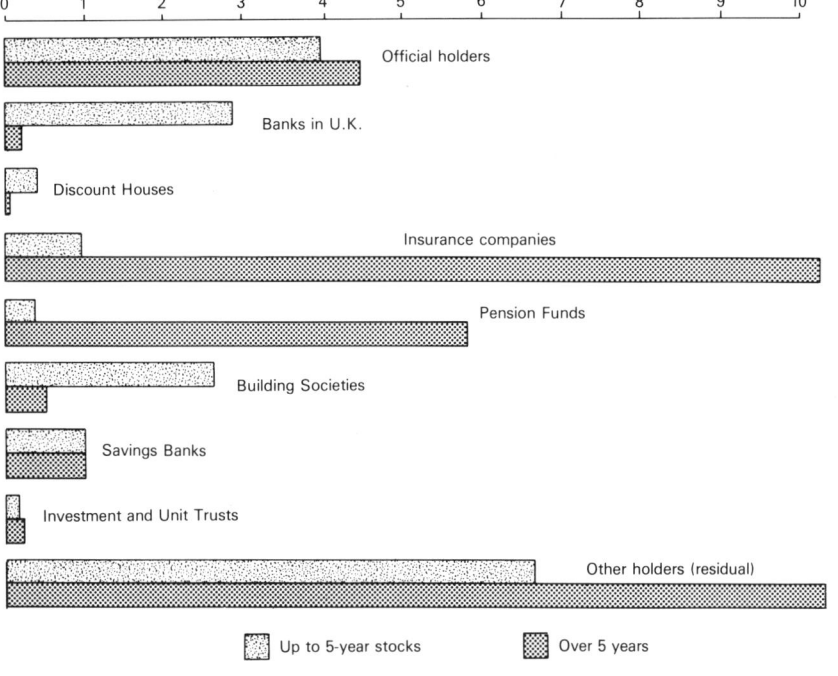

Figure 6 *British Government Stocks on the Stock Exchange Analysis by holders in £b*
Source: **Central Statistical Office,** *Financial Statistics* **(Dec 1979)**

Or to put it more forcefully, your grandfather could have bought a rather nice house in an exclusive London suburb for £200 in 1928. Suppose instead he had purchased £200 War Loan on which he had been receiving interest ever since - £7 per annum (less tax) to be precise. The house might be worth £30,000 or more at today's prices, while the War Loan is worth less than £100 in the stock market. The point is that all fixed-interest stocks fail to provide a hedge against inflation unless the net interest after deduction of tax exceeds the annual rate of inflation in the first year and the compound increase in subsequent years.

If the rate of inflation exceeds the interest earned the investor is actually penalised for making the investment. In classic economic theory interest is the reward for waiting. In times of rampant inflation a loss in the purchasing power of both capital and interest is the negative reward for delaying consumption.

Nevertheless, gilt-edged securities play a key role in the majority of investment portfolios and their popularity among institutional investors is apparent from an examination of Figure 6. You will note the preference of banks for shorts and the preponderance of longer-dated stocks in insurance company portfolios.

CORPORATION STOCKS

Local authorities (or corporations) sometimes acquire short-term funds from the banks through the medium of the discount market, but they also borrow funds from the public for varying periods. One avenue of investment for short-term funds are the so-called *Yearling Bonds*. These and other longer-dated Corporation Stocks are dealt in on the Stock Exchange and are subject to fluctuating prices in the same way as gilts. A few examples are given here:

London County Council $6\frac{3}{4}$ per cent 1988-90
Birmingham $3\frac{1}{2}$ per cent 1946 or after
Islington 14 per cent 1985-6

The divergent rates of interest are an indication that the stocks were issued at different times and are the result of continually changing levels of interest. The same effect is noted in the market for gilts. Another similarity to gilts in this small selection of corporation loans is that the Birmingham stock like War Loan is redeemable only at the option of the borrower. And redemption is unlikely while interest rates are in excess of $3\frac{1}{2}$ per cent per annum.

A large volume of loans are made through individual contracts be-

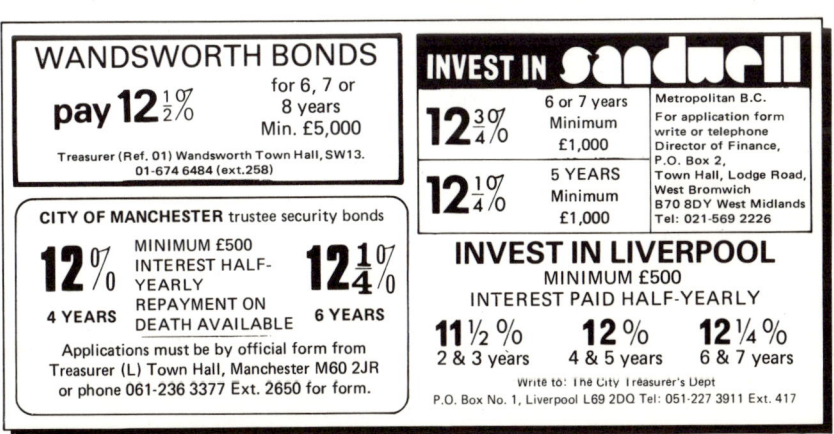

Figure 7 *Some typical advertisements for local authority loans*

tween the local authority and the investor, in which case the security is not listed on the Stock Exchange. The advertisements for such loans are familiar items in the local and national press. A recent selection appears in Figure 7.

You will note that the rates of interest offered and the terms generally differ slightly as between one authority and another. The smaller authorities are sometimes obliged to offer marginally better terms than some of their more illustrious counterparts. You will note that the City of Liverpool is offering slightly higher rates when the funds are lent for a longer period. It is usual for the authority to require a minimum deposit, and repayment is normally available only on the death of the investor during the stipulated period.

Local authority loans

Merits	*Demerits*
1. They give a slightly higher return than gilts.	1. Repayment of non-transferable loans may not be possible before completion of the term.
2. Secured against the authority's income from rates.	2. Any profit on the realisation of transferable stock is subject to capital gains tax.
3. The investor has an opportunity to support local developments.	3. Individual contracts for non-transferable loans vary and need to be studied before the rights of an investor can be determined.

COMMONWEALTH STOCKS

A number of overseas governments, particularly those in the Commonwealth, have floated loans on the London Stock Exchange. The numbers are now declining with the demise of the old sterling area, but there is still a small selection of stocks such as

New Zealand $7\frac{1}{4}$ per cent 1988-92

Bearing in mind a slightly higher risk involved and the fact that profits from these stocks are not exempt from capital gains tax, the investor could expect a higher return than that obtainable on gilts.

Assignment

Here are some multiple-choice questions for you to answer

1. *$8\frac{1}{4}$ per cent Treasury Stock 1987-90*

If interest rates fall to about 5 per cent per annum by the time the redemption period arrives, the Treasury could be expected to recommend

repayment of the stock in 1990	A
repayment of the stock in 1987	B
non-repayment of the stock	C

2. *6 per cent Funding Stock 1993*

Assuming that interest rates do not fall significantly below 6 per cent per annum, as the redemption date approaches we can expect the price to

rise above par	A
fall towards par	B
move towards par	C

3. *4 per cent Consolidated Stock (Consols)*

If the general rate of interest stands at about 10 per cent per annum, the price quoted on the Stock Exchange would be

about par	A
about 60	B
about 40	C

4. *3 per cent British Transport Stock 1978-88*

If the quotation for this stock is $51\frac{1}{8}-\frac{3}{8}$, the basic cost of purchasing £150 of stock will be

£77.07	A
£72.05	B
£85.00	C

5. *$10\frac{1}{4}$ per cent Exchequer Stock 1992*

If the price of this stock goes above par, it is likely to be because interest rates generally are

over $10\frac{1}{4}$ per cent	A
about $10\frac{1}{4}$ per cent	B
less than $10\frac{1}{4}$ per cent	C

6. *$3\frac{1}{2}$ per cent Conversion Stock 1961 or after*

If an investor anticipates a significant rise in interest rates in the near future he would be wise to

purchase the above stock	A
sell any of the above stock he holds	B
retain any of the stock he holds	C

7. *$3\frac{1}{2}$ per cent War Loan*

When the above stock stands at $52\frac{1}{2}$ one would expect to find $2\frac{1}{2}$ per cent Consols standing at

$41\frac{1}{2}$	A
$37\frac{1}{2}$	B
25	C

8. *12 per cent Exchequer Stock 2013-17*

If the price of this stock is quoted as $79\frac{7}{8}-80\frac{1}{4}$, what would the general interest rates be?

7 per cent per annum	A
10 per cent per annum	B
15 per cent per annum	C

4 Other Fixed-interest Securities

For an investor looking for safety coupled with fixed returns the choice extends beyond the range of company preference stocks and gilts. A number of the alternatives will be considered here.

Commerce and industry have insatiable appetites for loan capital and provide a variety of options for both large-scale investors and those of modest means. Of course the banks and similar financial institutions are great providers of finance for business, but investors have an important role to play in subscribing loan capital for companies.

But an investor lending to a company rather than the government is dealing with a different class of risk. Governments can meet their commitments on stocks by raising taxes or printing money. Local authorities can levy rates to cover the interest on their borrowings. By contrast, companies sometimes fail to meet their commitments and the investors lose their money. It follows that when a loan is being made to a company, or a loan stock is being purchased, the investor needs to consider a number of additional factors, viz.

(a) The resources of the company.
(b) The security (or collateral), if any, offered by the company.
(c) The company's other commitments.
(d) The company's past record.
(e) The integrity and acumen of the people who own and/or control the company.

DEBENTURE STOCKS

A Debenture is the written acknowledgement given by a company when accepting a loan. Debentures and loans are therefore, in one sense, synonymous. But Debenture Stocks issued by companies have additional features in that they are issued in units (usually of £1) and are transferable. The basic distinction between ordinary stocks (dealt with in Chapter 2) and debentures is that the former are subscriptions of capital and ownership confers membership of the company on the investor, while the latter are loans made to the company by outsiders.

The loan may be secured by any combination of fixed and floating charges on the assets of the company, but many loans are made without taking any security from the company. The investor may well feel that no security is necessary when the company in question has an excellent reputation. However, in the event of a winding-up of the company the secured creditors would be in a favourable position *vis-à-vis* the unsecured creditors. In view of the problems which even the largest companies run into, the value of a charge on the company's assets cannot be overrated.

A company will try to obtain any loan on the most favourable terms it can persuade the public to accept. If it has already issued secured debentures, perhaps against the security of buildings and property, it may be virtually precluded from issuing further loan stock. Of course, investors will look for an enhanced rate of interest in the absence of a fixed or floating charge on the assets. Any charges must be registered with the Registrar of Companies.

When the loan is floated - offered for sale to the public - the company will want to make sure the offer is attractive enough to ensure that it is well-subscribed. If the public do not find the offer sufficiently attractive it will cause embarrassment to the company. They may have to return all subscriptions if inadequate funds are offered because a minimum subscription will have to be stated. Their plans will be foiled if this happens, and the delay and disruption will inevitably prove expensive. It is no surprise, then, to find companies tending to err on the side of generosity. On the other hand, if they make the terms too attractive and the loan is heavily oversubscribed, the implication is that the interest rate could have been lowered without damaging the prospects for the issue. The sums involved could be considerable. For example, where a loan stock carries interest at 11 per cent whereas the public would have been prepared to accept a rate of 10 per cent, the avoidable burden for the company would be 1 per cent. This means that an additional burden of £10,000 per annum would have to be borne by the company for every £1 million of stock issued.

From the point of view of the company, one of the advantages of obtaining funds through an issue of loan stock or debentures is that the interest payments are deducted from profits before they are assessed for corporation tax.

Debenture stocks can be issued with redemption dates, much like gilts, which means the price will move towards parity as the maturity date approaches. They also suffer from the same defect as gilts in that the interest paid on them is fixed. The effect is that at times of rampant inflation the rate of interest is lower than the rate of inflation and so there is a negative return on the investment in real terms.

When company loan stocks are redeemable there is often provision for a sinking fund out of which stock is redeemed annually by purchases in the market or by annual drawings at a given price.

The use to which funds are put
The investor depends on the earning power of the company for the servicing of the interest payments. The use to which the additional funds are going to be put would be of concern to a stockholder who was being invited to subscribe for a new issue of debentures. Among the possible applications of funds are:

(a) The capitalisation of a programme of expansion with respect to
   (i) the development of new products,
   (ii) entering fresh markets, or
   (iii) increasing productive capacity.
(b) The provision of liquid funds to counter cash-flow problems.
(c) The coping with technological changes - either by replacing obsolete plant and machinery or by taking advantage of technological innovations.

The objective from the company's point of view will be to maximise the gap between the interest burden and the returns earned by the project.

Trust Deeds

When debentures are secured by a charge on the assets of the company, there will be a Trust Deed which sets out the rights of the stock-holders. The following matters are normally dealt with:

1. Restrictions on further borrowing.
2. Details of the assets charged.
3. The powers of the trustees particularly with regard to courses of action available to them if the interest payments are in arrear.

The trustees named will often be a bank or insurance company who can be expected to instil the necessary degree of confidence in the investors. But the danger remains that a company might dissipate floating assets such as stock and cash over a long period of time, leaving the trustees impotent so long as the company continues to pay the interest due on the stock.

Here are a few of the many company loan and debenture stocks available to the investor:

Guest, Keen & Nettlefolds Ltd 10½ per cent Debenture Stock 1990-5
House of Frasers 8 per cent Mortgage Debenture Stock 1986-91
Imperial Chemical Industries Ltd 5½ per cent Loan Stock 1994-04

CONVERTIBLE DEBENTURES/LOAN STOCK

Some loan stocks which are issued give the stockholder an opportunity to convert the holding into equities at a specified future date. An example would be a 10 per cent Convertible Loan Stock which gives the holder the right to convert the loan stock into ordinary stock on a one-for-one basis - at a price of par - at a date five years after the date of issue.

Case study

Eighteen months ago Claire Fenwick bought £1000 8 per cent Convertible Debenture Stocks in Convex Ltd at a price of 60p per £1 unit. She will shortly have an option to convert these debenture stocks into ordinary stocks on the basis of 2 ordinary stock units for every £1 debenture. The debentures are presently standing at 105p.

Under what circumstances will she be advised to exercise her option to acquire the ordinary stocks? And how would you account for the fact that the price of the debentures has gone over par?

Solution

Claire will be wise to exchange her debentures for ordinary stock if her future income from the ordinaries was likely to exceed her future income from the existing holding. She would need to concern herself with past records and future prospects. The only thing you need to know about the ordinary stocks at this stage is that the returns on them normally vary according to the profits made by the company. Furthermore, by opting for the ordinaries Claire would be jettisoning the right given by the debentures to interest payments whether or not Convex makes profits. Any protection given by a charge on the company's assets will also disappear.

However, Claire will no doubt be influenced by a straightforward comparison between the prices of the two securities on the Stock Exchange and if, for example, she has the chance of exchanging 1000 debentures standing at 105p each for 2000 ordinary stock units standing at, say, 65p each, she will be encouraged to exercise her option.

The fact that the debentures are standing at five points over par could be accounted for by either a general rate of interest of less than 8 per cent per annum in the stock markets, or by the market's valuation of the option.

MERITS OF CONVERTIBLE DEBENTURES/LOAN STOCK

From company's point of view
1. The options are likely to appeal to investors and the security is more likely to be taken up than a straight debenture, especially when there is a chance of substantial future profits.
2. The attractive feature of the option should allow the company to pay a lower rate of interest on the stock in the period leading up to the option date(s).

From investor's point of view
1. There is a secure investment even if the company fails to make the expected increase in profits and/or the ordinary stock does not rise in price significantly.
2. If the company prospers there is an opportunity for the stockholders to exercise the option and acquire a stake in the equity of the company. The ordinary stock acquired could be sold for an immediate profit if desired, and even the price of the convertible debentures would rise as it became obvious that the option was likely to prove of value.

DEMERITS OF CONVERTIBLE DEBENTURES/LOAN STOCK

From company's point of view
1. The existing ordinary stockholders will have to share future profits with the convertible debenture stockholders when the option is exercised.
2. If the Board of Directors own a narrow majority of ordinary stock carrying voting power, the new ordinary stock created when the options are exercised could take away the absolute control of the existing board.

From investor's point of view
1. Whether ordinary stocks or debentures are held the security for the investor is essentially the profitability of the company. The existence of the option rights can give the investor a false confidence.
2. The stockholders will not acquire voting rights in the period up to the option date. They will lack control over events in the meantime.

UNSECURED LOAN STOCK
When a company is highly rated by the investing public it may be able to issue loan stock which is not secured on the general assets or on specific properties as is the usual case with debentures.

WARRANTS TO SUBSCRIBE

When a company issues loan stock it may also issue warrants which give the holder a right to purchase ordinary shares at a fixed price at some future date. This is an alternative to the convertible debenture, but the distinction is that the warrant which gives the holder an option to purchase ordinary shares becomes separated from the loan stock. The warrants are quoted on the Stock Exchange and dealt with in the same way as shares, but they do not give the holder a right to attend or vote at company meetings. Any profits made are liable to capital gains tax.

COMPARISON WITH GILTS

There are certain disadvantages attaching to company fixed-interest securities (this term includes preference stock) compared to gilts. For example:

1. There is a risk of default by the company, however slight this might be in some cases.
2. Dealing costs are higher. Stamp duty of approximately 2 per cent is payable on the transfer of convertible stocks and preference shares (although not on straight debentures or loan stocks), and broker's commission is higher than for gilts.
3. Capital gains on company stocks are taxable.
4. There is a less active market for company fixed-interest securities. One would expect to find that returns were always likely to be higher on company fixed-interest securities in view of the disadvantages which have been mentioned. But while successive governments have issued new gilts on a massive scale, the finance directors of companies have shown a reluctance to issue new securities which carry a long-term burden of high interest rates. Furthermore, company fixed-interest stocks tend to be the preserve of tax-free institutions such as pension funds for whom a better net return is obtainable than from gilts. They buy large blocks of securities and hold on to them. Their assets are now estimated to exceed £40 billion and are growing by £5 billion a year (*Financial Times*, 26 March 1980). The overall result is that supplies of company fixed-interest securities tend to be in short supply.

EUROBONDS

Domestic issues of stocks are sometimes inadequate to meet the demands of big business and a market has developed whereby large institutions may invest (or borrow) funds in US dollars or major European currencies. The term 'bond' indicates that there is a loan evidenced by a document signed by the borrower. Surplus funds are deposited with European banks which either make them available to those seeking large-scale finance or underwrite the stocks issued by institutions such as national governments, nationalised industries, the World Bank and major corporations (companies).

Loans of around £500,000 and upwards can be obtained at short notice. The bonds are for fixed terms, the rate of interest being fixed for the term as with the other securities we have considered so far. The bonds are negotiable and the market is in sectors according to the currency in question. Thus there are dollar bonds, sterling

bonds, Swiss franc bonds, and so on. For example, among the Euro-
Deutschmark bonds are the following:

> 6 per cent European Investment Bank 1977-89
> 7 per cent Petrobras 1978-88

In both these cases repayment is by mandatory drawing by lot at par.
This is not an uncommon feature of Eurobonds.

  Business is done on the telephone between dealers scattered across
the world's major financial centres. Quotations and yields are
published monthly in the *Financial Times*. Interest is always paid
without deduction of withholding tax. Bonds are available in bearer
form, in which case there is no register of investors as the bond is
presumed to be owned by the bearer or holder.

  The primary market is that in which borrowers and lenders originally meet, while the secondary market is that which develops in the
stocks which are being bought and sold.

  Bonds with short lives are sometimes referred to as Notes.

  The international bond market includes Eurobonds and so-called
Foreign Bonds, which are issued by a foreign borrower in the domestic
market.

Assignment

Case study (for group work where possible)
Paul Saunders owns 300 convertible loan stock units in Gazebo
Electronics Ltd. On the first day of next month he will have an
opportunity to convert his stock into ordinary stock units of 25p
each on the basis of four units of ordinary stock for every unit of
loan stock.

The requisite data

Capital structure
>   10,000,000 Ordinary Stock units of 25p each
>   1,000,000 7½ per cent Preference Stock units of 25p each
>   1,000,000 8 per cent Convertible Loan Stock units of £1 each

Profits over the last three years

	Year 1	Last year	This year
	£	£	£
Annual profits before loan service	418,750	388,945	394,250
Annual loan interest	80,000		
Distributable profit	338,750		
Transfer to Reserve	50,000	40,195	20,500
Preference Dividend	18,750		
Available for Ordinary Dividend	270,000		
Percentage earnings for Ordinaries	10.8%		
Range of prices during the year	26-35p	25-32p	24-28p

Your task
Fill in the blanks and consider whether, on this evidence, you would advise Paul to convert his loan stock into ordinary stock units. Play the role of Paul's broker. Write him a letter giving your recommendations.

5 Investment Trusts

An Investment Trust is a limited company which has, as its main
business, the purchase of stocks with the purpose of holding them
for an extended period. The managers of such a company will be seeking stocks which show a potential for long-term growth. They will
seldom become involved with the day-to-day management of companies
in which they acquire an interest, though they would vet the manage-
ments carefully before making a large-scale investment. They often
choose to invest in the smaller successful companies, 'nursing' them
through the period when they would find it difficult to make an
issue of stock to the public. By the time these companies are strong
enough to bid for public support the investment trust will be able to
sell their stake at a substantial profit.

Some of the older investment trusts were able to make many useful
investments overseas, particularly in the New World. While overseas
investments tend to be risky in the sense that they can be burdened
by exchange-control restrictions, these were generally acquired
before the post-war explosion in the value of the US dollar. One can
gauge the benefit of holding US securities during a period when the
dollar appreciated from a rate of $5 to £1 sterling to the present
rate of $2 to £1. Even if the income from an American security had
remained static during this period the receipts in pound sterling
would have escalated. Thus a flow of dividends of, say, $1,000,000
would have been worth £200,000 initially, but would have appreciated
to £500,000 simply as a result of the changes in the exchange rate.

Prices of investment trust equities on the Stock Exchange are
usually at a discount compared to the value of the underlying
securities, partly because of the expenses of administering the portfolio and partly because turnover in the shares of investment trusts
is comparatively low as most buyers are long-term holders (see Table
1). But if the asset value gets too far out of line with the prices
quoted on the Stock Exchange the trust could become the subject of a
takeover bid.

The portfolios do not have to be particularly marketable. The
company can take a long position, i.e. they can acquire stocks with
a view to retaining them rather than aim at a quick profit.

Since investment trusts are looking for long-term growth stocks it
follows that their portfolios concentrate on equities. Inevitably,
the investment trust managers acquire expertise in particular areas
- geographical and otherwise - but diversification is the keynote of
their investment policy. A wide variety of equity stocks are purchased so that there is no danger of too many eggs being carried in
one basket. There are few portfolios of equities which have not
suffered casualties of one sort or another. The companies which
manufactured gas mantles must have looked good investment media at
the turn of the century. Then came cheap electricity and the super-

TABLE 1   DATA FROM A SELECTION OF INVESTMENT TRUSTS

| Total assets less current liabilities (£ million) | Company | As at close of business on 17.3.80 | | | Geographical spread 29.2.80 | | | | Total return on net asset value over 5 years to 29.2.80 (base=100) |
		Share price (pence)	Yield %	Net asset value (pence)	UK %	North America %	Japan %	Other %	
144	Alliance Trust	194	7.4	275	69	23	2	6	156
133	Scottish Invest. Trust	94	6.0	134	60*	27	3	10	167
112	Scottish United Investors	62	5.0	82	41	37	6	16	171
48	Second Alliance Trust	167	6.9	237	69	23	2	6	155
186	Foreign and Colonial Investment Trust	84	5.0	120	60	21	8	11	176
127	Philip Hill Investment Trust	90	7.7	122	81	16	–	3	206

* More than one-quarter in non-equity investments

+ The difference between the net asset value and the share price is termed 'discount'.

Source: The Association of Investment Trust Companies.

35

ior electric bulbs. Rayon stockings were an item of everyday use for females - until the advent of nylon hose. Changing technologies and fashions are the cause of many industrial failures. By investing in a wide range of securities the investment trust ensures that damage is limited to a small proportion of its total assets.

Diversification as a technique is not limited to investment trusts. Many companies have started off on a particular line of business and have diversified their interests over a period of time. It is not difficult to understand the reason for a tobacco group moving into the food industry. Anyone who has given up smoking will know the effect it has on one's appetite. A company can diversify vertically when it acquires stocks in companies which supply it or buy its goods. Or it acquires stocks in competing concerns. Rarely does a trading

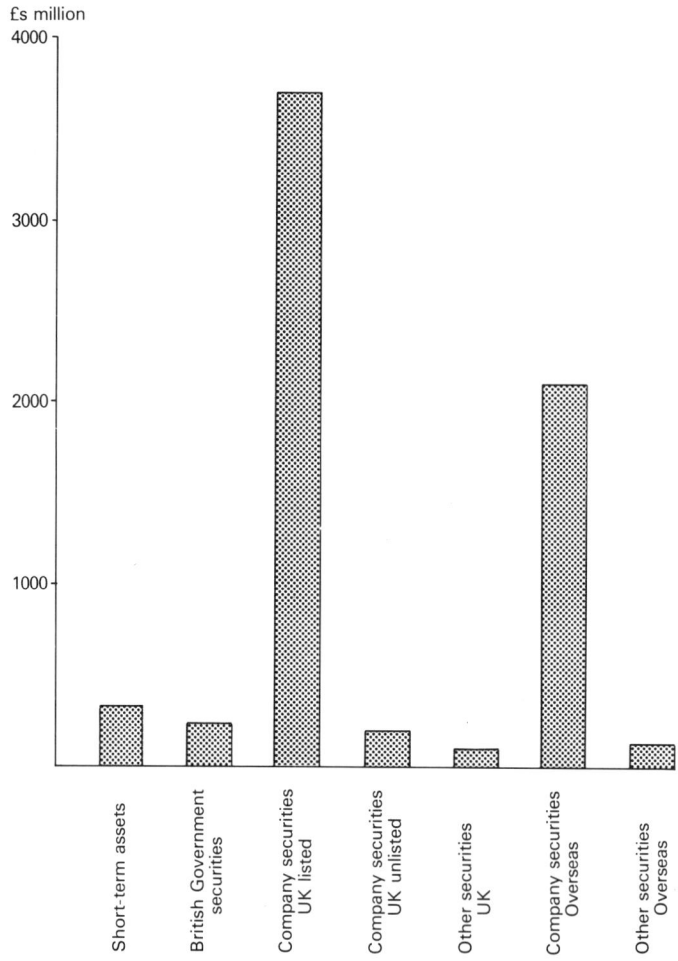

Figure 8 *Investment trusts*
analysis of Investments: Holdings in £m. at end of 1978
Source: Central Statistical Office, *Financial Statistics*
(Dec 1979)

36

company acquire stocks in another company simply because they represent a good investment. When they do this they are functioning in the same way as an investment trust. For the distinguishing feature of diversification as practised by the investment trust is that the investments are unrelated. Although there is a preponderance of company securities in investment trust portfolios (see Figure 8) there is no attempt to turn the concern into a holding company at the apex of a pyramid of subsidiaries and sub-subsidiaries.

The private investor may also wish to diversify in order to minimise the risk of losing his entire stake. He can achieve diversification quite effectively by buying stock in a first-class investment trust - even though his total stake is small. So the investment trust is often supported by the small investor which makes its board of directors more secure as a result of the diffusion of power among the remaining stockholders.

THE CAPITAL STRUCTURE
When an investment trust is first set up it will have a very simple balance-sheet. On the assets side there will be an item for premises, perhaps, but the principal assets will be the stocks it has bought in other companies. The stock certificates are valuable assets. If the customer of a bank requires a loan and can produce evidence of stock ownership he will no doubt get the accommodation he requires. Of course, the bank manager will look for a safety margin, but he may be prepared to grant a loan up to about two-thirds of the value of the securities - on the strength of a deposit of the certificates for safekeeping.

In the same way the investment trust can offer the stocks they have bought in other companies as security for an issue of loan or debenture stock. And what do the investment trust managers do with the additional funds they have acquired? Obviously they buy more stocks in other companies. Which give them the opportunity to acquire further funds by offering the next batch of stocks as security. These operations can take place quite a few times so that, in the end, the investment trust has a portfolio which exceeds by far the original stake of its own equity stockholders. If its reputation has also allowed it to issue preference stocks as well, the volume of stocks under the investment trust managers will be even further enhanced. This process is termed gearing and is an advantage not available to unit trusts.

SPLIT-LEVEL TRUSTS
Many investment trusts have two types of equity stock which cater for the differing requirements of investors. First, there is Income Stock which will entitle the holders to all the income earned on the underlying securities. At the end of the company's life the income stockholders will be repaid their capital - usually at par. The merit of this type of equity stock is that the growing returns over a period of time help to offset the effects of inflation. The major demerit is the inevitable pegging of the price to parity when the life of the company is drawing to a close - such companies normally have a fixed life.

By contrast the Capital Stock does not rank for dividends. The holders are entitled to share out the value of the underlying securities on termination of the trust. The main merit in capital stock is that it allows an investor who is paying high rates of tax on income to jettison dividends and concentrate on capital appreciation, the discount to assets reducing to nil by the date of winding-up. The main demerit of this type of stock for many investors is that there is a sacrifice of income in the hope of long-term profit.

A typical balance-sheet of a split-level
investment trust (as at 30 September 19..)

Assets employed	£000
Investments at valuation	
Listed on the British Stock Exchange	43,407
Listed on other Stock Exchanges	66,346
Unlisted as valued by Directors	7,623
Investment Funds on deposit	131
	117,507
Property at cost	163
	117,670
less net Current Liabilities	2,940
Net Total Assets	£114,730
Financed by	
Equity Capital Stock (units of £1 each)	25,000
Unrealised appreciation	4,616
Equity Income Stock (units of £1 each)	25,000
Dividend Account	114
7% Cum. Preference Stock (units of £1 each)	20,000
8% Debenture Loan Stock 1988	40,000
	£114,730

OTHER FEATURES OF INVESTMENT TRUSTS
1. The companies tend to be under the control of a group of specialist investment management concerns.
2. Investment trusts are not allowed to advertise. The result is they tend to be less well known to the public generally - compared to the more popular Unit Trusts.
3. Investment trust stocks are often highly favoured by instituional investors, who tend to hold them for extended periods. So the stocks are sometimes in short supply in the market.
4. Because of the high degree of diversification in the underlying securities the price of investment trust equities should fluctuate less than the majority of other equity stocks.

The effect of tax changes
A concession has been granted to investment trusts in that the Finance Act 1980 exempts authorised trusts from capital gains tax. However, to qualify for such concession:

(a) 85 per cent of the income has to be distributed, and
(b) not more than 15 per cent of its funds may be invested in another company other than another investment trust.

The shareholder remains liable to capital gains tax but since the limit for exemption has been raised to £3000 of gains, most small shareholders in investment trusts will not have to pay this tax.

When investment trusts were liable to capital gains tax their shares were unattractive to two very important categories of investors, namely, pension funds and charities, because these institutions were themselves tax exempt. Although they might have found the trusts' international spread of investment and management expertise attractive, they were discouraged by the unnecessary tax burden. This deterrent has now been removed, and pension funds and charities will no doubt be more prepared to include shares in investment trusts in their portfolios.

Theoretically, the investment trusts' liability to corporation tax might also deter tax-exempt bodies, such as pension funds and charities, from purchasing trust shares on the grounds that they are incurring unnecessary liabilities. The point is that, unlike other investors, these bodies are unable to claim back the corporation tax even though they are not subject to tax. However, many trust companies so balance income, management expenses and distributions that they are able to virtually eliminate liability to corporation tax.

Prior to the 1980 Budget shareholders received a 10 per cent credit against their capital-gains-tax liability. The effect of this concession was that when investors needed to raise funds they would tend to dispose of their investment trust holdings first. This tendency should now disappear since for capital-gains-tax purposes shares in investment trusts are on the same footing as other shares.

Another effect of the changes is that investment trust managers will no longer be constrained by capital-gains-tax considerations, which should lead to improved capital performance. There should also be beneficial effects on the income side because the trusts will be able to invest the sums which would otherwise be paid over in tax. According to the Association of Investment Trust Companies the effect of capital gains tax and exchange controls on a sale of a foreign investment could account for up to 20 per cent of the amount available for reinvestment.

The effect of the removal of foreign-exchange controls

In 1979 all foreign-exchange controls were lifted with the effect that investment trust managers can now increase their foreign portfolios without restriction. Previously there was a premium rate of exchange for overseas investments which acted as a disincentive. Similarly, foreign currency borrowings were penalised which restricted the overseas operations of the trust managers. They could be expected to use the borrowings to increase the gearing or to diminish exchange risks. By borrowing money at fixed interest and using the funds to purchase more securities the return to ordinary shareholders should be enhanced.

Quentin Lumsden, writing in the *Investor's Chronicle* (12 December 1980), indicates some of the effects of the removal of exchange controls as well as the tantalising difference for shareholders between the market price of their shares and the underlying value of the securities in the trust portfolio (see table 1):

Earlier most had consisted of massive chunks of money in 'blue chip'

shares which had underperformed in recent years. Now management
groups are re-orientating their trusts to specialise in glamorous
areas like the Far East or high technology . . . or concentrating
on the exciting smaller and unquoted companies which the pension
funds would like to invest in but do not have the time to investi-
gate. . . .

  There has been pressure for change from within and without. When
the typical investment trust is valued in the market at 80% or less
of assets which are most highly marketable quoted securities . . .
it is no surprise that shareholders become restive. Large trusts
have been taken over by pension funds looking for instant portfolios
or bought and liquidated by industrial companies as, effectively,
cheap rights issues. . . .

  The impressive performance of investment trusts generally can be
gleaned from Figure 9, which shows the record of dividend growth over
the past five years.

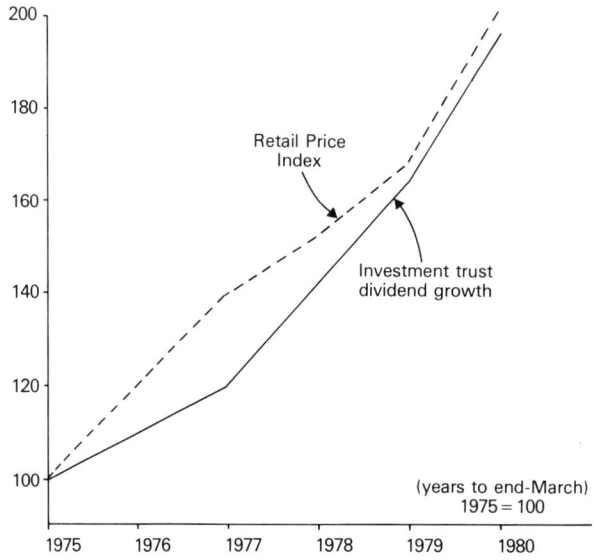

Figure 9 *Comparison between rises in Retail Price Index and*
              investment trust dividend growth 1975-80
              Source: The Association of Investment Trust Companies

Assignment

Task 1
Break up into small groups of 3 or 4. Play the role of a team of
executives in an investment trust who are looking for a selection of
equities in which to invest a total of £100,000. Reach a consensus
within each small group as to the type of stocks you would select.
Be as specific as possible and support your choices with reasoned
explanations.

Come together in the main group and compare the various investment proposals.

Finally, draft an individual report to the chief executive, Peter St Clair, giving your detailed recommendations for the investment of the sum in question.

The table that follows shows the existing pattern of investments in the company's portfolio. The Articles of Association do not contain any restrictions as to the investments which can be made.

Country/Industry		Percentage of total portfolio (by value — at cost)
Germany	– Motor industry	5
USA	– Banking	10
	– Railways	16
Canada	– Oil	8
UK	– Textiles	12
	– Insurance	10
UK	– Stores	3
	– Oil	18
	– Property	18
		100

N.B. The value of the portfolio at cost is £4,253,654.

6 Unit Trusts and Life Assurance

The private investor with only a small sum available and having
little or no understanding of the mechanisms of the Stock Exchange
may be reluctant to stake the whole of his capital in one company.
It will be little comfort for him to learn that prices of stocks and
shares rise as well as fall, if he is forced to sell his holding to
meet a commitment just at the time when the stock market is depressed.
Yet the savings of the small investors, when aggregated, represent
a large sum and it was with this in mind that Unit Trusts were
created. In essence, a large batch of specified stocks, usually
equities, is purchased in a block, or unit. The unit is then broken
down into a large number of marketable sub-units which are offered
to members of the public.

Through the medium of a unit trust an investor can achieve a
considerable measure of diversification with a very small outlay -
though most unit trusts (or funds, as they are more correctly called)
require a minimum initial holding. While the price of the sub-units
will still vary over time, the fluctuations will be dampened because
of the diversity of the underlying stocks.

Under the Prevention of Fraud (Investments) Act 1958 the control of
a unit trust is diffused in that for each fund there must be a
management company and a trustee company which are independent of
each other.

THE ROLE OF THE MANAGERS
The management company is responsible for the day-to-day administration of the fund. They must have a paid-up capital of at least
£50,000. The management company will set up the fund and market the
securities within the limits laid down by the trust deed. There will
be a prescribed list of securities with which they can deal and it
will be their function to buy and sell stocks within these para-
meters - for the advantage of their clients the sub-unit holders.
If the managers are successful their reputation will grow so that
when they are looking to set up another fund the public can be
expected to support them. Most of the management companies are
involved in a number of different funds and in this way can achieve
various economies of scale. In a highly competitive market some of
these economies will benefit the investors.

The managers are permitted to take a limited amount from the fund
to cover their expenses. Briefly these amount to:
  Up to 5 per cent for an initial charge, and thereafter
a maximum of $13\frac{1}{4}$ per cent over a period of twenty years.

The charges are described as front-loaded when the management
company has taken its full entitlement to charges at an early stage
in the life of the trust. One of the effects of possible front-
loading is that management companies will be encouraged to think of

increasing the scope of their operations rather than concentrating
their efforts in obtaining the best performance for existing funds.

One of the management company's functions will be to review the
value of the fund periodically. This is usually done on a daily
basis. The managers calculate two values for the fund - the buying
and the selling price for the underlying securities. Duly adjusted
to take account of the costs of brokerage and duties, the accrued
income in the fund, and the management charges, these values divided
by the total number of units held represent the dealing prices for
the public.

Bid and *offered* prices are quoted. The bid is the price at which
the managers will buy back the securities from the unit-holders.
The offered price is that at which the managers are offering
securities to new unit-holders. The bid price will obviously be
below the offered price.

Another function of the managers is to expand or contract the units
according to fluctuations in demand and supply. While changes in
price will dampen fluctuations to some extent, there are bound to be
times when there is a residual inflow or outflow of cash. At such
times the managers will either create more units (where funds are
pouring in) or liquidate units - by selling some of the securities
held (where there is a flood of sales).

It is normal practice to pay away all available income to the unit-
holders, but a few funds are 'accumulating' and plough back dividends, while most have an arrangement whereby distributions can be
used to purchase further holdings.

Although some funds have obtained Stock Exchange quotations,
nearly all buying and selling of units by the public is done through
the management companies. Bid and offer prices for the leading funds
are quoted in newspapers such as the *Financial Times* and the *Daily
Telegraph*.

THE ROLE OF THE TRUSTEES
The majority of unit trusts are Authorised Funds having Department
of Trade approval and are formed in accordance with a trust deed,
which is a formal legal document setting out the actions which are
to be taken by the various parties. The trust deed will name the
trustees for the fund who will be either a large bank or insurance
company, since the trustees are required to be part of a group with
paid-up capital of at least £500,000. All the fund's securities and
other assets will be vested in them and they will be responsible for
ensuring that the terms of the trust deed are complied with. If the
trustees fail to carry out the terms of the trust, they will be at
risk to any claims made by aggrieved investors. But they are not
responsible for the choice of shareholdings within a unit trust, nor
can they exercise control over the performance of the fund.

However, the specific functions of the trustees usually include the
following:

(1) To maintain a Register of unit-holders. This would also
    necessitate recording all sales and purchases.
(2) To issue share certificates to new unit-holders.
(3) To distribute dividends at the appropriate times. When the
    register of unit-holders is closed so that the distribution
    warrants can be prepared the prices are quoted x.d. (or ex
    dividend), which means that someone purchasing units at this

stage does not receive payment. The price quoted will be lower to compensate.

(4) To vet advertisements inviting subscription to the fund. Under the Prevention of Fraud (Investments) Act 1958 all advertisements must be approved by the trustees and there must be no misleading statements.

(5) To ensure that no investments are acquired of a type not authorised by the trust deed or in excess of the permitted proportion of the total portfolio. For example the trust deed may restrict investment in any one particular company to, say, 10 per cent of the total funds invested. If losses are incurred as a result the trustees will be liable.

Among their other duties the trustees may also:

(a) ensure that an adequate cash reserve is maintained by the management company to guard against the contingency of a cash outflow resulting from large-scale withdrawals by unit-holders.

(b) check that the trust income is not artificially boosted by the managers buying securities just before a dividend is declared - as a matter of policy.

(c) check from time to time the calculation of unit prices being quoted by the management company.

TAX CONCESSIONS

Both investment trusts and unit trusts receive favourable treatment in respect of taxation so long as the trusts are authorised by the Department of Trade. First, Section 81 of the Finance Act 1980 exempts both from capital gains tax on the sale of their securities. Of course this exemption does not extend to the investor in investment trusts or unit trusts who remains liable for capital gains tax on any profits on the disposal of his holdings.

A second concession is related to corporation tax paid by the trusts. The bulk of the income they receive will already have suffered corporation tax and the trusts will not be required to pay any further tax on this so-called franked income. Until the 1980 Budget, interest received from the trusts on holdings of gilts or local authority stocks would not have been subject to corporation tax and so would be liable to this tax in the hands of the trust. This explains why these trusts have chosen preference shares rather than gilts or corporation stocks in their portfolios. However, for unit trusts dealing in only UK fixed-interest securities, the Finance Act 1980 limits the rate of tax to 30 per cent, the standard rate, rather than 52 per cent which is the current rate for corporation tax (40 per cent for the smaller trusts). As a result, unit trusts will now be encouraged to introduce funds specialising in the management of gilts.

At the end of 1978 there was some £4 billion invested in unit trusts of which approximately five-sixths was related to equity investments, mainly in the United Kingdom. The overall break-down in terms of the types of securities held by unit trusts is shown in Figure 10.

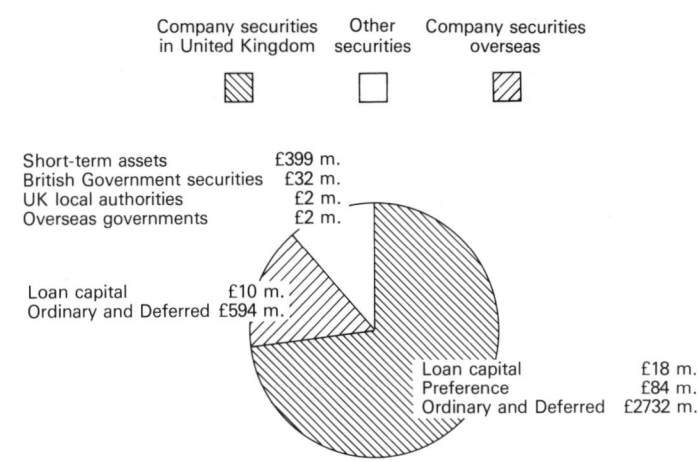

Company securities in United Kingdom   Other securities   Company securities overseas

Short-term assets   £399 m.
British Government securities   £32 m.
UK local authorities   £2 m.
Overseas governments   £2 m.

Loan capital   £10 m.
Ordinary and Deferred   £594 m.

Loan capital   £18 m.
Preference   £84 m.
Ordinary and Deferred   £2732 m.

Total investments: £3873 m.

Figure 10 *Unit trusts*
analysis of 375 trusts by type of securities held at the
end of 1978
Source: Central Statistical Office, *Financial Statistics*
(Dec 1979)

FLEXIBILITY v. SPECIALISATION

There are a considerable number of unit trusts and they offer the
investor a wide range of options. In order to differentiate their
'product' they often offer the investor stakes in companies within
a particular industry - or geographical area. Thus an investor might
choose a fund which appeals to him from the following:

(a) A fund specialising in gold-mining equities
Such stocks would be likely to rise in value broadly in line with
inflation.

(b) A fund purchasing equities in the United States
This would be attractive when the exchange rates were likely to move
in favour of the dollar and against sterling.

(c) A fund investing in Japanese industrial stocks
This would be a useful investment if there was expected to be a
further strengthening of the yen on the foreign exchanges over a
period of time.

(d) A fund dealing exclusively in banking and insurance company
stocks
Banking and insurance stocks can be expected to be comparatively
stable in terms of price and dividends - with prospects of long-term
growth - especially when the holdings are well-spread.

The investor decides what sort of company he wants a stake in and
purchases his units accordingly.

But there are disadvantages in this situation. In some ways the
managing company's hands are tied. It could be that they can forecast a rise in the price of oil shares. They could invest profitably in such shares, but they are not allowed to do so because of
the constraints laid down in the trust deed. They might equally

foretell a fall in prices in that sector of the market in which the fund is operating. Indeed it could be argued that inflexibility is one of the inherent problems for unit trusts though the degree of flexibility will vary between the funds. However, investors are now able to switch from one specialist trust to another.

THE ROLE OF THE BANKS
There are around 400 different unit trusts functioning in the United Kingdom. Bearing in mind the expertise available within their ranks and their connections with potential investors of modest means it is no surprise to find each of the Big Four commercial banks actively involved in the unit trust business. It may help to convey an impression of the various types of unit trust available to the investor if we study a selection of those on offer by one of the Big Four, viz. National Westminster. They include the following trusts on their list:

Title	*Aim*	*Special features* *
1. Capital Trust	To produce a high level of capital growth.	Income earned by the trust is not distributed but held and applied to the purchase of further securities.
2. Growth Investment Unit Trust	To provide overall growth of both capital and income through investment in a wide range of high-class ordinary shares both in the United Kingdom and overseas.	Invested in over 132 high-class securities with over one-fifth in North America.
3. Income Trust	To provide an increasing income together with a measure of capital growth.	Portfolio weighted towards income rather than capital growth but about one-tenth of the portfolio is in banks and insurance.
4. Extra Income Trust	To provide investors with a high and progressively increasing income.	7-8 per cent of the portfolio is invested in preference shares to boost the income. The balance of the fund is invested in companies which offer a high yield
5. Financial Trust	To produce long-term capital growth by investing in an international spread of financial shares.	Nearly half the portfolio is taken up in UK banking and insurance equities. Approximately one-quarter of the securities are overseas mainly in North America.
6. Universal Fund	To provide capital growth from world-wide investment.	The bulk of the portfolio is in US securities.

| 7. Portfolio Investment Fund | To provide an overall growth of both capital and income for the larger unit trust investor. | The minimum initial investment is £1000 enabling the managers to adopt a low initial management charge. |

*these will vary from time to time depending upon the state of the market generally.

Apart from the Capital Trust investors may choose whether to receive income distributions or have them automatically reinvested in the purchase of further units.

All four of the banks operate what are described as General Trusts, which have high income or capital growth, or a combination of both, as the main aim. They also operate various Selective Trusts such as the Nat West Financial Trust mentioned above. These funds concentrate investment within specified industries or geographical locations. Thus Barclays Unicorn '500' Trust invests mainly in the shares of smaller companies, while Lloyds International Technology Trust concentrates on companies involved in advanced technology, energy conservation and the pioneering of alternative energy sources.

Investment in a unit trust usually takes the form of a lump sum paid over to the management company. The minimum investment varies from fund to fund. But many funds, including those managed by the banks, operate a monthly savings plan whereby relatively small sums can be invested on a regular basis. The banks also operate share exchange plans which allow the investor who holds his own shares to exchange these for a holding in the unit trust.

Case study
During the course of the morning the Manager of National Westminster Hightown branch discusses the possibility of investment in unit trusts with four different customers:

Miss Elizabeth Hart is in her late sixties. She has a life interest in the estate of her late father which includes the house in which she lives and which provides her with an income of about £1500 per annum. Her only other income is her old-age pension from the state. She has been advised of a legacy of £5000 which is shortly to be paid to her from a friend's estate. She is considering investing part of the legacy in a unit trust.

George Parry is a 52-year-old professional earning approximately £15,000 a year. He is at present financially self-sufficient but would like to boost his income on retirement in eight years' time.

Peter Webb is the proprietor of a small engineering works producing specialised farming equipment. He already has a portfolio of U.K. equities, mainly in banks and insurance, with a current market value of £40,000.

Delia Carter wishes to make a gift of £2000 to her ten-year-old grandson. She is thinking of investing the money in a unit trust for him.

Your task
Consider which of the unit trusts listed the bank manager would be most likely to recommend to each of these customers - on the evidence available.

Note

No doubt when the manager interviews his customers he will draw their attention to the merits of investment in unit trusts such as these. First, the trusts offer skilled management. The offer price of units in the Growth Investment Trust, for example had risen by 85 per cent between launching in June 1967 and 30 June 1978. This compared with a rise of 31 per cent in the *Financial Times* Industrial Ordinary Share Index over the same period. The difference between 85 per cent and 31 per cent is in part a measure of the managerial skill deployed. Second, the trusts offer a spread of risks and a choice of objectives to suit a variety of individual requirements. Third, the investor acquires a selection of stakes in the different companies without having to become involved in the tedious paperwork associated with share transfers, takeover bids, rights issues, etc. Someone like Miss Hart may have little understanding of these matters.

The popularity of unit trusts as investment media can be gauged from Figure 11, which shows the growth in the value of unit trusts generally between 1972 and 1978, and the steady sales of units during this period.

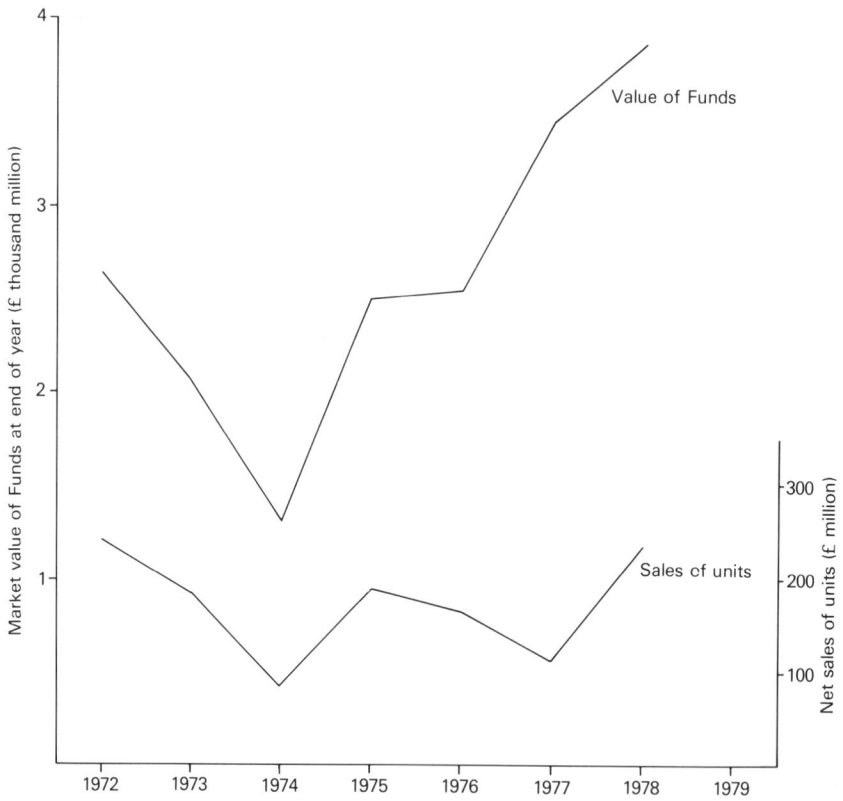

Figure 11 *Unit trusts: total funds and net sales 1972/9*
Source: Central Statistical Office, *Financial Statistics*
(Jan 1980)

LIFE ASSURANCE

Protection and investment are the two main elements in life assurance. Protection is given by a sum payable to dependants on death, while the investment element is related to the appreciation resulting from the investment of the premiums by the insurance company. Brokers talk of Life Assurance Plans. Term Plans provide a high level of protection only, for a limited period of years. There is no investment element in this type of policy. By contrast Endowment Plans provide protection for a limited number of years plus an element of investment which varies as between the different contracts offered by the life offices.

THE ENDOWMENT POLICY

The policyholder pays regular premiums to the insurance company over a fixed period and on the due date receives an enhanced capital sum from the insurers. The weakness of this form of investment is that where there is inflation the premiums are paid out of 'high-value' money, while the eventual capital payment from the life office is in 'low-value' money.

It is possible to take out a policy 'with profits' and with this sort of contract the insurance company agrees to pay out an additional sum on the maturity of the policy, this sum being related to the profits made by the company during the period of the insurance. The share in profits is a hedge against inflation and is particularly useful when a compound interest rate of bonus is offered.

Apart from the benefit of life cover, the policyholder is afforded tax relief up to one-half of the basic rate of income tax and this relief is immediate, being deducted from his payment of premiums to the insurance company.

If the policyholder is unable to continue paying the premiums or the circumstances change so that there is no benefit to be gained by continuing payment of the premium, it is possible with most contracts to surrender the policy for a cash sum. The surrender value is usually much less than the sum of the premiums paid to the date of surrender because the assured has enjoyed life cover in the intervening period.

Another concession available to some policyholders is the possibility of obtaining a loan from the insurance company, if required, against the security of the policy. The rate of interest is usually favourable and the loan limit will increase as the policy comes closer to maturity.

THE ANNUITY

A wide variety of contracts involving an element of investment are offered by the life offices. One such is the Annuity, whereby a capital sum is paid to the insurance company in return for which the company pays out fixed sums either for the remainder of the annuitant's life or for a fixed number of years. The payments are usually made half-yearly. In the case of an annuity for life there is not usually an apportionment on the death of the annuitant. If death occurs, say three months after the last instalment, no further payment will be due to the annuitant's estate. However, it is possible to purchase an annuity 'with proportion' and/or to have the instalments paid more frequently than half-yearly.

The table below indicates some of the rates currently available for an annuitant aged 70.

Annuity: Purchase price £10,000: Payable monthly in arrears

	Male (£)	Female (£)
Legal and General	1936	1746
London Life	1922	1714
Eagle Star	1910	1730
English	1905	1703
Scottish Amicable	1899	1712
Royal	1897	1699

For a male aged 70, basic-rate taxpayer, taking out an annuity with Legal and General, the net return after tax is as follows:

Total annuity	£1936	£1936
less Capital Content	891	
Tax payable at 30% on	£1045 =	313.50
Net annuity		£1622.50

Source: *Money Management Magazine* (January 1980).

The different rates for males and females result from the fact that females have a longer life-expectancy. The longer your life-expectancy the smaller the instalments you can expect from the company. The table also illustrates the advisability of comparing the terms offered by different companies in any insurance business, though the reputation and soundness of the company are other considerations to bring into account.

The annuity is a particularly valuable form of investment for an elderly person who has no close family or friends he would wish to benefit from his estate.

One can see that each of the payments received by the annuitant is part interest and part capital. The danger from the annuitant/investor's point of view is that inflation will erode the value of successive payments.

EQUITY-LINKED ASSURANCE POLICIES

An equity-linked assurance policy is essentially an endowment policy. Premiums are paid, on a regular basis. Insurance cover is given in the form of a fixed minimum sum payable to the policyholder's estate in the event of his death, and a fixed minimum sum payable at the end of the Selected Period (say, fifteen years). But to these minimum sums may be added an amount which is calculated by reference to a unit trust managed by the insuring company.

When each premium is paid an amount representing an agreed and fixed proportion of the premium is notionally allocated to the purchase of units in the unit trust. The notional holding grows in time and is valued on the death of the policyholder or at the end of the selected period. If the value of the notional holding exceeds the minimum benefit mentioned then, in most contracts, this sum is substituted for the minimum sum and is paid out by the insurance company.

In compiling the notional holding of units all the usual unit trust conventions are applied. Units are 'bought' at the offer price. Valuations of the holding are made at the bid price. Annual management charges are deducted.

The effect can be seen in Figure 12. In this example:

If the policyholder had died during the first eight years his estate would have received £3000.

If the policyholder had died at the end of year 9 his estate would have received £3750.

At the end of the full term the policyholder would have been able to take £4375 either in cash or in the form of units in the trust.

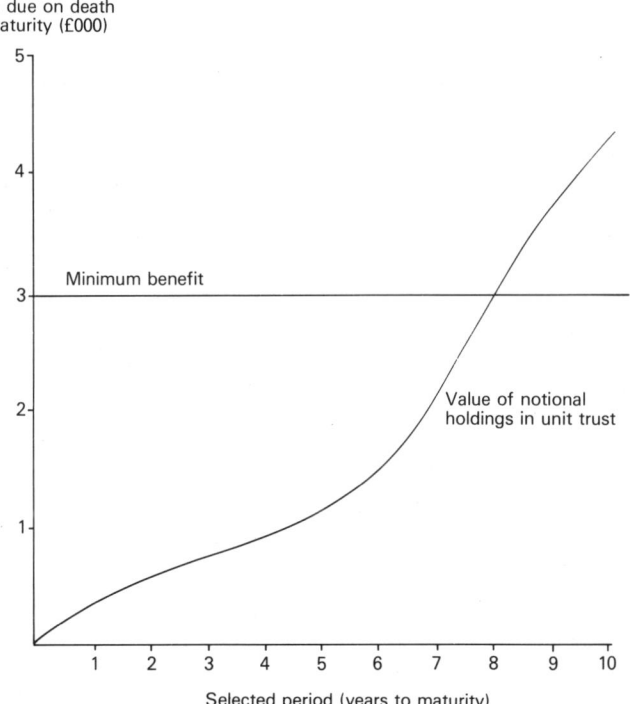

Figure 12 *Benefits on death or maturity during term of unit-linked assurance policy*

The Abbey Life Assurance Company is one of the institutions in the linked assurance business and offers the assured, in a typical contract, a choice between linking the policy with investment in
(a) Equity Units
(b) Property Units, or
(c) A Selective Fund, to be invested in equity units and in property units in such proportions as the company from time to time determine in their absolute discretion.

Advantages to the policyholder/investor
(1) There is immediate life cover.
(2) At the end of the selected period (perhaps before) when the
    value of the notional holding exceeds the sum assured a degree
    of protection against inflation is afforded. The assumption is
    that growth stocks will increase in value over time at broadly
    the same rate as inflation.
(3) For all practical purposes the notional holding might be an
    actual holding. The policyholder is making regular savings which
    are being invested in unit trusts. He has the holding at his
    disposal at the end of the selected period. But he enjoys the
    security of a minimum realisation value below which the value of
    the holding cannot fall.
(4) The bulk of the premiums rank for tax relief.
(5) The policy can be surrendered or converted to a paid-up policy
    if the policyholder is unable to proceed. In some cases the
    insurers will also be prepared to grant loans against the
    security of the policy.

Disadvantages
(1) The policy is essentially a long-term saving plan, and if the
    policyholder runs into financial difficulties and wishes to with-
    draw he can only do so at a price - the surrender value will tend
    to be punitive.
(2) If the policyholder opts out there are claw-back provisions for
    the tax relief - the tax has to be paid back to the Revenue.
(3) As a hedge against inflation the equity-linked assurance policy
    may be no more effective than a with-profits endowment policy.
(4) Judging the policy as an investment it is decidedly illiquid and
    leaves the investor very much at the mercy of the unit trust
    managers over a long period of time.
(5) It could prove to be both a rather expensive form of insurance
    and a mediocre form of investment, but this would depend very
    much on the terms offered and the skill of the managers of the
    unit trust.

Investment Bonds
These are unit-linked insurance contracts with a variety of forms.
Nevertheless there are certain common features. An Income Bond is
purchased either with a single premium (a lump-sum payment) or a
series of premiums. A proportion of each premium payment is set
aside to cover the risk that the policyholder might die. This
normally amounts to about 5 per cent of the total sum invested. The
remainder of the sum is invested by the life office (insurance
company) in much the same way as if they were unit trust managers.
  Typically, the bonds are offered with the underlying securities in
the form of property, equities (home and overseas), or fixed-interest
securities. A recent innovation is to offer bonds for trading in
commodities. *Managed bond funds* mix their purchases of properties
and Stock Exchange securities to take advantage of changing trends,
though this flexibility relates to incoming investments rather than
existing holdings because properties can be neither acquired nor
disposed of quickly.
  The income from the funds invested takes the form of rents,
interest or dividends according to the nature of the underlying

securities. This income does not belong to the bondholders. It is
retained by the insurance company and adds to the value of the bond.
If the bondholder wishes to make withdrawals he must make sure the
contract allows this. There are no tax consequences on the withdrawal of capital so long as (a) withdrawals are limited to 5 per
cent of the value of the bond and (b) the bondholder is neither a
higher-rate taxpayer nor subject to an investment income surcharge.

It is important for an investor to choose a life office with a good
record because, unlike unit trusts, there are no guarantees of
diversification, no approved valuation formulae and no controlled
charges. The investor depends very much on the integrity of the life
office managing the bond funds.

Assignment
Working together in twos or threes complete the following table,
placing the factors in what you regard as their order of importance
from the investor's point of view. When you have completed your
discussion, compare your findings with the other groups.

	Merits	Demerits
Unit Trusts	1.	1.
	2.	2.
	3.	3.
Endowment Policies	1.	1.
	2.	2.
	3.	3.
Annuities	1.	1.
	2.	2.
	3.	3.

7 Property

When we talk about shares of a particular class in a specific company,
we are referring to homogeneous and identical items. The price of
one share is exactly the same as the price of the others. The rights
of the respective shareholders are identical. The term *'pari passu'*
is an indication of this feature in shares. By contrast, no two
houses or office blocks can occupy the same site. Nor are they
likely to be in an identical state of repair, or occupied by the same
people. There is one further distinction in property which needs to
be understood. Property is a legal concept and the world of property
is a world of rights and obligations. There are restrictive
covenants and rights of way, planning permissions and compulsory
purchase orders, tenancy agreements and schedules of dilapidation.
The legal problems are not our concern but we might take note of
D. R. Denham's explanation of one of the basic features of the
property market:

> As it was in the beginning, so now. Land deals are transactions
> not in land but in rights in and over land. . . . Land is not cut
> up like linen cloth. More than one interest may exist in the same
> parcel of land. Picture a Neapolitan ice-cream, the horizontal
> layers - vanilla, strawberry and coffee. Peculiar to the owner of
> 'vanilla' property may be the right to occupation of the land; to
> the owner of 'strawberry' property the right to reserve rent from
> the 'vanilla' interest; and peculiar to the 'coffee' property the
> right to sanction or prohibit the development of the land.
> (Institute of Economic Affairs, *Land in the Market* - Hobart Paper
> 1964.)

If there are complications with property there are also compensations. One of them is that property can be inspected before purchase.
Another is the psychological satisfaction derived from the ownership
of property.

HOUSE OWNERSHIP
House ownership is one of the most common and effective forms of
investment for the private investor. Typically the property is freehold and the purchase is financed with the aid of a building society,
local authority, commercial bank or insurance company. The favourable features for the investors are fourfold:

(1) Property prices can be expected to rise in line with inflation
    in the long run. The cost of materials and wages for the
    construction of new homes can be expected to relate to increases
    in prices generally and if building land is scarce property prices
    might outstrip inflation. Some people would say that the ready

availability of building society funds also tends to make for spiralling property prices.
(2) The interest element in the mortgage repayments is subject to tax relief. Furthermore, owner-occupied houses are free of capital gains tax on realisation (sale).
(3) The money advanced by the building society or other institution is 'high-value' money, but the repayments by the borrower are 'low-value' money - since wages and prices generally can be expected to rise over a period of time. This can be seen as the opposite case to the investment in an endowment policy (see previous chapter).
(4) An individual needs accommodation of one sort or another and this asset gives him shelter and personal satisfaction during the period of the investment, though against this must be set the costs of maintenance and rates.

The less-favourable features of residential property are:

(a) The property may take time to sell.
(b) The costs of dealing in property are much higher than those in connection with stocks and shares.
(c) If the accommodation is rented to a tenant, the rent may be difficult to raise.

LEASEHOLDS
A property can either be freehold or leasehold. The person in occupation of a leasehold property is described as 'the lessee' while the person who grants the lease is called 'the lessor'. If X owns the freehold title to land (and the buildings if any thereon), he may grant possession to another party for a term of, say, 99 years. The lessee will then take legal possession of the property for this period but at the end of the 99 years the property will revert to the lessor/freeholder. Many leases are granted for as long as 999 years which means in effect that the freeholder has given up possession of the property permanently. The justification for this action is that the freeholder will obtain:

(a) a price for the lease which is approaching the full freehold price and
(b) a regular income from the ground-rent which the leaseholder is required to pay as part of the price.

The lessee will incur certain obligations under the terms of the lease. Normally these will include an obligation to keep the buildings in good repair. On the termination of the lease the lessor (or freeholder) will serve a schedule of dilapidations on the lessee for any repairs which are necessary. Fair wear and tear is excluded.
Leasehold property is a wasting asset as far as the lessee is concerned and at the termination of the lease the title reverts to the lessor (or freeholder).
Flats are commonly leasehold because by this means the freeholder can retain responsibility for communal maintenance. To fragment the responsibility among a large number of tenants could lead to chaos.

THE LEASEBACK

Many industrial and commercial firms - with cash-flow problems - and valuable properties among their assets - have taken advantage of a modern innovation in the property market - the leaseback. A property company is found who are prepared to buy the freehold from the firm at a realistic price, but the purchase is coupled with a long lease which is granted to the firm. In this way the firm retain possession of the property and at the same time receive a large injection of cash from the property company.

Rates

One of the outgoings on all properties is the rates which are paid to the local authority. Each property is given a rateable value and the local authority levies a rate of so much in the £ to meet its various commitments (refuse-collection, street lighting, education, etc.).

For example, Dominique's Restaurant in the High Street may be assessed for rates at £1200. If the rate levied by the local authority is 90p in the £, the restaurateur will be required to pay

$$\frac{90}{100} \times £1200 = £1080 \text{ per annum (normally in half-yearly instalments)}$$

Sales of property

A contract for the sale of land has to be in writing or be evidenced in writing. When the vendor and would-be purchaser agree on a price the agreement is said to be 'subject to contract' and until the respective solicitors draw up and formally exchange contracts either party may drop out of the transaction.

Estate agents are usually employed to sell a property and they charge a commission for their services. Scales of fees vary, but tend to be about 2 per cent of the sale price. A typical scale of fees would be:

The first £10,000 of sale price to be charged at $2\frac{1}{2}$ per cent
The next £10,000 of sale price to be charged at $1\frac{1}{2}$ per cent
The remainder to be charged at 1 per cent.

In which case the estate agent's fee on property sold for £30,000 would be about £500.

Where a property is sold at a public auction the services of an estate agent become indispensable. A reserve price may be put on the property and if bids do not reach this price the property is withdrawn. But when the auctioneer brings down his hammer the bid is accepted and the effect is the same as if contracts had been exchanged.

A solicitor's services are also normally required whenever property is being disposed of. The solicitor will check on the validity of the vendor's title to the property and make appropriate searches to ensure that there are no plans for developments which will affect the property adversely.

The usual document of title to land (and the buildings thereon) is the Land Registry Certificate, which shows who owns the property and also indicates the main encumbrances such as rights of way across the land and restrictive covenants which debar the owner from doing

certain things such as carrying on business from the premises.
   Stamp duty is also payable on the purchase of property where the
price exceeds £20,000. The scale of duty at present is as follows:

£	%
0-20,000	nil
20,001-25,000	$\frac{1}{2}$
25,001-30,000	1
30,001-35,000	$1\frac{1}{2}$
above 35,000	2

A typical Completion Statement presented by a solicitor to his client
on the completion of a property sale might be:

Completion Statement
for sale of F/H 6, Roxy Crescent, New Wickstead

	£
Sale Price	29,000
less Mortgage outstanding to New Wickstead Building Society	12,000
	17,000
less Solicitor's Costs and disbursements	460
	16,540
less Estate Agent's agreed commission	560
Cheque herewith	£15,980

INDUSTRIAL AND COMMERCIAL PREMISES
Property booms are not limited to private accommodation and many of
the larger investors stake their funds in the purchase of blocks of
shops and flats, offices and even industrial premises. The returns
on the investment take the form of rents from long or short leases.
   Increasingly investors are seeking suitable properties in a world-
wide market. Publicity often accompanies the purchase of British
properties by the oil sheikhs but the traffic is by no means one way.
The following snippet from Edward Rushton Son & Kenyon's *Review*,
Winter. 1979, indicates the scope of the market:

   A completed shopping centre in Landover, Maryland, will be of
   particular interest to institutions and pension funds seeking
   established and profitable American investments. A price of six
   million dollars is being sought for this 144,460 sq. ft. shopping
   centre, which is fully tenanted except for one 1,600 sq. ft. unit.

PROPERTY BONDS
These were briefly referred to under the heading of Investment Bonds
on page 52.   They are technically life assurance policies, usually
involving the payment of a single premium. The first property bond

was launched by the Westminster Friendly Society in the late 1960s
but the market is now dominated by the Big Three, viz. Hambro Life,
Abbey Life and Property Growth. They function similarly to unit
trusts except that commercial and industrial properties are purchased
instead of stocks and shares. The fund is divided into notional
units which are allocated to bondholders with a weighting according
to age - favouring the younger investor.

The properties are professionally valued once a year with monthly
adjustments so that bid and offer prices can be established. The
managers must maintain adequate reserves of cash to meet any substantial withdrawals of funds by the bondholders. In some cases the
managers reserve the right to defer encashment for a stipulated
period.

To accommodate the needs of the smaller investor some companies
allow the withdrawal of regular amounts from capital on the basis
that this is in line with a long-run appreciation in the value of
the properties.

The main merit of property bonds would appear to be that, by
combining with others, the small investor is able to acquire a stake
in the purchase of the more attractive and expensive properties. In
the words of James Rowlatt: 'This is an instance where big is
beautiful - partly to give you a reasonable spread of assets in the
portfolio, partly for the group to have enough power to arrange good
property acquisitions. . . .'

He goes on to explain that property funds usually carry a cash
reserve of 20 to 30 per cent of the total in any case - to meet
claims for redemption. This is a large slice of the fund to be out
of circulation. But there is another limitation to bear in mind:

> Prices have to be fixed by valuations, not by reference to published
> quotations, as with a share portfolio . . . the result has to be
> fixed by reference to someone's subjective experience of the current
> state of the market, and his assessment of a sensible yield basis
> on which the properties might change hands. (James Rowlatt, *A
> Guide to Saving and Investment* (Pan, 1979).)

SHARES IN PROPERTY COMPANIES
Another way of acquiring a stake in real property is to purchase
equities in a property company. There are a number of companies
whose operations centre on the purchase, leasing and sale of a wide
variety of properties, and where the companies have highly geared
capital structures (see Chapter 9) this may more than compensate for
the fact that the company's profits are subject to corporation tax
before becoming available for distribution to shareholders.

In other words, much as investment trusts are able to use the
shares they purchase as security for further loans, property
companies are able to charge their freehold and leasehold properties
as security for loans. The result should be that the property
companies are able to extend their portfolios and increase profitability for the benefit of their equity owners. However, there are
two presumptions, namely, that property prices and rents will
continue to rise, and that interest rates will not be punitive.

BUILDING SOCIETIES
The public are invited to deposit funds with a building society in

return for which they will receive a rate of interest which varies
with interest rates generally. This is a net rate to the majority
of investors because the society pays the income tax before paying
over the interest, but taxpayers who pay above the standard rate of
tax will be subject to an additional assessment. Investors who do
not pay income tax are not able to claim a rebate of tax and they may
get a better return in other forms of investment.

The funds are used to lend to house purchasers. The building
society takes security by way of a deed of mortgage on the property
until full repayment is made. The amount lent will normally be
limited to about two and a half times the borrower's annual earnings,
but husbands' and wives' earnings will be combined to make the computation. The borrowers will repay the loan - together with interest -
over a fixed term, commonly 25 years.

The building society is not a profit-making organisation and uses
the margin between the interest allowed to its depositors and the
interest charged to the borrowers to cover its management and
administration expenses and to build up reserves.

Both borrowers and lenders are investors in the sense that the
house purchasers are investing in property, while the depositors are
investing funds in the society with the properties as a safeguard
for their investments.

Societies offer a variety of terms to their depositors. A typical
selection would be:

    On Deposit Accounts - 8 per cent p.a.
    On Share Accounts   - 8½ per cent p.a.
    On Term Shares   - 9 per cent p.a.

The depositor who chooses the higher rates of interest will find
he has to forfeit a degree of liquidity. The share accounts normally
require more notice for withdrawal, and the term shares are only
repayable after a fixed period. The shares would also be repaid
after the deposits in the event of the society's insolvency.

The fundamental weakness with the building society account as a
form of investment is that it provides no hedge against inflation so
long as the rate of inflation exceeds the rate of interest offered
by the building society.

Assignment

Multiple-choice questions for you to answer
1. Someone investing in a ground-rent will be acquiring:

    a long lease for the property   A
    ultimate possession and an income in the meanwhile   B
    a rent for the ground but not the property itself   C

2. When a building society gives a loan to a housebuyer against the
   security of the property deeds the society is described legally
   as

        mortgagee   A
        freeholder   B
        mortgagor   C

3. Property investment is a hedge against inflation

> only when property prices are rising
> faster than prices generally   A
> at any time   B
> only when the cost of living is rising
> faster than property prices   C

4. If you owned equities in a property company which of the following events would be most likely to see your shares rise in value?

> news of high levels of unemployment in
> the building industry   A
> a rise in interest rates   B
> a reduction of corporation tax   C

5. Which of the following events would be most likely to produce a fall in the price of houses?

> a worldwide shortage of timber   A
> a substantial reduction in the building
> programme by local authorities   B
> a rise in interest rates   C

6. Which of the following investments are likely to be the least effective hedge against inflation?

> debentures in a property company   A
> industrial and commercial premises   B
> property bonds   C

8 Company Formation and Capitalisation

If an investor is prepared to tie up capital in a company he would be well advised to have at least a basic understanding of the nature and structure of such an organisation. A limited company, normally a company which has been registered under the Companies Act, might be formed with two purposes in mind:

(1) The proprietors of the business acquire limited liability, which is to say they stand to lose only their stake in the company and cannot be compelled to pay debts incurred by the company. In the case of a sole trader or a partner the proprietor(s) are fully liable for the debts of the business even if this means disposing of all their personal assets.
(2) Investors will be unlikely to subscribe capital if by doing so their personal assets are placed at risk. A limited company will find it easier to raise funds because this danger is eliminated for its stockholders.

A company is regarded by the law as a legal entity - an artificial or juristic person. It can own land and other property, sue and be sued, enter into contracts and borrow money from others - with certain restrictions. The Memorandum and Articles of Association which are drafted on the inception of the company define the internal rules and regulations. Together with the Companies Acts these documents prescribe the relationships between the company, its shareholders and outsiders.

The Memorandum of Association usually contains an express power to borrow money, but a trading company has an implied power to borrow unless this is prohibited in the Memorandum of Articles. In contrast a non-trading company requires express power to borrow. If the company exceeds its borrowing powers the borrowing is described as *ultra vires* and the borrowing and any security given for it is void.

The Articles of Association regulate the company's internal affairs and deal with matters such as the appointment of directors and the allocation of voting powers among the members.

Limited liability is obviously a valuable protection for shareholders, but the Company's Act 1948 closely prescribes the procedures which must be followed by officers of the company including the directors, the company secretary and the auditors.

If a company does not issue its own Articles then Table A will apply. This is a *pro forma* set of rules for a company - other than a private company - set out as an Appendix (First Schedule) to the Companies Act 1948. A sample of the provisions in Table A follow:

Variation of rights

4. If at any time the share capital is divided into different classes of shares, the rights attached to any class (unless other-

61

wise provided by the terms of issue of the shares of that class)
may, whether or not the company is being wound up, be varied with
the consent in writing of the holders of three-fourths of the
issued shares of that class, or with the sanction of an extraordinary resolution passed at a separate general meeting of the
holders of the shares of the class.

Alteration of capital

44. The company may from time to time by ordinary resolution
increase the share capital by such sum, to be divided into shares
of such amount, as the resolution shall prescribe.

Rotation of directors

89. At the first annual general meeting of the company all the
directors shall retire from office, and at the annual general
meeting in every subsequent year one-third of the directors for
the time being, or, if their number is not a multiple of three,
then the number nearest one-third, shall retire from office.

As a general rule the rights attaching to all stocks and shares
are governed by the terms of issue and/or the relevant clauses in
the Memorandum and Articles of Association. While a small-scale
investor cannot be expected to pay attention to such minutiae this
does not mean they are irrelevant.

Among the problems facing the EEC is the need to harmonise the
company laws of its member states. The Companies Act 1980 is a
response to the EEC Second Directive on the formation of public
limited liability companies and the subscription and maintenance of
their share capital. The act envisages two types of company. The
public company is one which meets various conditions set out in the
act. One of these conditions is that there must be a minimum
authorised share capital of £50,000 which must be issued in full
though only a quarter needs to be paid up.

Any company which is not registered as a public company will be
deemed a 'private company' and a criminal offence would be committed
if the shares or debentures of such a company were issued to the
public.

It follows that only public companies are quoted on the stock
exchanges. But of course many public companies are not quoted. The
importance of this to the investor is that a quotation will make his
stocks more easily marketable - and the marketability of the stocks
will reflect in the price which can be obtained for them. If a
stockholder wishes to dispose of his stocks in a non-quoted company
he may well have to ask the company secretary whether there is anyone
who would be prepared to buy the stock. This is a very different
matter from simply giving instructions to a broker and finding a
purchaser through the medium of a stock exchange. And with stocks
or shares in a private company the directors may be empowered to
refuse to accept a transfer even when a purchaser has been found.

PROMOTERS

People who are involved with the formation of the company are called
promoters and they stand in a fiduciary position towards the company.
They are in a position of trust and must act accordingly. For

example, if a profit is made on the sale of the promoter's property to the company, this must be disclosed, otherwise the company will have a right to rescind the contract and recover the purchase money. Alternative remedies are to claim the profit made from the promoter or to sue for damages for breach of a fiduciary duty.

PROSPECTUS
A document which invites the public to subscribe for shares is called a prospectus. Because there is a danger that the public could easily be misled by falsely glowing accounts which would not stand up to scrutiny, the law attempts to protect the investor. Information required in the prospectus as set out in the Fourth Schedule of the 1948 Act include:

1. The names of the directors and details of their remuneration.
2. Any profit which is being made by the promoters.
3. The minimum amount of capital to be subscribed, the amount actually received in cash, and the consideration given for the remaining capital. If the minimum subscription is not received by the company all subscriptions will have to be returned to the subscribers.
4. Details of outstanding contracts and preliminary expenses including commission.
5. Details of the voting and dividend rights of each class of shares.
6. Where the company is already in existence and is seeking additional funds by a new issue of shares, the company's financial record is required including details of profits and losses in each of the preceding five years. Similar details are required for any subsidiary companies.

One of the most interesting prospectuses in recent years must be that issued by Thermo-Skyships Ltd. On 19 November 1979 they published a prospectus to cover an issue of 2,560,000 ordinary shares of 25p each. This was part of a scheme aimed at raising £6.4 million to build flying-saucer-shaped airships to carry 100 passengers a trip between the centre of London, Paris, Amsterdam and Brussels at fares and timings competitive with the airlines. The money was required in two parts, with the first £1.9 million to complete the design stage and to start building the prototype (on the Isle of Man). The next £4.5 million was expected to take the airship up to a certificate of airworthiness which should be received by mid-1982. The prospectus was admitted to have a risk on every page and there was a warning in heavy black type that all the money could be lost.
In two situations a full prospectus is not required, viz.

(1) Where the prospectus or form of application is issued to existing members or debenture holders, or
(2) Where it relates to an additional issue of existing shares which have a quotation on a prescribed stock exchange.

In either case 'an abridged prospectus' may be issued in lieu of a full prospectus.

PURCHASE OF SHARES BY INSTALMENTS
Many people who would like to invest in a company's shares have their

funds tied up elsewhere. It takes time to arrange for a substantial sum to be made available and, with this in mind, a company often offers the purchaser of its shares the opportunity to produce the purchase money in stages. It is not unlike interest-free hire purchase or credit selling which occurs elsewhere in commerce. Thus a company might offer its 25p shares at £1.25 each, of which 25p is payable on application and allotment, 50p is payable in two months' time (the date being prescribed), and the final instalment of 50p is payable in four months' time (again on a prescribed date).

An individual who wishes to buy 10,000 shares would have to find £12,500 rather quickly if the purchase money was payable in full on application and allotment, whereas when the purchase money can be paid in instalments only £2500 has to be found immediately. The investor has a chance to sell other investments in his portfolio and obtain the proceeds from them without undue haste. The company which sells its shares in this way will no doubt be able to raise the price in much the same way as a retailer who offers credit terms on his goods.

UNDERWRITING

When a company invites the public to buy its shares it is an expensive operation and, perhaps more importantly, its reputation may suffer irreparable harm if the market gives the 'thumbs down' to the offer. One way of ensuring that all the shares offered are taken up is to employ underwriters. The underwriters agree to take any shares which the public do not take up. As compensation for this risk the underwriter receives a commission of, say, 5p, which is payable whether or not he is obliged to purchase any of the shares.

Let us suppose that Zeta Ltd are issuing 1,000,000 new £1 shares at par, i.e. £1 each, and that a stockbroker, John Brown, has agreed to underwrite 10,000 of these shares at a commission of 5p per share. First assume that the public take up all the shares. In this case John Brown will simply collect a cheque from the company for £500 underwriting commission (10,000 × 5p).

Then assume the public have only taken up 600,000 of the shares. This is 60 per cent of the total and leaves the underwriters to take up the remaining 400,000 shares. John Brown will now be required to take up 40 per cent of the 10,000 shares he has underwritten. The 4000 shares will cost him 87½p each (£4000 less £500 = £3500).

It is common practice for underwriters (usually brokers, banks or issuing houses) to pass on part of the risk and with it part of the commission to sub-underwriters.

The legal constraints for underwriting are set out in detail in Section 53 of the Companies Act 1948.

OVERSUBSCRIPTION

One sometimes hears of new shares being issued which attract so many applications that only a small proportion of the applicants receive allotments. Bearing in mind the possible damage to a company's reputation when shares are left unsold it is understandable that the company's advisers should err on the side of caution. But some years ago a very prestigious company issued stock which was over-subscribed approximately 200 times. In other words for every stock unit on offer there were 200 applications. While this was heralded as a sign of the company's strength, it could also be seen as a costly error in that it would have presumably been possible to offer much less favourable terms and still obtain more than enough applications for the stock. If we are thinking of an issue of, say, £5 million then the avoidable cost to the company could be considerable (see also page 28).

INSOLVENCY
When an individual is unable to meet his financial commitments he is made bankrupt, while a company in this situation becomes insolvent. For the company there are three possibilities:

1. *A receiver may be appointed.* This would happen where, for example, there was a loan or debenture stock and the company failed to keep up the payments of interest. The debenture-holders would have the right to appoint a receiver under the terms of the trust deed. The receiver would take possession of the assets and dispose of them in order to repay the debenture-holders' capital. The receiver has no need to consider the interests of the shareholders. His responsibility is solely to the debenture-holders, though when the latter have been fully repaid, surplus assets must be passed over to the directors.

2. *A liquidator may be appointed.* A liquidator is appointed either at the request of the shareholders or of the unsecured creditors. The liquidator will take over control of the company from the board of directors. He will deal with the assets which remain after the secured creditors have been satisfied. First he will need to satisfy the company's unsecured creditors. Then he can distribute the residue to the shareholders according to the terms of issue or the Memorandum and Articles of Association.

3. *The quotation may be suspended.* If either a receiver or liquidator is appointed it is common practice to close the company's share register. In this case new shareholders cannot be registered and the Stock Exchange quotation is withdrawn.

Protection to the stockholder
Inevitably some recent purchasers of shares are going to feel aggrieved when a company fails but a broker cannot be held responsible for mistaken advice given through an error of judgement. However, where a broker defaults and fails to meet his commitments, an investor may claim on the Stock Exchange Compensation Fund for any losses suffered.

ANALYSIS OF COMPANIES
According to the Department of Trade (*Companies in 1978:* HMSO) the number of companies registered at 31 December 1978 were as follows:

Public Companies

On registers	16,954
Of which, in liquidation or in course of removal	1,129
Effective number on registers	15,825

Private Companies

On registers	727,487
Of which, in liquidation or in course of removal	51,130
Effective number on registers	676,357

It is apparent from these figures and Figure 13 that the vast
majority of companies are both private and small.

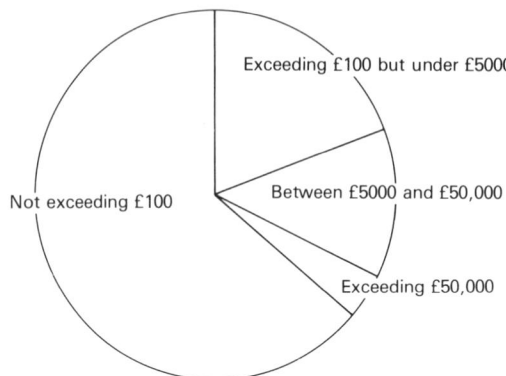

Figure 13 *Numbers of new companies registered in 1978 analysed by*
nominal capital
Source: *Companies in 1978* (HMSO)

Assignment

Case study (for group work)
John Kendrick comes from a long line of distinguished yachtsmen and
it was no surprise when he started his own boat-building business.
At first his yachts were custom-made but he has now designed a
racing catamaran which is beginning to rouse a lot of interest around
the world. For some time he has depended on his bank to finance his
expansion but he is beginning to look for more permanent finance.
It has now been suggested that he might form a limited company –
Kendrick Catamarans Ltd – and sell ordinary shares and/or debentures
to forty or fifty friends and fellow enthusiasts who have indicated
a willingness to acquire a stake in the business.
   The firm's net assets have been valued at £200,000 and John is
prepared to recognise this as his present stake in the business.
The inflow of £300,000 cash will be provided by the purchasers of
the new ordinary shares and/or debentures which are issued on the
formation of the company.
   The net profits over the past five years have averaged £70,000 and
with the new injection of capital this figure is expected to increase
to £120,000 per annum.
   A firm of local stockbrokers have advised that if debentures were
issued they should be secured on the freehold boatyard – recently
valued at £150,000 – and would then attract a rate of interest about
2 per cent below bank lending rates. If convertible debentures
were issued with an option to convert at the end of five years, the
brokers consider the rate of interest could be reduced by a further
1 per cent.

Consider the sort of shares which Kendrick Catamarans Ltd might issue in these circumstances. Bear in mind the following points:

(a) John Kendrick will want to remain in control of the business.
(b) The prospective investors will need to be offered attractive terms.
(c) John Kendrick will still wish to maximise his returns from the business.

When you have considered the problems together, write your brief individual reports to John Kendrick, setting out your personal recommendations.

9 Capital Structures and Gearing

When stocks or shares are issued by a company there are two distinct groups whose differing interests have to be catered for. First, there are the people and institutions who are being invited to subscribe for the securities. They will be looking critically at the prospectus and forming their own judgements as to the company's future prospects. If they have surplus funds they will find there are numerous options open to them and this company's offer is but one of many competing claims for their cash. Further, they will have their own personal requirements for a suitable investment. Long-term growth may be less appealing to an older investor than high present income. And present income may be of little value to someone who pays a high rate of tax. Some investors will accept a high-risk stock so long as there is a hope for high profits, while others will wish to eliminate risk as far as possible. When a company decides to offer stocks or shares to the public it will be necessary to consider the market - in all its aspects.

The second group of people to be considered are the existing proprietors. From their point of view the situation could be expressed quite simply. They require funds. They will have to pay for those funds. But they will want to pay as small a price as possible. It is the classic trading situation. And so when different proposals are being considered for raising funds, the existing proprietors will prefer to issue debentures without charging the company's assets - if they can persuade the investors to accept such an arrangement. Or they will prefer to issue non-voting equities so they can be certain of retaining control of the company. Their problem is to make the offer sufficiently attractive without being unnecessarily generous. We saw an example of these machinations in the last assignment.

When securities enjoy a stock exchange quotation the Stock Exchange Council prescribes certain rules which have to be complied with by the company. For example, where proxies are issued (see Chapter 12) the stockholder has to be given the opportunity to vote against a resolution. And in a prospectus the Council requires a company to disclose audited profits over the past ten years rather than the legal requirement of five years. If a quotation is being sought then all subscriptions will have to be returned if permission to deal is refused by the Council of the Stock Exchange.

The existing proprietors will benefit from a quotation. It will increase the value of existing shares because they will be more easily disposed of. Furthermore, any new shares will be more marketable and therefore a higher price can be asked for them. But before a quotation will be permitted a sufficient number of stocks and shares will have to be made available to the members of the Stock Exchange so that a proper market in the securities can be created.

In other words the stocks or shares will have to be acceptable to the Stock Exchange.

Thus the capital structure of any company issuing stocks or shares to the public will be shaped by three different forces, viz.

1. The dictates of the market.
2. The designs of the present proprietors.
3. Stock Exchange requirements where the securities are quoted or to be quoted.

An example showing the effect of alternative capital structures
Gamma PLC has the following capital structure at present:

£500,000 Ordinary Stock (£1 units)
(For the significance of PLC see the Compendium, p. 192.)

The company require £1,000,000 additional capital and the directors have the choice of issuing either

£250,000 new Ordinary Stock units of £1 each at £4.00 per unit, or £1,000,000 12 per cent Debentures secured against the company's freehold premises and its floating assets.

Brokers advise that either of these alternatives are likely to be taken up in full by investors.

Let us assume these other features in the case:

(a) Edward Droy and his immediate family own 60 per cent of the existing equities which carry one vote per unit. The Board of Directors is composed of him and his nominees.
(b) Another faction of the family own 25 per cent of the equities and is opposed to Edward.
(c) With the new capital the level of distributable profit is expected to reach £300,000 per annum (previously £100,000 per annum).
(d) The new equities will rank *pari passu* (on an equal footing) with the existing stock.

With these features in mind which of the alternatives should Edward Droy pursue? The test is essentially how much of the new inflow he can retain for himself and the existing equity owners. How much of the profit will belong to the existing equity owners if equities are issued?

$$\frac{\text{existing equities}}{\text{existing + new equities}} \times \text{profit} = \frac{£500,000}{£750,000} \times £300,000$$

If ordinary stocks are issued the existing equity owners stand to take £200,000 profit/dividends.

How much could they expect if debentures were issued instead?

	£
Profit	300,000
payment of 12 per cent p.a. to debenture-holders	
(12 per cent on £1,000,000)	120,000
remainder to existing equities	180,000

On this evidence it would be better to issue new ordinary stock -
there would be £20,000 more passing to the existing equity owners.
But that ignores the problem of keeping control in the hands of
Edward Droy. His percentage of the total voting power will fall to
40 per cent, i.e.

$$\frac{300,000}{750,000} \times 100$$

Even assuming the opposing faction in the family do not acquire any
of the new equities Edward Droy's control of the company has become
precarious. In these circumstances he may prefer to choose the 'less
profitable' option - especially when the difference is only marginal.

CAPITAL GEARING
The extent of fixed-interest borrowings has a magnifying effect on
the fluctuations of trading profits. The relationship between
equities on the one hand, and debenture and preference stocks on the
other, is described as the capital gearing of the company. The
general gearing factor can be obtained through the use of the formula

$$\frac{\text{total capital}}{\text{equity capital}} = \text{gearing ratio (to 1)}$$

Thus, in the case of a company with the following capital structure

£200,000 equities
£800,000 debentures

the capital gearing would be

$$\frac{1,000,000}{200,000} = 5 \text{ to } 1$$

This is an example of a highly geared capital structure. As a rough
guide a ratio of up to 1.5 to 1 could be regarded as low-geared.
Between 1.5 and 2.5 to 1 could be regarded as moderately geared and
anything over this would be highly geared.
    The effects of capital gearing can be gauged by a study of three
companies with differing capital structures. We can assume they are
otherwise identical and we will consider the effects of the different
gearing on the dividends and prices of ordinary stock in each of the
companies at six different levels of profit. For the purpose of the
calculations we shall assume that all profits are distributed. We

shall also assume that investors in equities such as these are looking for yields of 8 per cent - so that where they can obtain a dividend of 12 per cent, for example, they will pay £1.50 for a £1 ordinary stock unit ($£\frac{1\frac{1}{2}}{8} \times 100$).

Alpha Ltd

	£
Ordinary Stock (£1 units)	200,000
10% Preference Stock (£1 units)	800,000
Total stock	£1,000,000
Capital Gearing	5 to 1

	Level of profit (before payment of Preference Dividend)	*Available for Ordinary Dividend*	*Rate for Ordinary Dividend*	*Price of Ordinaries (based on expectation of 8% yield)*
	£	£		£
1.	80,000	nil	nil	nil
2.	100,000	20,000	10%	1.25
3.	120,000	40,000	20%	2.50
4.	140,000	60,000	30%	3.75
5.	160,000	80,000	40%	5.00
6.	180,000	100,000	50%	6.25

Beta Ltd

	£
Ordinary Stock (£1 units)	500,000
10% Debenture Stock (£1 units)	500,000
Total stock	£1,000,000
Capital Gearing	2 to 1

	Level of profit (before Debenture service)	*Available for Ordinary Dividend*	*Rate for Ordinary Dividend*	*Price of Ordinaries (based on expectation of 8% yield)*
	£	£		£
1.	80,000	30,000	6%	0.75
2.	100,000	50,000	10%	1.25
3.	120,000	70,000	14%	1.75
4.	140,000	90,000	18%	2.25
5.	160,000	110,000	22%	2.75
6.	180,000	130,000	26%	3.25

Gamma Ltd

		£
Ordinary Stock (£1 units)		1,000,000
Total stock		1,000,000
Capital Gearing		1 to 1

	Level of profit (no prior charges)	*Available for Ordinary Dividend*	*Rate for Ordinary Dividend*	*Price of Ordinaries (based on expectation of 8% yield)*
	£	£		£
1.	80,000	80,000	8%	1.00
2.	100,000	100,000	10%	1.25
3.	120,000	120,000	12%	1.50
4.	140,000	140,000	14%	1.75
5.	160,000	160,000	16%	2.00
6.	180,000	180,000	18%	2.25

These statistics are shown graphically in Figure 14.

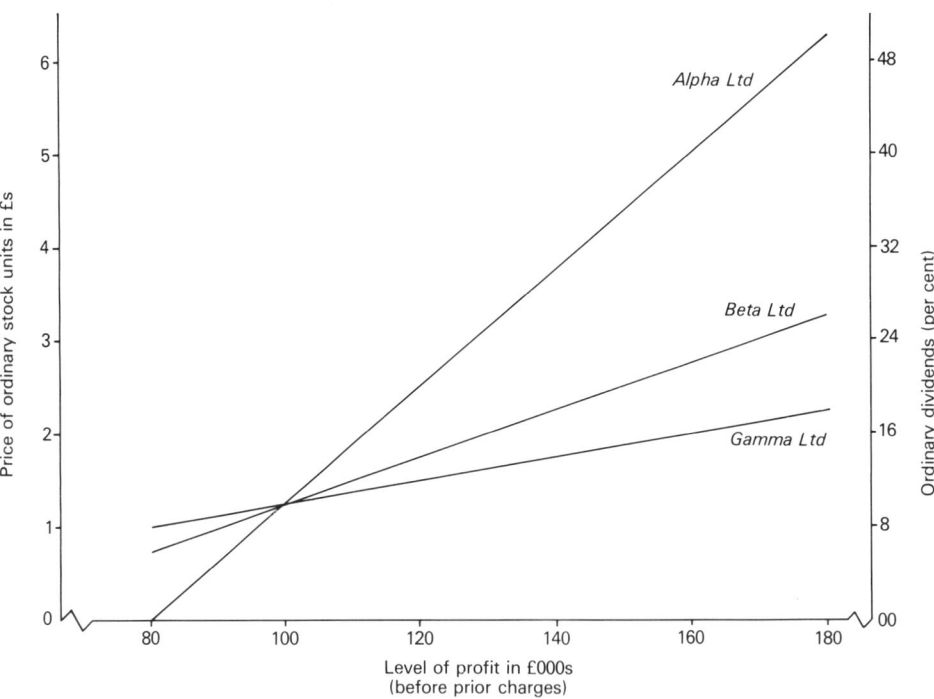

Figure 14 *Relationship between prices, dividend rates and profit levels for companies with different capital gearing*

In the highly geared company the variation of dividends (and there-fore of prices) is intensified with changes in the profit level. Thus, when profits increase from £100,000 to £140,000 (40 per cent), the increases in dividends and prices for the three companies are:

```
Alpha Ltd 200 per cent
Beta Ltd   80 per cent
Gamma Ltd  40 per cent
```

This intensification of fluctuations in highly geared companies means
that their equities are likely to be popular with speculators.
Consider the case of X who buys 100 ordinary stock units in Alpha Ltd
(for £125) at the same time as Y buys 100 ordinary stock units in
Gamma Ltd (for £125). Ignoring the costs of purchases and sales,
when both companies increase their profits by 40 per cent and X and
Y decide to sell their stocks, their personal profits will be

for X, £375 (the new price) less £125 (the cost) = £250; and
for Y, £175 (the new price) less £125 (the cost) = £50

Naturally the converse is true so that when there is a fall in
profits the reaction is magnified for the highly geared equities.
For example, where profits fall from £160,000 to £80,000, X's stock
will move from £5 towards a nil value, while Y's holding in Gamma Ltd
will drop in value - proportionately - from £2 to £1.

It does not follow that any company which has a highly geared
capital structure will have a highly volatile record of equity prices
and dividends. If such a company enjoys comparatively stable profits
this will tend to negative the effects of the high gearing. Similarly, a low-geared company may be operating in an industry where
fluctuating profits are the norm, and this will reflect in equity
prices and dividends in spite of the low gearing.

There are two particular types of company which tend to have
highly geared capital structures. As explained in Chapter 5,
investment trusts expand their operations by pledging existing
securities to purchase further equity stocks. And property companies
are in a similar situation except that they have property deeds
instead of share certificates to charge as security for fixed
interest loans.

Assignment

Your first task (for group work)
Here are some statements which can be made about the statistics
represented in Figure 14. Working in small groups, draw up a list
of six similar conclusions from the evidence available. Then compare
your lists with those of the other groups.

1. If an economic recession were forecast Alpha Ltd equity share
   prices would fall faster than those of Beta and Gamma - other
   things being equal.
2. When investing in highly geared equities it is increasingly
   important to buy when the share prices are at the bottom of the
   downswing.
3. If profits for Alpha Ltd fall from £160,000 to £120,000 the price
   of the shares will tend to be halved.

Your second task

Here are the capital structures of two companies:

	Etna Ltd		*Zeta Ltd*
1,600,000	Ordinary Shares of 25p each fully paid	£600,000	Ordinary Stock units of £1 each
250,000	6% Preference Shares of £1 each fully paid	£50,000	7½% Mortgage Debenture Stock
£550,000	Bank Loan (Long-term) currently at 14% p.a.		

Last year the trading profits were

Etna Ltd £200,000   Zeta Ltd £100,000

Assume that 50 per cent of all trading profits are distributed to the shareholders, the other 50 per cent being transferred to reserves. What effect would it have on ordinary dividends if trading profits fell by 12 per cent in both companies?

10 New Issues

When a company issues new securities the purpose is usually, but not invariably, to obtain additional capital. We have already looked at the types of stocks which might be issued. We have also considered the effects of different capital structures. In this chapter we are going to examine the methods by which the securities might be issued.

DIRECT ISSUE TO THE PUBLIC
If a company enjoys a sufficient reputation, it may be possible to advertise to the public directly for subscriptions. The company will consult with an issuing house to determine the type of security to be offered, the price to be asked, and the timing of the issue. The latter factor is not inconsequential. At times there are ample funds available for investment. At other times there is a dearth of funds. And the company could face problems if it transpires that there are other companies offering securities on more favourable terms during the same period. An issuing house will protect a company from making errors such as these, and will no doubt arrange for the necessary underwriting contracts.
   This method is likely to be expensive in that:

(a) A detailed prospectus will have to be prepared and published in the financial press.
(b) A large number of applications might be received, many of them not being allotted stocks, others receiving partial allotments. The cash received and returned will need to be controlled carefully at this time.
(c) Underwriting commission will be incurred. Under Section 53 of the Companies Act 1948 the commission must not exceed 10 per cent of the price at which the shares are issued.
(d) Fees will be required by the issuing house.
(e) If the minimum subscription set out in the prospectus is not received the company will have to return all the cash subscribed. The company's financial reputation will also suffer.

   These factors no doubt explain why this method is only used by the larger companies.

Companies Act 1980
Under Section 16 of the Act the minimum payable on application is 25 per cent of the nominal value of the shares plus the whole of any premium. Section 21 prohibits shares being allotted at a discount.

OFFER FOR SALE
An issuing house may acquire a block of shares from the company or its principal shareholders which are subsequently offered to the

public at a fixed price. The issuing house will normally make its profit by purchasing the shares at a lower price than that charged to the public. Alternatively, they may sell the shares at the same price as they were purchased, but charge the company a fee. Many companies make their ordinary shares available to the public for the first time through an Offer for Sale. A Stock Exchange quotation is usually obtained at the same time.

The public may have no previous knowledge of the company whose shares are being offered. They would probably lack confidence in the company but are reassured by the intervention of a reputable issuing house.

ISSUES BY TENDER

One of the problems for a company issuing new securities is to find a price at which demand and supply are broadly in balance. In order to avoid substantial oversubscription, which is expensive, and at the same time avoid an overoptimistic price, which could be disastrous, some companies choose to make an issue by tender. This is a form of auction. The public are told the minimum price at which the stocks or shares can be acquired, but they are invited to bid a higher price. Thus, if Zeta Ltd offered 3,000,000 ordinary shares of 25p at a minimum price of 100p - bidding to be for blocks of 100 shares - in steps of 10p - the response might be as follows:

Applications (in 000s)	*Price Bid*	
100	150p or better	
600	140p "	"
1200	130p "	"
2500	120p "	"
3000	110p "	"
5000	100p "	"

In this case the 'striking price' would be 110p and all applicants offering 110p or more would be allotted the new shares at this price.

There are two disadvantages in this method of floating stock. From the point of view of the private investor it will be difficult to assess the value of the securities and make a realistic bid. And from the company's point of view the inflow of funds will not be able to be gauged accurately in the initial stages.

PLACING

A company may find that it does not need to go to the public at large for the sale of new stocks and shares. If the company's broker or issuing house can find a sufficient number of clients to take up the securities the operation is described as a placing. The clients might include institutions such as insurance companies, investment trusts and pension funds. The ordinary investor will not be invited to subscribe but can purchase the securities in the normal way through his broker.

A placing is administratively cheaper than an offer for sale.

AN INTRODUCTION

The directors may seek a quotation for their securities in which case the Stock Exchange will require a sufficient allocation of stocks or

shares to jobbers before a quotation is granted. A common reason
for seeking a quotation is to avoid a situation where a principal
shareholder is likely to be deemed to be in control of the company
under Section 55 of the Finance Act 1940 in the event of his death.
In this case his holdings will be valued for death duty (Capital
Transfer Tax) 'by reference to the net value of the assets of the
company'. By contrast, if the shares are quoted they will be valued
at $\frac{1}{4}$ up, i.e. if the price quoted on the Stock Exchange is 10-12p
the shares will be valued for probate at $10\frac{1}{2}$p. The difference
between the two valuations can be considerable and with high rates
of death duty can make all the difference between keeping a company
in the control of the family and losing control to outsiders.

RIGHTS ISSUES
One of the most popular methods for a company to acquire funds
through the issue of stocks is by means of a Rights Issue. The
existing stockholders are sent a Provisional Allotment Letter (see
Figure 15) which offers them the new shares on favourable terms
pro rata with their existing holdings. A rights issue would operate
like this.

   Delta Ltd has the following capital structure:

   500,000 ordinary shares of £1 each fully paid (currently quoted
   on the Stock Exchange at 220p each)

   The directors wish to raise funds to the extent of £150,000 in
order to modernise the plant. They therefore send a provisional
allotment letter to their shareholders offering 1 new ordinary share
at 150p for every five shares held.

From the company's point of view
Because the shares are offered at a favourable price the company can
be sure of receiving the funds they require. If they have been too
generous with the terms it is only the existing equity owners who
will benefit. It is an inexpensive and effective method of raising
additional funds which is likely to prove acceptable to the shareholders - so long as proportionately large sums are not required.

From the shareholder's point of view
Consider the case of Mark Stone, who was holding 1000 ordinary shares
in Delta Ltd. He would have been invited to take up 200 of the new
ordinary shares at a price of 200 × 150p, i.e. £300. If he wishes
to acquire all the new shares to which he is entitled, all he needs
to do is to send a cheque for this sum together with the allotment
letter.
   If he only wants to take up part of the shares comprised in the
allotment letter he will send it back to the company registrar -
having signed the Form of Renunciation - and ask the company
registrar for what is called a 'Split Letter'. He may then sell the
rights of sufficient shares to enable him to take up the remainder.
   If he does not want to take up any of the new shares he may sign
the form of renunciation and give the allotment letter to his broker,
who will then sell the rights on his behalf.
   How much can Mark Stone expect to receive from any rights he wishes
to dispose of?

```
┌─────────────────────────────────────────────────────────────┐
│                 Provisional Allotment Letter                  │
│                      from Delta Ltd                           │
│                                                    Page One   │
│                                                               │
│  Holding of Ordinary Shares      Number of new Shares         │
│         of £1 each                    of £1 each      Amount payable │
│   in the name of Mark Stone      provisionally allotted  at 150p per share │
│                                                               │
│          1,000                        200                £350 │
│                                                               │
│  Dear Sir (or Madam),                                         │
│                                                               │
│          The Directors have provisionally allotted to you the number of new Ordinary Shares │
│  of £1 each set out above. The Shares have been allotted to the holders of existing Ordinary Shares on the │
│  basis of one new Ordinary Share for every five Ordinary Shares previously held. │
│          If you wish to take up the Ordinary Shares provisionally allotted to you, you must send an appropriate │
│  remittance for the amount shown above.                       │
│          If payment is not made by 15 January 198X this provisional allotment will be deemed to have been │
│  declined and will lapse.                                     │
│                    By Order of the Board of Directors,        │
│                         K. C. Green                           │
│                         Secretary.                            │
│                                                               │
│                    Form of Renunciation           Page Two   │
│                                                               │
│  To the Directors of                                          │
│      Delta Ltd                                                │
│                                                               │
│  I/We hereby renounce my/our right to the Shares comprised in the within-mentioned Allotment Letter in │
│  favour of the person named in the Registration Application Form. │
│                                                               │
│      Signatures of person(s)      .................................................... │
│      named on page One.                                       │
│                                                               │
│      All Joint Holders must sign.   .................................................... │
│                                                               │
│      In the case of a corporation   .................................................... │
│      its Common Seal must be                                  │
│      affixed.                                                 │
│                                                               │
│               Registration Application Form                   │
│                                                               │
│  This form is only completed where there has been a renunciation. It is used to identify the purchaser(s) │
│  so that the company can record the ownership of the shares.  │
│                                                               │
│  Christian Name(s)............................................................................................ │
│                                                               │
│  Surname.................................................Mr/Mrs/Miss/Title................................ │
│                                                               │
│  Address........................................................................................................ │
└─────────────────────────────────────────────────────────────┘
```

Figure 15 *Key features in a provisional allotment letter*

The stock market has assessed the value of the equity in Delta Ltd as 500,000 × £2.20, i.e. £1,100,000. With the new inflow of cash from the rights issue the amended value of the equity would be £1,100,000 + £150,000, i.e. £1,250,000. Divided between 500,000 old shares and 100,000 new shares (600,000 in total) the value of each share (ranking *pari passu*) would be £1,250,000/£600,000, i.e. approximately £2.08.

So if shares costing £1.50 each are worth £2.08 the value of the rights to each share must be around 58p. In practice the rights may go over 58p where the extra injection of cash is expected to benefit the company. You will recall that Delta Ltd wanted the cash to modernise their plant.

If Mark Stone sells all his rights he will receive a cheque for 200 × 58p less the broker's commission. If he decides to sell sufficient to take up the remainder, he will have to sell about 150 shares in order to be able to take up the other 50.

Pre-emption rights

Under Section 17 of the Companies Act 1980 a company proposing to issue equity shares of convertible debentures for cash must first offer them to existing shareholders in proportion to their existing holdings. These so-called 'pre-emption rights' are not given in respect of preference shares, equity shares issued for other than cash, or those relating to an employees' share scheme.

Section 18 of the Act allows these rights to be varied so long as the exclusions or modifications are covered in the Articles of Association or by Special Resolution.

The effect of this legislation is likely to be that Rights Issues will become an increasingly popular method for companies raising funds.

BONUS OR CAPITALISATION ISSUES

Over a period of years Delta Ltd might have been a very successful company. Substantial portions of trading profits might have been transferred to reserves which is what is called 'ploughing back profit' and is how most companies expand their operations. But consider what happens when there are very large reserves.

Balance-sheet of Delta Ltd

	£		£
Ordinary Shares of £1 each fully paid	500,000	Net Assets	2,000,000
General Reserves	1,500,000		
	£2,000,000		£2,000,000

If distributable profits on this capital of £2,000,000 were £400,000 (a 20 per cent return) the dividend would be £400,000/£500,000 × 100 = 80 per cent for the year. This could be considered an inflammatory rate of dividend where, for example, the company is attempting to resist employees' claims for wage increases. Of course such a rate of dividend could be justified, but the situation can be defused by formally converting the general reserves to ordinary shares. In Delta's case the Board would allot, say, 2 new ordinary shares (fully paid) for every one existing share held. In due course the shareholder would receive a share certificate for the additional holding. The ordinary dividend would be declared as $26\frac{2}{3}$ per cent (£400,000/£1,500,000 × 100) rather than 80 per cent.

After the entries were passed in the company's accounts the balance-sheet would read:

	£		£
Ordinary Shares of £1 each fully paid	1,500,000	Net Assets	2,000,000
General Reserves	500,000		
	£2,000,000		£2,000,000

There would be another advantage in capitalising reserves in that the quoted price per share would fall to about one-third of its previous price. This would tend to make the shares more attractive to the small investor.

ISSUES BY THE SMALLER COMPANIES

When a company is not large enough to warrant a quotation on the Stock Exchange it is unlikely that the public will be prepared to subscribe for stocks and shares. However, there are a number of specialist institutions which have been formed to aid the smaller company seeking expansion.

One of the most important of these institutions is Finance for Industry (FFI) with its major subsidiaries, the Industrial and Commercial Finance Corporation and the Finance Corporation for Industry. Finance for Industry is owned by the Bank of England (15 per cent) and the English and Scottish Clearing Banks (85 per cent). The nature of the group's contribution can be gauged from the following extracts from the ICFC booklets – *How We Can help Private Enterprise* – and *Briefing* for 1980-81.

> Our business is to provide the small to medium-sized company with money for expansion. It may be a new production line, a move to larger premises, additional working capital, or to develop export potential. Or any sound proposition requiring long-term funds from £5,000 to £2 million or more. It can be any business and in any part of Britain. . . .
> In a typical year 70% of our customers will require £100,000 or less. The diagram below [Figure 16] shows how we cover the needs of companies, both small and medium sized.

A Loans up to £50,000
B £50,000 to £100,000
C £100,000 to £250,000
D Over £250,000

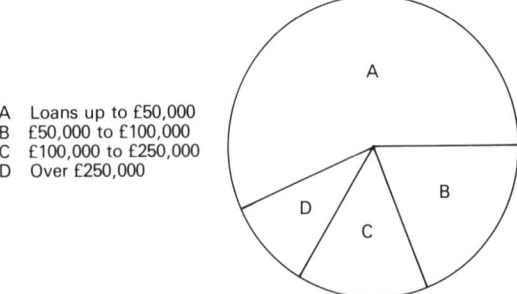

Figure 16

In 1980-81 ICFC has continued to make a major contribution to the risk financing of small businesses by agreeing 1,014 advances for £96.7m. . . . ICFC now has a total of £400m in 3,400 companies. . . . During the last three years ICFC has developed new solutions to management buy-outs. . . . Our funds have helped managers purchase the division or company they work for where they have demonstrated the skill to lead a growing company. Buy-outs often occur when a profitable division is threatened with closure by the parent group.

One of the more recently formed institutions designed to support the medium and smaller companies is Equity Capital for Industry (ECI). It was set up in 1976 with a capital of £40 million raised in the City, and will take equity stakes between £1 million and £3 million in suitable companies. After the injection of additional equity the company should be able to raise additional loan capital elsewhere.

Assignment

Case study (for group work where possible)
Hypothetico Ltd has an issued capital of £1 million ordinary stock in units of £1 each. The shares are currently quoted at £2.50 each on the Stock Exchange. The company has made a bonus (capitalisation) issue of one new share for every existing share held. This is immediately followed by a 1 for 8 rights issue of new £1 shares at par. What is the most likely price of the new shares when fully paid, on this evidence?

Your second task
Play the role of a bank manager whose customer, Miss Amelia Trelawney, has £1000 ordinary stock in Hypothetico and has just received documents from the company which she does not understand. Write a suitable letter to Miss Trelawney explaining the courses of action open to her. Be as helpful and as specific as you can be, on the evidence available.

11 Interpretation of Accounts

When one is assessing a company for investment purposes the most obvious source of data is the company accounts. These must be prepared in compliance with the Companies Acts of 1948 and 1967 which lay down minimum disclosure requirements. The Eighth Schedule of the 1948 Companies Act gives the detailed requirements for accounting procedures but the approach is epitomised in Section 149, viz.: 'Every balance sheet of a company shall give a true and fair view of the state of affairs of the company as at the end of its financial year, and every profit and loss account of a company shall give a true and fair view of the profit or loss of the company for the financial year.'

It would be easy to be lulled into a false sense of security by the mass of detailed provisions, supported and reinforced though they are by a highly competent accountancy profession, and a Stock Exchange whose Council is determined to protect its reputation with regard to the securities with which it deals. However, there are certain problems which are inherent in any attempt to evaluate a company's performance simply through an examination of its accounts because, *inter alia*:

(1) *The historic cost forms the main valuation base.* You might already have found out from personal experience that something like a cassette recorder purchased yesterday for £50 has dropped its value by half when you come to sell it second-hand a few weeks later. Conversely, businessmen often find that when they come to replace machinery which cost them, say, £10,000 a decade ago the cost of replacement has escalated to £30,000 or more. Any attempt to assess the 'true' value of assets in these circumstances is likely to prove difficult enough for the accountant let alone the lay investor who is attempting to interpret the accountant's assessment. Indeed it might be said that the accountant's problem in a large company is that he has too much detail to interpret meaningfully, while the problem for the lay investor is that he has too little comprehensible data.

(2) *It is difficult to assess and evaluate profit levels with accuracy, at least in the short run.* Share prices rise or fall in line with profits. Investors are very sensitive to fluctuations in profits. And yet profits are capable of manipulation - to an extent. Consider just a few examples:

(a) The company buys a computer costing £300,000. It is obviously necessary to calculate depreciation on this valuable asset. The depreciation will range over the life of the asset. But who is to say how long it will be before the computer becomes obsolete? It is not a question of accounting rules and procedures or of personal integrity. The effective life of the asset can only be estimated and this will determine the rate of depreciation to be used. If the rate turns out to have been too high profits will have been deflated, while if the life of the computer is overestimated the profits will have been inflated.

(b) An advertising campaign costing £500,000 commences in June and continues for the next six months. The benefits will presumably show up in a subsequent period. How should the advertising campaign be charged as between the two years' accounts? One can make rational estimates, but there is no 'right' and 'wrong'. So long as there are imperfections in the allocations there must be inaccuracies in the measurement of profits.

(c) An engineering company is spending millions of pounds on a long-term project to save energy. How is the work in progress to be valued in the accounts? Accounting conventions allow some allocation of overhead expenses to be included in the valuation. They also allow a proportion of the profit to be anticipated in the accounts. But the amounts are essentially at the discretion of the directors.

(3) *Group Accounts, which are required by law when a company owns subsidiaries, make an analysis more difficult.* It is an increasingly common situation to find a holding company with dozens of subsidiaries and sub-subsidiaries, many of them overseas. A glance at a selection of annual reports and accounts will demonstrate this tendency. The complexities in terms of accounting are enormous. Dennis Parkinson shows both sides of the coin - the purpose of group accounts - and, by implication, the dangers:

> If the requirement to produce group accounts was not present, it would be possible for unscrupulous owners and directors to fragment their groups to conceal the true position. Many possibilities could be introduced. Profits could be manipulated to make it appear that a main company was making a loss while another subsidiary took the profits to distribute them for personal gain. It is only when there are some overseas subsidiaries which would encourage trading difficulties if there was disclosure, or where the activities in the subsidiary are so different the resulting consolidation would be misleading, can exception be made. . . . What goes on inside, between the various companies does not affect the outsiders and so needs to be ignored in the final presentation of information. . . . (*Finance* (Blandford Press, 1979).)

The law encourages full disclosure and insists on the provision of auditors' certificates, qualified where the need arises, and also insists on suitably qualified auditors. The Stock Exchange and the accountancy profession make strenuous efforts to ensure that the appropriate accountancy conventions are applied by those whom they have power to influence. The standards of integrity are obviously very high in general but it would be unrealistic to assume that individuals in control of companies will never behave like politicians and hold back unpalatable truths.

(4) *It is difficult to assess the effects of inflation from an examination of the accounts.* Accounts can be misleading to the

extent that they fail to reflect the effects of inflation. Thus a balance-sheet may show net assets which appear to have appreciated during the course of a year, but far from making a profit the company may have made a 'real' loss after the effects of inflation are brought into account. And the problem is aggravated when the company is able to borrow funds which disguise the effects on the erosion of the company's 'real' assets.

The problem can be seen in a simple example. Consider a machine purchased for £10,000 ten years ago which is being written off (depreciated) at £1000 per annum. At the end of ten years a virtually identical machine is bought as a replacement at a cost of £30,000. On this evidence it could be argued that the asset should have been depreciated by an additional £2000 per annum but this would have reduced profits by this amount during the intervening period.

In an attempt to cope with this problem the UK and Irish accountancy bodies have introduced SSAP 16 (Statement of Standard Accounting Practice 16), which will apply to the accounts of all listed companies and large unquoted companies from 1 January 1980. Exceptions include:

(a) companies which have no stocks quoted on the Stock Exchange providing they satisfy at least two of the following three criteria:
   (i)   a turnover of less than £5 million per annum
   (ii) a balance-sheet total of less than £2.5 million according to the historical cost ('normal') accounts
   (iii) less than 250 employees
(b) wholly owned subsidiaries
(c) authorised insurers, property investment companies, investment trusts, unit trusts, charities, building societies and pension funds.

For the companies obliged to comply with SSAP 16 it will be necessary to produce current cost accounts (CCA). These will show adjustments for price changes on cost of sales, working capital and depreciation as well as an adjustment for gearing (related to the volume of business financed by borrowing).

Listed companies will be expected to show the current cost earnings per share based on the current profit attributable to equity shareholders (see page 87).

Pre-tax profits under the CCA system will generally be much lower than previously. Dividends may also be affected.

Having signposted some of the limitations of the annual reports and accounts we can now turn our attention to acknowledging their virtues and attempting to understand some of the analytical techniques available to interpret the information they provide.

The accounts provide us with:

(1) A financial record of the trading results of the company and the financial situation at a particular point of time.
(2) A facility to compare results over a period of time and to compare performances with other businesses.
(3) Data which allows us to draw projections of past figures and trends in a number of key areas.

(4) An opportunity to study the results critically with a view to discovering whether there are any apparent flaws in the financial structure of the business.

From what has been said so far it is clear that the analysis of published accounts is not likely to prove a fruitful pastime for the layman, but we shall now turn our attention to a comparatively straightforward set of accounts such as might be received by a shareholder:

Group Profit and Loss Account of Omega Ltd
for the year ended 30 June 1981

	1981 £000	1980 £000
Turnover	1,135,336	974,062
Trading profit	50,019	37,906
Share of profits of associated companies	495	491
	50,514	38,397
Interest payable (net)	7,150	7,090
Profit before taxation	43,364	31,307
Taxation	8,164	6,070
Profits after taxation	35,200	25,237
Attributable to outside shareholders' interests	265	402
	34,935	24,835
Extraordinary items	187	74
	35,122	24,909
Dividends	8,000	7,000
Profits retained	27,122	17,909

Balance Sheet of Omega Ltd at 30 June 1981

	1981 £000	1980 £000
Net Assets Employed		
Fixed assets	150,290	124,703
Goodwill	40,344	42,845
Investments	1,420	2,342
Current assets	250,372	222,674
Total assets	442,426	392,564
less Current liabilities	165,139	136,335
	277,287	256,229
Financed by		
Ordinary shares of £1 each	50,000	50,000
Reserves	180,584	159,765
	230,584	209,765
Outside shareholders' interest in subsidiaries	2,231	2,502
Loan capital	40,108	40,007
Deferred taxation	4,364	3,955
	277,287	256,229

The accounts would be accompanied by a series of notes explaining special features such as the extraordinary items included in the Group Profit and Loss Accounts.

A variety of analytic techniques can be applied to evaluate the company's shares and loan stocks and a number of companies are producing statistics like these in the annual statements for the information of their members.

ASSET VALUE PER SHARE
This is of interest to the equity owners and is derived from the formula

$$\frac{\text{Net assets (after repaying preference and debenture capital)}}{\text{Number of ordinary stock units}}$$

In the case of Omega the book value of the equities would be
arrived at thus:

	£000
Total assets	442,426
less Current liabilities and Goodwill	205,483
	236,943
less Other liabilities	46,703
	190,240

$$\frac{\text{Net assets}}{\text{No. of shares}} = \frac{£190,240,000}{50,000,000} = £3.80 \text{ per share}$$

EARNINGS PER SHARE
This is used to measure a company's performance in relation to the
equity.   The ratio is calculated by dividing the earnings available
to ordinary shareholders by the number of shares.   In Omega's case
the EPS would be

	£000
Profits retained	27,122
Dividends	8,000
Profit available to ordinary shareholders	35,122

$$\text{EPS} = \frac{£35,122,000}{50,000,000} = 70p$$

PRICE/EARNINGS RATIO
This ratio uses the EPS as a base.   The formula is

$$\frac{\text{Market price}}{\text{EPS}}$$

If we assume the market price of Omega ordinaries to be £2.10 per
share the Price/Earnings ratio would be

$$\frac{£2.10}{70p} = 3.0 = \text{P/E Ratio}$$

This result shows that the purchaser would have to wait three
years before the capital outlay was recouped from earnings, or
alternatively that the capital outlay would purchase three years
earnings.
   While one should be looking for a low price in relation to earnings
(i.e. a low P/E ratio), since this indicates 'value for money', this

is but one dimension, and the low price could be accounted for by the market assessment of the risk associated with the share.

The value of this ratio is that it gives the investor an opportunity to compare shares of a similar nature in terms of performance and price relationships.

COVER FOR ORDINARY DIVIDENDS

Two companies might each declare an ordinary dividend of 10 per cent, but the earnings from which the dividends are paid might be very different. The amount of times the dividend was covered by earnings is obviously of interest to an investor. The cover is calculated by the formula

$$\frac{\text{Maximum dividend which might have been paid}}{\text{Dividend paid}}$$

In the case of Omega the ordinary dividend was covered

$$\frac{£35,122,000}{£8,000,000} = 4.4 \text{ times for } 1980$$

PRIORITY PERCENTAGES/TIMES COVERED

Preference and loan stockholders also benefit by knowing to what extent their warrants are covered by earnings. The margin of safety can be expressed as times covered or as a percentage range within the total earnings for the year.

The Priority Percentage is calculated by relating the interest or dividend on a particular stock to the range of earnings, while the Times Covered represents an inversion of the result. Take a simplified example of a company with the following capital structure:

100,000 Ordinary shares of £1 each
100,000 10 per cent Preference shares of £1 each

The earnings for last year were £50,000, of which half were distributed. Thus £10,000 was paid to the preference shareholders and £15,000 to the ordinary shareholders. The dividend cover can be expressed in the following manner.

	Calculation		*Priority Percentage*	*Times Covered*
10% Preference shares	$\frac{£10,000}{£50,000}$	=	0-20%	5
Ordinary shares	$\frac{£10,000 + £15,000}{£50,000}$	=	20-50%	2
Reserves (remainder)			50-100%	

88

WORKING CAPITAL (OR CURRENT RATIO)

Modern businesses are run on credit. In a typical manufacturing
company raw materials are obtained months before they are paid for,
and finished goods are delivered months before payment is received
for them. If ever a company were unable to meet its commitments,
its creditors would lose confidence and credit facilities would be
withdrawn with catastrophic results. This is the reason for concern
about Working Capital (the margin between liquid assets and current
liabilities). More specifically the formula reads

$$\frac{\text{Stocks + Debtors + Cash}}{\text{Current liabilities}}$$

   If the ratio is less than 1 the company cannot meet its obligations,
so we are looking for a result in excess of unity.

QUICK RATIO (OR ACID TEST)

This is an alternative measure of solvency which eliminates the
stocks from the calculation, bearing in mind that stocks may be
difficult to dispose of. The formula then becomes

$$\frac{\text{Debtors + Cash (or near Cash)}}{\text{Current liabilities}}$$

THE FLOW OF FUNDS STATEMENT

This is a more sophisticated measure of solvency. Quoted (or listed)
companies are now required to produce a statement indicating for
their shareholders the flow of funds which has occurred within the
business during the course of the year. From this statement it will
be possible to derive certain basic aspects of the financing policy
of the company through the year. The description of this type of
statement varies from 'sources and application of funds' through to
'funds flow' and 'cash flow', but the purpose is the same, namely to
trace the major inflows and outflows of cash throughout the period
in question.

   The information is valuable in that it supplements the data
contained in the annual accounts. It gives the accounts another
dimension and concentrates attention on one of the most vital aspects
of any business. When a business is disgorging more cash than it is
generating it is heading towards insolvency and external borrowings
may be simply delaying the eventual outcome.

   While the profit and loss statement shows the details of revenue
and expenses during the year (or other period), and the balance-sheet
shows the company's assets and liabilities at a particular point of
time, the Flow of Funds Statement shows the sources from which the
inflows of cash have come and the destinations of the outflows. So
long as there are no complications the statement can be drawn up from
a comparison between the latest and the previous balance-sheets,
excluding adjustments such as depreciation, tax provisions and bonus
issues, each of which are 'paper entries' as distinct from movements
of cash.

   In the case of Omega the statement might take the following form:

	1981 £000	1980 £000
Source of funds		
Profit before taxation	43,364	31,307
Depreciation	15,008	13,938
Extraordinary items (gross)	276	112
Funds generated from operations	58,648	45,357
Funds from other sources		
Disposal of fixed assets and goodwill	2,850	1,860
Disposal of investments	1,305	–
Loan capital	101	84
	62,904	47,301
Application of funds		
Fixed assets	29,652	26,856
Acquisitions of fixed assets and goodwill of new subsidiaries	2,317	1,057
Investments	208	59
Decrease in outside shareholders' interest in subsidiaries	387	264
Increase in working capital:		
Increase in stock	20,642	5,270
Increase in debtors	21,543	18,889
Increase in creditors and provisions	(17,919)	(21,103)
	24,266	3,056
	56,830	31,292
Dividends paid	5,900	5,012
Taxation paid	4,865	4,345
	67,595	40,649

Movement:
Increase/Decrease in net liquid
  funds   (4,691)   6,652

RETURN ON CAPITAL EMPLOYED (ROCE)

It is fairly meaningless to talk about profits without knowing how much capital is being employed to produce the profits. This formula interrelates the two variables.

$$\frac{\text{Total earnings before tax}}{\text{Net assets}} \times 100$$

    Analysts differ on the items to be included in these reckonings but the debate is not important so long as the treatment is consistent over a period of time so that meaningful comparisons can be made.
    Results can also be compared with those found in similar companies and with averages for the particular industry. By this means comparative strengths and weaknesses can be identified. Where there is a group of companies, results can be compared between the different companies in the group and explanations for deviations can be sought.

TURNOVER TO CAPITAL EMPLOYED

Bearing in mind that all businesses should aim to maximise the gap between revenue and costs, sales need to be carefully monitored. Where additional capital is employed in the business, one ought to expect an appropriate volume of sales to be generated.

$$\frac{\text{Turnover (or Sales)}}{\text{Capital employed}}$$

TURNOVER TO WAGES

Since wage claims escalate costs, it is important to determine whether sales are increasing at the same pace as wages or whether the two variables are getting out of line with each other. If the ratio is rising the explanation could be either that proportionately more capital equipment is being used or that labour efficiency has been increased. If the ratio is falling it could mean that wage demands are outstripping earning capacity in which case there could be serious problems ahead for the company.

$$\frac{\text{Turnover (or Sales)}}{\text{Wages}}$$

WAGES TO NUMBER OF EMPLOYEES

It is useful to monitor average wages to see how the company's wages fluctuate over a period of time and as compared with those of other workforces. Wages are often the most vital element in the cost structure of a company's operations.

$$\frac{\text{Wages for the year}}{\text{Number of employees}}$$

DIFFERENT EXPECTATIONS

Before it is possible to interpret accounts purposefully it is necessary to consider the industry or industries in which the company is involved. The accounts of an insurance company will take a different form from the accounts of a manufacturing company and in assessing the companies' well-being we will be bearing different factors in mind. By the nature of their business, bankers need to inspire the confidence of their depositors as well as their share-holders. Their accounts should be seen to display a high degree of liquidity and their conservative approach will be expected to produce steady growth and stability, though high interest rates and inflation ought to enhance profits and (to a lesser extent) dividends.

Likewise when we look at the accounts of a mining company we need to adjust our frame of reference because the mines are wasting assets and every dividend should be seen as a part return of capital. And when we look at companies in the capital goods industries it has to be recognised that their performance is bound to be affected by the upturns and downturns of the business cycle and changes in business confidence generally.

Each type of industry has its own special features and any evaluation of performance needs to bear these differences in mind.

Extel Statistical Services

This company provides detailed data on individual companies for use by investors and investment analysts. Each company covered has an Annual Card and most of them have a News Card. The annual card contains basic facts about the company's formation and history, its main activities, its subsidiaries etc. It shows who is on the Board of Directors and summarises the latest annual report and accounts. The details given include:

    (i) the price records of shares
   (ii) the priority percentages
  (iii) earnings per share
   (iv) balance-sheets for recent years
    (v) source and application of funds statements
   (vi) the net asset (or book) value of the ordinary shares
  (vii) profit and loss accounts for up to ten years past
 (viii) the accounting procedures used to cope with inflation

A subscriber receives a complete set of cards which are updated daily. A news card is issued whenever something special is happening such as an acquisition or merger. Several different services are available. The British Company Service covers 3000 companies listed on the British and Irish Stock Exchanges, while the Unquoted Companies Service offers data on 2000 of the larger unquoted companies. There are also services for Australian companies and other specialist services.

Assignment

Working in small groups calculate, from the data below, (a) the Priority Percentages, (b) Earnings per Ordinary Stock unit and (c) the Price/Earnings Ratio.

	Athena PLC	*Spartacus PLC*	*Zeus PLC*
Ordinary Stock	£150,000	£200,000	£300,000
10% Preference Stock	£100,000	£50,000	£50,000
5% Debenture Stock	£100,000	£100,000	–
Ordinary Dividend (gross)	15%	15%	15%
Earnings available for debenture service and distribution as dividends	£50,000	£50,000	£50,000
Present Ordinary Stock, price per £1 unit	£1.10	£1.20	par

(d) Consider the evidence jointly and decide

(i) Which of the preference stocks would you prefer, and why?
(ii) Which of the ordinary stocks would you prefer, and why?

Did each of the small groups reach the same conclusions?

Written work
Write a report to Mr Gordon Wright, an influential client, who is asking for advice. He is considering investing a substantial sum in one of these companies but wants to know the results of your analysis, on the evidence here, before making up his mind.

12 Shareholders' Rights

When a person buys ordinary or preference shares in a company he/she becomes a member of the company and acquires certain rights. The details of those rights vary from company to company and from share to share. Nevertheless certain basic rights attach to shareholdings generally, and a shareholder is entitled *inter alia:*

1. To a dividend if a dividend is declared on the class of shares held.
2. To vote at the meeting of members unless the shares do not carry voting rights.
3. To receive an appropriate portion of the capital on distribution of the assets in the event of a winding up.

In addition there is a battery of what might be described as ancillary rights, the shareholder's entitlements being

4. To receive a notice of general meetings, unless the articles provide otherwise. A typical notice convening an Annual General Meeting is shown in Figure 17.
5. To receive a copy of the Memorandum and Articles of Association on request.
6. To receive a copy of every balance-sheet with documents annexed prior to their being laid before a general meeting.
7. To inspect and/or receive copies of the minutes of all general meetings - on request.
8. To inspect copies of any of the directors' contracts of service with the company.
9. To inspect free of charge the various registers maintained by the company.
10. To requisition an Extraordinary General Meeting under Section 132 of the Companies Act 1948. The directors must call such a meeting if requisitioned by the holders of not less than *one-tenth* of such of the paid-up capital of the company as carries the right to vote at general meetings. If the meeting is not convened within 21 days the requisitionists or any of them representing half their total voting rights may themselves convene such a meeting.
11. Under the general law the wishes of the majority of members normally prevail over the minority (*Foss* v. *Harbottle* (1843)), but under Section 222 of the Companies Act 1948 an oppressed minority shareholder has a right to petition the Court for a winding up of the company where there is inequity or injustice.
12. Any one member of an oppressed minority may petition the Court, seeking a remedy other than the winding up of the company, where the affairs of the company are being conducted in a manner oppressive to some part of the members (Section 210 of the Companies Act 1948).

Notice of Annual General Meeting

Notice is hereby given that the eighty-seventh Annual General Meeting of Fantasia Fashions Limited will be held at the Confederation of British Industry, Council Chamber, 21, Tothill Street, London SW1 on Tuesday 25 November 1980 at 11.30 a.m.

1. To receive and consider the statement of accounts and the reports of the Directors and Auditors thereon and to declare a dividend.

2. To elect Directors.

3. To authorise the Directors to fix the remuneration of the Auditors.

4. To transact any other business that may be transacted at an Annual General Meeting.

By Order of the Board
G. G. Carruthers
Secretary

NOTES

1. Only holders of Ordinary shares are entitled to attend or be represented at the meeting. A member entitled to attend and vote may appoint one or more proxies to attend and vote instead of him. A proxy need not be a member.

2. No Director has a service contract which does not expire, or which is not determinable by the Company without payment of compensation, within one year.

3. Warrants will be posted on 2 December if the proposed dividend is approved.

Registered Office:
Hambledon House
London W6

31 October 1980

A PROXY CARD IS ENCLOSED FOR HOLDERS OF ORDINARY SHARES

Figure 17 *Notice of Annual General Meeting*

13. *Prima facie*, shares rank *pari passu* both as regards *dividend* and *capital*, but the detailed entitlements will normally be spelt out in the Memorandum and Articles of Association or in the terms of issue.

14. Class meetings have to be held whenever required by the Companies Acts, the Memorandum and Articles, or the terms of issue. The most frequent case in which class meetings are required arises when it is proposed to alter, vary or affect the rights of a particular class of shares, e.g. Table A requires 'the consent in writing of the holders of three-fourths of the issued shares of that class' before rights attached to any class of share can be varied.

RESOLUTIONS

A Resolution is the normal means by which the members of a company reach a formal decision. A resolution can only be passed at a meeting which has been duly convened in accordance with the company's articles, and is duly constituted with the requisite quorum. Upon the resolution being proposed and seconded and put to the meeting, the persons entitled to vote do so - in the first place by a show of hands. They raise a hand either to show they are 'in favour' of the resolution, or 'against' - when the question is put by the chairman. Upon a show of hands only persons present can vote and not proxies, unless the articles provide otherwise.

According to Section 136 of the Companies Act 1948, 'Any member of a company entitled to attend and vote at a meeting of the company shall be entitled to appoint another person (whether a member or not) as his proxy to attend and vote instead of him . . . but a proxy shall not be entitled to vote except on a poll. The term 'proxy' then is used to describe the person appointed to vote on the member's behalf. But it is also used to describe the document which appoints the substitute (see Figure 18). The Stock Exchange encourages the

---

For use by Ordinary Shareholders only

Fantasia Fashions Limited

I/We (Block capitals please) ....

of...

a member/members of the above-named Company hereby appoint Sir Wilfred Mack* or, failing him, the duly appointed chairman of the meeting, as my/our proxy to vote for me/us on my/our behalf at the Annual General Meeting of the Company to be held at 11.30 a.m. on Tuesday 25 November 1980 and at every adjournment thereof.

Dated...1980   Signature..

Please indicate with ticks in the spaces below how you wish your votes to be cast. If no indication is given, your proxy will vote for or against each resolution or abstain as he thinks fit.

Resolutions	For	Against
1. Receiving the reports of the Directors and Auditors and declaring a dividend.		
2. Re-electing as Directors: Mr James Melhuish		
Mr Harold Brinkman		
3. Reappointing Messrs Haslett, Taylor & Co. as Auditors and allowing the Directors to fix their remuneration.		

Notes

1. If any other proxy is preferred, strike out the name* inserted above, add the name of the proxy you wish to appoint and initial the alteration.

2. If the appointer is a corporation, this form must be under its common seal or under the hand of some officer or attorney duly authorised in writing.

3. The signature of any one of the joint holders will be sufficient, but the names of all the joint holders should be stated.

4. To be valid this form must reach the Registrars of the company at the address given overleaf by 11.30 a.m. on 24 November 1980.

Figure 18 *A typical proxy*

use of two-way proxies which give the delegating member the option
to instruct his proxy to vote 'for' or 'against' the resolution.
  Before, on, or immediately after the chairman's declaration, a
poll may be demanded, in the manner and subject to the limitations
provided under the articles. The difference between a 'show of
hands' and a 'poll' is that in the latter

(a) members have voting power related to the numbers of voting
    shares they hold.
(b) proxies may be used.
(c) share registers will be required to confirm holdings.

Ordinary resolutions
Apart from any contrary provisions in the 1948 Companies Act or in
its Memorandum or Articles of Association, the company in general
meeting makes decisions by means of Ordinary Resolutions. These are
resolutions which require a simple majority of the persons entitled
to vote doing so affirmatively, either in person or through their
proxy.

Extraordinary resolutions
An Extraordinary Resolution is a resolution which has been passed by
a majority of not less than three-quarters of the voting members.
The resolution, in the form in which it is passed, should be set out
in the notice convening the meeting. If it is to be proposed at an
annual general meeting, not less than twenty-one clear days notice
is required, but if it is to be proposed at an extraordinary general
meeting, fourteen clear days notice is required - unless a Special
Resolution is also proposed. In the latter case twenty-one clear
days notice is required. The extraordinary resolution is most
commonly used on the winding up of a company.

Special resolutions
A Special Resolution requires the same majority as an extraordinary
resolution (viz. three-quarters) and, in addition, notice must have
been given of the intention to propose it as a special resolution.
Twenty-one clear days notice is required. It is by the use of
special resolutions that a company is empowered to take a wide range
of important decisions such as

(a) amending its Objects Clause so as to allow new business to be
    undertaken,
(b) altering its articles, or
(c) reducing its capital.

THE ANNUAL GENERAL MEETING
The board of directors exercise complete control over the day-to-day
running of the company. It is they who appoint the senior executives,
select appropriate targets for the company, and choose the *modus
operandi*. They even select their own nominees for appointment to
the board and determine their own remuneration. But once every year
they are legally obliged to account for their stewardship and the
ultimate 'sovereignty' rests with the shareholders. If the shareholders are sufficiently peeved at the director's performance - and
can muster a sufficient number of votes between them - they will be

able to oust the existing board. However, this is easier said than done because

(i) the shareholdings in most public companies are widely diffused with the result that opposition to the board is difficult to muster,
(ii) many of the private investors with stakes in the company are comparatively unversed in the intricacies of business finance,
(iii) much of the data which would be required to make a reasoned assessment of the board's performance is unavailable to the shareholders, and
(iv) by the time the shareholders have evidence of a poor performance it is often too late to take any effective action.

Bearing in mind the strictly limited powers of the average shareholder the Annual General Meeting's significance becomes apparent. It is the occasion when the board of directors have to ensure that the shareholders are at the very least placated - and more positively that the shareholders are both enlightened and satisfied. To this end the annual report and accounts are instrumental in conveying selected information to the members of the company. The ordinary business of an annual general meeting depends upon the articles but according to Table A it should consist of

(a) the declaration of a dividend,
(b) consideration of the accounts and the report of the directors and auditors,
(c) the election of directors and auditors, and
(d) the fixing of the auditors' remuneration.

THE AUDITORS
The Auditors are the watchdogs for the shareholders and the Companies Acts recognise the importance of their role. The 1948 Act established their basic role, but it is significant that both the 1967 and 1976 Acts have set out to increase substantially the powers of the auditors. Section 14 of the Companies Act 1967 gives the auditor wide investigatory powers and allows him to qualify his report or even refuse to certify the accounts. And much of the Companies Act 1976 strengthens the hands of the auditors. For example:

S.15: An auditor who has been removed from office has a right to be heard at any meeting which he would otherwise have been able to attend.
S.16: An auditor's resignation must be notified to the Registrar of Joint Stock Companies, and the members must be informed of the circumstances if the auditor thinks this is warranted.
S.17: A resigning auditor can also call on the directors to convene an extraordinary general meeting.

REDUCTION OF CAPITAL
In certain circumstances a company may wish to reduce its capital, but this can only be done with the sanction of the Court. There are two basic explanations for a reduction. There may be a surplus of assets which cannot be effectively employed within the company. This situation could arise where a company has sold off a substantial portion of its assets. A second explanation is that the company has

lost a substantial portion of its assets through deficits on the profit and loss accounts. The object here is to enable the accounts to present a realistic picture of the company's financial position. The role of the Court is to ensure that the company's creditors are not jeopardised in such an operation. The procedure for reducing capital is set out in Section 66 of the Companies Act 1948.

ALTERATIONS IN SHAREHOLDERS' RIGHTS

The directors of a company may decide that some form of capital reconstruction is required. They may wish to

1. Issue new shares not provided for in the Articles of Association and which will rank *pari passu* or ahead of existing shares.
2. Reduce the degree of the company's capital gearing, or otherwise improve the capital structure.
3. Modify the rights of preference shareholders as part of a scheme to write down capital.

Wherever the rights of any class of shareholders are to be revised, the changes have to be approved by postal ballot or at a separate meeting by three-fourths in value of the particular class of shareholders whose rights are affected (Section 206, Companies Act 1948). The approval of the Court is required but this will not normally be withheld unless there has been an irregularity in the proceedings.

Assignment

You are invited to play the role of a group of preference shareholders who have been summoned to an Extraordinary General Meeting of Theseus Marine Equipment Ltd to consider a Special Resolution put forward by the directors in the following terms:

'The holders of the existing 8 per cent Cumulative Preference Shares of £1 each fully paid, accept in exchange one new Ordinary Share of 50p fully paid for each Preference Share held, such new Ordinary Shares to rank *pari passu* with the existing Ordinary Shares for all purposes including dividend distributions, voting rights, and distribution of surplus assets on dissolution.'

Available data

1. The profits available for distribution over the past five years have averaged £80,000 but the directors transfer the bulk of these funds (50-100 per cent) to general reserve as a matter of policy. The level of profits is unlikely to change in the foreseeable future according to the chairman's last report.
2. There have been no ordinary dividends declared during the past five years. The price of the ordinaries on the Stock Exchange has been static at 15-20p for the past two years.
3. The preference dividends have been paid in full until two years ago. Since then they have not been paid. The price of the preference shares on the Stock Exchange has been static at 10-20p over the past two years.
4. The Articles of Association specify that preference shareholders rank before ordinary shareholders in the event of a distribution of assets in a dissolution. The Articles also specify that the ordinary shares carry one vote each and that the preference shares do not carry voting power.

5. The latest balance-sheet (as at 31 December last) in abbreviated form reads:

	This year (£000)	Last year (£000)
Use of Capital		
Fixed Assets	1000	1000
Net Current Assets	2000	1950
	£3000	£2950
Source of Capital		
Shares (Authorised and Issued)		
Ordinary (50p each)	1000	1000
Preference (£1 each)	500	500
General Reserves	1250	1200
10% Debentures	250	250
	£3000	£3000

Your task

Appoint a chairman and conduct the meeting on as formal a basis as possible. Vote on the resolution and assume that each member present holds 40,000 preference shares and that the chairman holds proxies for absent preference shareholders as follows:

    For the Resolution   100,000 shares
    Against the Resolution   20,000 shares

13 Takeovers and Amalgamations

The takeover is one of the more dramatic events in business. The direct result of a takeover is that the directors who have been the supreme decision-making body in the company - possibly over a long period of time - find their powers taken over by outside interests. The effects can be widespread. It is not only the directors who are at risk. Senior executives and even rank-and-file workers may find their life-styles threatened by a new board of directors who have acquired the authority to change the direction of the company, if they so wish. The owners of the company's equity stocks will certainly not escape the effects of the takeover operation. They will no doubt find the prices of their securities climbing even before the bid is announced. They will receive attractive offers for their stocks but will probably be told by the existing board that their stocks are even more valuable than the offer suggests. The equity owners might also find that the value of their holding falls sharply if the takeover bid fails and the bidder's interest wanes, though their eyes will have been opened as to the 'true value' of their securities.

The takeover situation arises out of two salient facts:

1. Whoever owns a majority (50 per cent plus) of the votes attaching to stocks and shares, is able to control the election of directors, and the directors determine the company's objectives and policies.
2. In large public companies, while directors are usually required to hold a minimum number of stocks or shares, in most cases the board between them exercise only a minority of the voting power.

A simple case study might be used at this point to explain the mechanics of a typical takeover bid.

SQUIRES FAMILY HOLIDAYS LTD
This company operates from six different sites along the south coast of England. It offers holidays in individual chalets (mainly timber) with communal catering and entertainment. The company has been in business since 1946 when the founder, Jim Squires, bought his first seaside site and built a holiday camp to cater for homecoming troops and their families. Jim has now retired as chairman and managing director and his son Colin has taken over from him. The essential financial data is as follows:

Epitomised Balance-Sheet as at 31 May last

Liabilities	£m.	*Assets*	£m.
Ordinary Stock (25p units)	1.5	Land and Buildings	2.5
General Reserves	1.5	Net Current Assets	0.5
	£3.0		£3.0

Results over the past five years:

Trading profits have averaged £800,000 (last year the figure
topped £1 million)
Ordinary dividends: 20 per cent for four years - last year
25 per cent
Price of ordinaries on the Stock Exchange has varied between
30p and 40p per unit but has risen to 50p since announcement of
record profits.

Among those looking with interest at the fortunes of the Squires
company is Mark Wyvern, Chairman of Goodlife Estates Ltd. His
company has developed a new style of living module for people who
have retired. The modules are interlocked in a variety of ways to
form panoramic landscapes. The basic problem is that they require
fairly large sites on which to be built. Mark has successfully
built and disposed of a number of sites in Spain and he is now
turning his attention to England. He would like to acquire any or
all of the Squires holiday camps. In his view the land would fetch
£10 million in all in the open market, but there was no need to make
a direct offer. The land could be acquired more surreptitiously -
and cheaply.

Mark notes the price of the Squires Ordinaries on the Stock
Exchange. If he were able to purchase the whole of these at the
current price, he would be able to acquire the land for £3 million.
He decides to make a takeover bid for the Squires company.

Stage One

Mark Wyvern begins to buy ordinary stock of Squires Family Holidays
Ltd through his stockbroker. He buys in three different names so as
to allay suspicion, viz. Goodlife Estates Ltd, a nominee, and his
own name. The orders are small enough to avoid pushing up the prices,
but over a period of time they mount up until approximately 30 per
cent of the Squires equity stock is in Mark Wyvern's hands.

Stage Two

Goodlife Estates Ltd make a formal offer to the remaining owners of
Squires equity on the following terms:

For each four Squires Family Holidays Ltd Ordinary Stock units of
25p Goodlife Estates Ltd *offer* one new ordinary share of 25p in
Goodlife Estates Ltd presently standing at 60p on the Stock Exchange
plus £2.50 cash.

Colin Squires, who owns 25 per cent of the Squires equity stock, is
also offered a seat on the board of directors of Goodlife Estates.

Stage Three

The offer is accepted by the Squires equity owners and Mark Wyvern's
company acquire the land they require for development at around £4.2
million made up as follows:

	£m.
1.8 million units acquired at 50p each (Stage One), cost	0.9
4.2 million units acquired at $\frac{60}{4}$p + $\frac{250}{4}$p = 77½p, each cost	3.3
	£4.2

Whether the deal was good from the Squires stockholders' point of view is debatable, but units which were worth 50p each before the takeover bid finally fetched the equivalent of 77½p, which represents a capital appreciation of over 50 per cent.

Squires Family Holidays Ltd has now become a fully-owned subsidiary of Goodlife Estates Ltd and the latter will appoint directors as and when required. They may decide to wind up the Squires company or, more likely, in the circumstances given here, let the holiday business continue but gradually close down the sites as they are required for development.

When the shares of another company are acquired in this fashion it is not uncommon for the bidding company to offer a mixture of cash and its own securities in exchange. This is particularly true where the amounts involved are large, but the proportions of cash and securities in the total mix have been surprisingly similar over a period of years (see Figure 19).

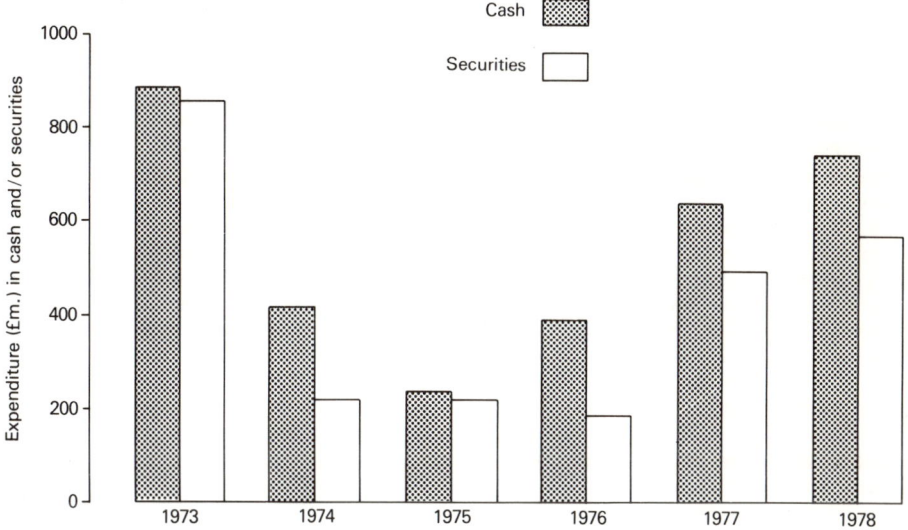

Figure 19 *Acquisitions and mergers of companies within the United Kingdom, 1973-8: total expenditure as between cash and securities*
Source: Central Statistical Office, *Financial Statistics* (Dec 1979).

Dissenting shareholders
In the Squires case study we conveniently assumed that all the equity owners accepted Goodlife's offer, but in a real-life situation more resistance can be expected. While some will be happy to take a windfall profit without asking too many questions, others will be more demanding. However, under Section 209 of the Companies Act 1948, where 90 per cent by value of the holders of shares subject to an offer accept it within four months, the bidding company may within a further two months acquire the remaining shares compulsorily. In

calculating the 90 per cent any holdings previously acquired by the bidding company have to be excluded. Thus in the Squires case study the 90 per cent would be related to the 4.2 million stock units under offer and not the 6.0 million in total.

THE CITY CODE ON TAKEOVERS

When a takeover bid develops share prices are likely to rise sharply and fortunes can be made by anyone who has 'inside information'. The directors in the company which is being bid for may be approached before their shareholders receive notice of the offer. Of course they are in a position of trust and must put the share-holders' interests first, but there have been occasions when both companies and individuals have behaved reprehensibly and it is to cope with this sort of situation that leading institutions in the city of London published the *City Code on Takeovers and Mergers*. A permanent Takeover Panel has been appointed to implement the Code. Among the rules are the following:

1. All shareholders of the company being bid for (called the offeree company) must be treated similarly - no favourable treatment being accorded to influential individuals or groups.
2. Shareholders in the offeree company must be given sufficient evidence, facts and opinions on which to judge the issues.
3. Any action taken to frustrate the bid by the offeree company's directors must be formally approved by the shareholders in general meeting.
4. All documents must be lodged with the Panel secretariat contemporaneously with dispatch or announcement.
5. When an offer is made to acquire a controlling interest, accep-tance cannot be made unconditional unless the offeror company (making the bid) has acquired or agreed to acquire more than the 50 per cent of shares which would give it control.
6. If an offeror company decides not to proceed with a bid which has been formally made, an explanation is required by the Panel.

The weakness of the Code is that it lacks the force of law, but the Stock Exchange will withhold quotation from any new securities emerging from the operation and the Panel can issue a public repri-mand and ask for sanctions from any association of which the offender is a member. The Panel might also refer the case to the Department of Trade where action under the Prevention of Fraud (Investments) Act 1958 is called for.

The Companies Act 1976

Section 26 of this Act endeavours to regulate takeover bids involving companies on the Stock Exchange lists. It requires that anyone acquiring 5 per cent or more of the voting shares must notify the company in writing within a period of five days. This provision makes it more difficult to 'warehouse' shares by distributing them among a number of holders acting in collusion.

Section 27 reinforces this regulation by giving the company a statutory right to demand information from a stockholder as to the beneficial ownership of any shares standing in his name. This allows the company to make formal inquiries if it has suspicions that a particular holding is being used in connection with a takeover bid.

Dealings by insiders

In any company there are individuals, such as directors, who have confidential information. There are times when the knowledge they have could be turned to their own advantage by dealing in the company's shares in an appropriate fashion - selling prior to the announcement of dramatic losses - or buying shares in the company knowing that a favourable takeover bid is about to be made. *Inter alia*, the Companies Act 1980 attempts to protect investors whose interests might otherwise be abused in this situation. By Section 68 such an 'insider' is prohibited from dealing in the securities of the company if he has information which is 'unpublished and price-sensitive' including information relating to a takeover. The maximum penalty is set at imprisonment for two years or an unlimited fine.

REASONS FOR TAKEOVERS AND AMALGAMATIONS

A company may acquire a stake in another company for a variety of reasons. Among the most common explanations for a takeover or an amalgamation (or merger) are the following:

(a) *Undervaluation of assets*

When there is a high level of inflation land and buildings particularly can easily become undervalued in the books of the company. We saw in Chapter 11 how investors might judge a company's performance by the return on capital employed. But what appears to be a healthy return can be transformed when the assets are revalued realistically. A company which takes over another may hope to use the assets more efficiently within the framework of its own business.

(b) *Asset stripping*

Having acquired control the new board may have in mind the sale of the company's assets, the taking of the profit, and the winding up of the company.

(c) *A conservative dividend policy*

While adequate transfers to reserve and dividend restraint safeguard cash flows and liquidity ratios, the effect may be to depress the price of the company's equity on the Stock Exchange, and this facilitates a takeover.

(d) *Resurrection of an ailing company*

Takeovers are usually associated with prosperous businesses but occasionally a company in the doldrums will actively seek a sponsoring company to take it over and provide desperately needed funds.

(e) *Economies of scale*

Many economies of scale can be achieved by companies combining resources. For example, advertising expenses and research costs can be spread over a larger number of units. If unit costs can be reduced the scope for profits will be increased.

(f) *Elimination of competition*

A smaller and yet vigorous competitor may be eroding a company's share of the market. A takeover can eliminate the competition or absorb the competing company and benefit from its successes. If the takeover or amalgamation reduces competition within a particular industry below an acceptable level, the Monopolies Commission may take appropriate action.

(g) *Securing supplies*
This involves what economists call 'vertical integration'. A company can ensure for itself an adequate supply of comparatively cheap raw materials - industrial disputes apart - by acquiring a controlling interest in an appropriate company.

(h) *Securing markets*
Another example of vertical integration. For example, a shoe manu-facturing company may acquire retail outlets by acquiring control of a company with a chain of shoe shops.

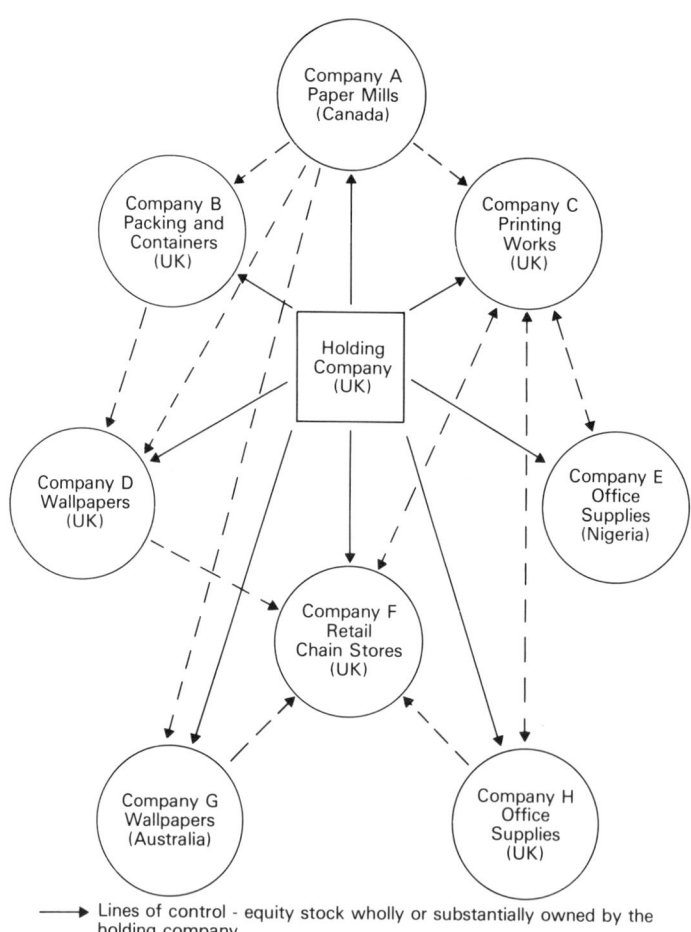

Figure 20 *An example of a multinational group of companies*

In both (g) and (h) the objectives might be achieved through the
use of interlocking directorates or the formation of new companies
rather than by takeover or amalgamation. Supplies and markets are
also commonly secured by incursion into overseas territories.
Foreign companies are acquired wholly or partly. Overseas subsidiaries are set up. The whole operation becomes international (see
Figure 20).

Assignment
Here is a letter received by a bank manager from one of his wealthy
elderly customers. Draft a formal reply to the letter for him.

White Lodge
Faversham
13th January 198X

The Manager
Midchester Bank Ltd
Faversham

Dear Sir,
You will recall that I recently purchased 10,000 ordinary shares in
Xanthu Products and Sparta Holdings are now making a takeover bid
for the company. They are offering Non-voting A Ordinaries in part
payment. I am concerned that the shares do not carry votes and
would welcome your opinion. I have never voted at a meeting yet,
either in person or by proxy, but I seem to remember your predecessor
mentioning that non-voting shares had some distinct drawbacks.

Yours sincerely,
Charles Dobing

14 The London Stock Exchange

The London Stock Exchange dates back to the late seventeenth century. From the beginning there have been two separate strands in the dealings, the stocks of the government and the securities of various companies. Borrowings by the Crown were evidenced by means of tallies or wooden sticks with notches to show the amount of the sum lent by the holder. In 1694 a syndicate of merchants lent the government - as distinct from the Crown now - £1.2 million in perpetuity in return for interest at 8 per cent per annum and the right to do banking business and issue their own notes. This was the birth of the National Debt.

The earliest example of a permanent joint-stock company was the Russia Company, formed in 1553. The largest and most famous of the era was the East India Company, which received its Royal Charter in 1600. Early trading in the shares of these and other companies took place on a private basis, but during the last decade of the seventeenth century an organised market began to develop in both government and company stocks. By the turn of the century the stockbrokers, who arranged purchases and sales of stocks on behalf of their clients and themselves, were frequenting the coffee houses in Change Alley, particularly Jonathan's and Garroway's. By 1802 the first Stock Exchange was built - in Capel Court. It is interesting to note that the term 'Waiters' is still used in referring to Stock Exchange staff acting as messengers, etc., on the floor of the Stock Exchange.

With the advent of the Industrial Revolution came the need for a steady influx of capital and the spate of legislation in the middle of the nineteenth century ensured that there was an increasing variety of company shares in which to trade. The Joint Stock Companies Act of 1844 provided for the formation of companies by means of registration with the Registrar of Companies, and the Limited Liability Act of 1855 enabled registered companies to limit the liability of their members to the nominal value of their shares. This encouraged a wide range of investors to put up stakes in the ever-growing numbers of joint-stock companies. The effect can be gleaned from the statistics for company registrations between 1853 and 1913:

1853	1865	1883	1897	1913
339	900	1416	4750	6900

The scale of present-day business on the Stock Exchange can be gauged by the following statistics (see also Figure 21):

Stock Exchange Transactions (1978)

	Turnover £m.	*Transactions* (000s)
British government securities	103,678	751
Irish government securities	9,672	60
Local authority securities	4,247	99
Overseas government, provincial and municipal securities	273	24
Fixed interest, preference, and preferred ordinary shares	1,684	426
Ordinary shares	19,216	4,130
	138,767	5,489

Source: Central Statistical Office, *Financial Statistics* (HMSO, Dec 1979).

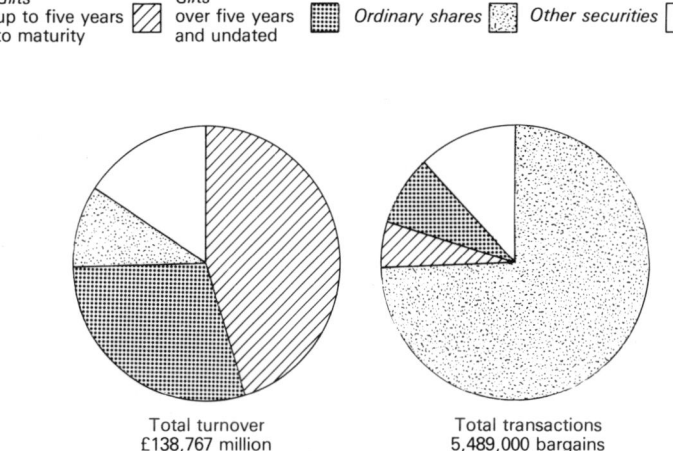

Gilts up to five years to maturity ▨ Gilts over five years and undated ▦ Ordinary shares ▩ Other securities ☐

Total turnover
£138,767 million

Total transactions
5,489,000 bargains

252 business days

Figure 21 *Stock Exchange transactions 1978: analysis by type of security*
Source: Central Statistical Office, *Financial Statistics* (Dec 1979).

The extent of the trade in Irish government securities is explained by the fact that the British and Irish Stock Exchanges amalgamated in 1973. In volume of business the London Stock Exchange ranks after New York and Japan, but it offers the largest range of securities of any stock exchange in the world.

Until 1965 there were 22 local stock exchanges outside London. In that year they joined forces on a regional basis. They subsequently formed a federation and finally, in 1973, merged formally with the London Stock Exchange to become the United Stock Exchange. The separate physical markets still retain their individual names.

THE COUNCIL OF THE STOCK EXCHANGE

The Stock Exchange is governed by a Council elected by ballot by the members. They have a three-year term of office. The Government Broker is an ex officio member. The Council annually elects a chairman who becomes known as the Chairman of the Stock Exchange, but the responsibility for day-to-day administration rests with the Secretary of the Stock Exchange. Among the more important departments under his control are the Share and Loan Department, the Settlement Department and the Official Lists Department.

THE MEMBERSHIP OF THE STOCK EXCHANGE

A unique feature of the London Stock Exchange is the division of membership between brokers and jobbers. Under Rule 22, every applicant for re-election, admission or readmission must declare whether he proposes to act as a broker, jobber or clerk. Until 1962 brokers and jobbers were allowed to trade as individuals but since that date they have been required to amalgamate into firms with at least two partners.

Brokers are agents: they are intermediaries between their clients and the jobber. They buy and sell securities on the instructions of a client, being paid a commission for this service. The rate of commission tends to be around $\frac{5}{8}$ per cent of the value (or consideration money) for gilts, around $\frac{3}{4}$ per cent of the value for debenture and loan stocks, and around $1\frac{1}{2}$ per cent of the value for ordinary and preference shares. Larger transactions are understandably charged at lower rates. One of the useful services provided by brokers for their clients is the preparation of a report which will offer suggestions for a specific programme of investment (with alternative suggestions). In this way the expertise of the broker is made available to the client.

Jobbers are principals and act on their own account: they deal only with brokers and other jobbers, never with the public. The jobbers will quote double-barrelled prices for their securities. This margin, or Turn as it is called, represents the difference between the price a jobber pays for the securities he buys and the price he receives for those he sells. From the investor's point of view it is the difference at any point of time between what a buyer has to pay for a particular share and what a seller will receive. As there are likely to be competing jobbers this is often less than the spread quoted by any one jobber.

The jobber's price is determined in the long run by the flow of demand and supply, but in the short run he may try to increase his profits by anticipating the trend of supply and demand. He will raise his price when he expects an increased demand and lower the price when he expects a surfeit of sellers.

A TYPICAL TRANSACTION

John Doe already holds a portfolio of Stock Exchange securities and has an additional £2000 he is wanting to invest. He approaches his broker who suggests the funds be invested in Fisons Ltd £1 Ordinary Stock units which are currently quoted at 270-300. The client agrees to the suggestion and gives instructions to invest £2000 in Fisons Ordinaries at the best price possible.

The broker or his clerk goes to the Exchange and approaches one of the jobbers dealing with industrial securities. 'What are Fisons?'

he asks. It is important to note that the jobber does not know at this stage whether the broker is buying or selling for his client. The jobber replies, '294 to 300p'. The broker then approaches a second jobber and asks the same question. The second jobber replies '296 to 302p'. When he tackles a third jobber the reply is '292 to 298p'.

While the jobbers do not know whether the broker is buying or selling, the broker knows his client wants to buy shares and so for him the jobbers' prices are 300p, 302p and 298p respectively. It is obviously cheapest for him to buy from the third jobber and he will now disclose to the third jobber that he wishes to buy the appropriate number of shares for his client. The bargain will be made when each records the transaction in his dealing book.

How is it that the three jobbers offered different prices for the same stock? The first jobber was comparatively short of Fisons stock. By raising his price to 302p he discouraged buyers. But if a broker had been selling, then his offer of 296p for Fisons ordinaries would have been enough to ensure that the broker sold the stock to him.

By contrast the third jobber had more Fisons ordinaries than he required and by lowering his prices he discouraged brokers from selling further stocks to him, but encouraged them to take the surplus stocks off his hands.

The broker will send John Doe a Contract Note on the day that the bargain was made (see Figure 22). This sets out the details of the transaction, identifying the securities bought or sold, the price, and the net amount due or payable after bringing into account the brokerage, the contract stamp and, in the case of purchases, the Government Transfer Duty. Under the rules of the Stock Exchange John Doe is regarded as the owner of the Fisons securities from the moment the deal is made between the broker and the jobber.

Bought	Bargain No. 0024		Bargain date and tax point 20 March 1981
A. N. BROKER & CO			IN ACCOUNT WITH Mr. John Doe
	Fisons Ltd £1 Ordinary Shares		
Amount	Price		Consideration
647	298p		£1927.06
	1.5% on £1927.06	TRANSFER STAMP CONTRACT STAMP COMMISSION VAT AT 15%	39.00 .60 28.91 4.35
		TOTAL	£1999.92
	For settlement 27 March 1981		

Figure 22 *A contract note*

The contract note will show the date on which the transaction is due for settlement. In the case of gilts this is usually the day after the transaction, but in the case of the Fisons stocks settlement will normally be for the Account. Dealings for an Account commence on a Monday and finish on a Friday, either two weeks or three weeks later. They are known as a Fortnightly Account or a Three Weeks Account (covering a Bank Holiday). Six working days after the close of dealings is the Settlement Day (or Account Day). So John Doe will have between one and three weeks before he is charged for his purchase.

The broker acting for John Doe can expect to receive the form of transfer duly signed by the seller, together with the stock certificate on or shortly after the settlement date. The transfer is a document instructing the company registrar to remove the seller's name from the register of shareholders and to substitute the name of John Doe. On receipt of the duly executed transfer, with appropriate stamp duty affixed and the stock certificate, the registrar will record the new ownership in the books of the company and issue a new certificate to John Doe.

TALISMAN SETTLEMENT SYSTEM

During 1979 a new computerised central settlement system was set up by the Stock Exchange. The earlier system had operated for nearly 100 years and was based on the passing of tickets between brokers and jobbers. The new system is known as Talisman (Transfer Accounting Lodgement for Investors, Stock Management for Jobbers) and is expected to bring economies in staff and equipment for all those dealing with the transfer of stocks and shares.

A Stock Exchange nominee company called Sepon Ltd (Stock Exchange Pool Nominees) has been established with a single undesignated shareholding account in the register of every company participating in the scheme. All stocks coming under the Talisman System are delivered to the Central Settlement Department and are registered in the name of Sepon. Buying brokers send their clients' registration details to the Stock Exchange who then transfer the stock out of their nominee into the individual clients' names. Within the 'pool', separate accounts are kept for each jobber dealing in the stock and these record transfers of ownership during the settlement process.

On Account Day, stock for sale already deposited is transferred to the jobber's trading account and the selling broker receives payment for it. At the same time, stock in the jobber's trading account is allocated to his sold bargains in 'shapes' or blocks and buying brokers are required to pay for them. This process is known as apportionment. Once apportionment has taken place the stock is held to the order of the respective buyers and Talisman Bought Transfers are issued allowing the stock to be withdrawn from the Sepon account and lodged for registration. When the Talisman Bought Transfer is registered the legal title passes to the buyer and a stock certificate is issued by the appropriate registrar.

A Talisman Transfer - in this case for the sale of company securities - is shown in Figure 23.

TALISMAN
SOLD
TRANSFER

This transfer is pursuant to a Stock Exchange transaction, and is exempt from Transfer Stamp Duty.

Above this line for Registrar's use only

Bargain Reference No.

Certificate lodged with Registrar

Name of Undertaking

Description of Security

(for completion by the Registrar of Stock Exchange)

Amount of Stock or number of Stock units or shares or other security in words

Figures

Names of registered holder(s) should be given in full: the address should be given where there is only one holder.

If the transfer is not made by the registered holder(s) insert also the name(s) and capacity (e.g. Executor(s)) of the person(s) making the transfer.

In the name(s) of

Account Designation (if any)

PLEASE SIGN HERE

I/We hereby transfer the above security out of the name(s) aforesaid into the name of SEPON LIMITED and request the necessary entries to be made in the register.

Bodies corporate should affix their common seal and each signatory should state his/her representative capacity (e.g. 'Company Secretary' 'Director') against his/her signature.

1 _____

2 _____

3 _____

4 _____

Balance Certificate Required for (amount or number in figures)

Stamp and Firm Code of Selling Broker

Date

SEPON LIMITED is lodging this Transfer at the direction and on behalf of the Member Firm whose stamp appears herein ('the Original Lodging Agent') and does not in any manner or to any extent warrant or represent the validity or genuineness of the transfer instructions contained herein or the genuineness of the Transferor's signature. The Original Lodging Agent, by delivering this Transfer to SEPON LIMITED, authorises SEPON LIMITED to lodge this Transfer for registration and agrees to be deemed for all purposes to be the person(s) actually lodging this Transfer for registration.

Stock Exchange Operating Account Number (if applicable)

Figure 23 *A Talisman transfer*

DIVIDEND MANDATES

When a new stockholder is placed on the register, instructions can be taken for the payment of interest/dividends. A typical Dividend Mandate for company securities is shown in Figure 24.

REQUEST for Payment of INTEREST or DIVIDEND

Insert name and address of Company

To: The Secretary or Registrar   *Date* _____

Please forward, until further notice, all Interest and Dividends that may from time to time become due on any Stock or Shares now standing, or which may hereafter stand, in my (our) name(s) or the name(s) of the survivor(s) of us in the Company's books to:—

Full name and address of the Bank, Firm or Person to whom Interest and Dividends are to be sent

or, where payment is to be made to a Bank, to such other Branch of that Bank as the Bank may from time to time request. Your compliance with this request shall discharge the Company's liability in respect of such interest or dividends.

This form must be signed by ALL the Registered Holders, Executors or Administrators as the case may be

(1) *Signature* _____   (3) *Signature* _____

Name in full _____   *Name in full* _____

(BLOCK *Capitals*)   (BLOCK *Capitals*)

Address _____   *Address* _____

Any change of address may be notified by quoting former and present address

(2) *Signature* _____   (4) *Signature* _____

Name in full _____   *Name in full* _____

(BLOCK *Capitals*)   (BLOCK *Capitals*)

Address _____   *Address* _____

NOTE (i) Directions to credit a particular account MUST be given to the Bank direct and NOT INCLUDED in this form.

(ii) Where the stock is in the name of a deceased Holder, instructions signed by Executor(s) or Administrator should indicate the name of the deceased.

Where the instructions are in favour of a Bank, this form should be sent to the Bank branch concerned for the insertion of the following details:—

Bank's Reference Numbers and Details:—

(1) Sorting Code No. _____

(2) Name of Bank and

Title of Branch _____

(3) Account Number (if any)

(Please quote all digits including zeros)

STAMP OF BANK BRANCH

Figure 24 *Dividend mandate for company securities*

BULLS

Because Stock Exchange dealings for each Account Day settlement normally last for two weeks a particular type of speculation becomes possible. Bulls are speculators who feel that a particular share is likely to rise in price during the course of an Account. They will therefore buy shares which they have no intention to take delivery of, and they will sell them within the same Account. If their judgement is correct they will simply receive a cheque from their

114

broker representing the difference between the buying and selling price, less expenses. Conversely, if a loss results the client has to pay his broker.

BEARS

These are speculators who foresee a fall in the price of a share during the period of an Account. They therefore sell shares which they do not hold and in doing so accept that they will have to produce the shares by the end of the Account. If their judgement is correct they will sell the shares at a comparatively high price, and buy them in at a comparatively low price. As in the case of a Bull, the successful Bear speculator will simply collect a cheque from the broker representing the difference between the buying and selling price.

However, if the shares have moved up, the seller will have to repurchase as he cannot deliver the shares he has sold. If the jobbers suspect the sellers are in this position they may raise their prices to much higher levels causing heavy losses to the bears (this situation is known as a Bear Squeeze).

Covered Bears

This type of dealing is more frequently engaged in by investment trusts and other funds. Sales are carried out in part of a holding if a downward trend in markets is anticipated, with the intention of repurchasing at a profit before the shares need to be delivered. If the shares move higher then delivery can be effected and a different investment purchased.

THE STOCK EXCHANGE DAILY OFFICIAL LIST

This is a list of all the main securities quoted on the Stock Exchange (some extracts are shown in Figure 25). A tabloid form has recently been introduced but the data presented is essentially similar. A Supplementary List gives details of shares changing hands less frequently. The List gives the following particulars, *inter alia*:

(a) Due dates for interest payments for government stocks.
(b) The last dividend for company securities.
(c) The official quotation (double-barrelled) for all stocks, which represents the range within which business might have been done throughout the day.
(d) Notes of any bargains which have been 'marked', i.e. publicised, though there is no indication whether the bargain is a sale or a purchase. Marking is intended to aid the establishment of a market price.
(e) The amount of the issued capital for British and other government bonds. (This information is not given in the new form.)
(f) Code number (for computer checking and Talisman).
(g) The date the security was last quoted ex-dividend (this date establishes whether the buyer or the seller of shares is entitled to the next dividend).

The Stock Exchange Daily Official List, Wednesday, April 2, 1980

BRITISH FUNDS

Amount Listed	INTEREST DUE	When Last xd		CODE †† NO.	CLASS. GROUP	NAME	QUOTATIONS Apr. 2	BUSINESS DONE
400,000,000*l*. 400,000,000*l*.	15J. 15D. 5A. 5O.	8 Nov. 3 Mar.	5¼ 5¾	355–766 355–681	1 1	5¼% Funding Ln. 78–80........................(1k) 5¼% Do. 87–91....................................	97¼–98¼ 58 –60 xd	97.70 59½ Φ $8\frac{7}{8}$ Φ $\frac{7}{8}$ $\frac{13}{16}$ $\frac{3}{4}$
599,998,940*l*.	15M. 15S.	7 Feb.	6	355–647	1	6 % Do. 1993....................................	55¼–57¼	$56\frac{1}{8}$ Φ $\frac{1}{2}$ $\frac{13}{16}$ $\frac{1}{8}$ $\frac{3}{8}$ $6\frac{1}{4}$
559,287,803*l*.	1M. 1N.	25 Mar.	6½	355–807	1	6½% Do. 85–87....................................	70¾–72¾xd	$71\frac{1}{8}$ Φ $\frac{3}{4}$ Φ 2 Φ $1\frac{5}{8}$ 2 $1\frac{1}{4}$
443,269,992*l*.	14J. 14J.	10 Dec.	3½	355–722	1	3½% Funding Stk. 99–2004 (Reg.).....................	34½–36½	$35\frac{1}{4}$ Φ $\frac{1}{4}$ $\frac{1}{2}$
500,138,251*l*.	15J. 15J.	10 Dec.	5½	355–788	1	5½% Do. 82–84........................(1k)	77 –78	$77\frac{3}{8}$ Φ $\frac{9}{16}$ Φ $\frac{3}{4}$ $\frac{5}{8}$ $\frac{3}{8}$
1000,000,000*l*.	1M. 1N.	25 Mar.	6¾	903–262	1	6¾% Treasury Ln. 95–98..............................	54½–56½xd	55 Φ $\frac{3}{4}$ Φ $\frac{1}{2}$ $\frac{3}{8}$
500,000,000*l*.	26J. 26J.	20 Dec.	7¾	902–623	1	7¾% Do. 85–88..............................	74 –76	$74\frac{7}{8}$ Φ $\frac{3}{4}$ $\frac{5}{8}$

FOREIGN STOCKS, BONDS, &c. (Coupons payable in London)

The currency of the amount of capital issued and listed is the same as the quotation is expressed in, except where otherwise indicated

Amount (000s omitted)	Amount Listed (000s omitted)	INTEREST DUE	When Last xd	Per Ct.	CODE NO. ††	CLASS. GROUP	NAME	QUOTATIONS Apr. 2	BUSINESS DONE	With Coupon No.	With Coupon Due
25000	942	15J. 15J.	15 Jan.	7	889–522	8	Thorn Int. Finance B.V. 7% Cnv. Gtd. Bds. 1988........	$US 90–100	8 (9/1/80)	4	15/1/81
30000	30000	15A. 15O.	15 Oct.	$7\frac{3}{4}$	896–856	6	Toray Inds. Inc. (Tor Kabushiki Kaisha) 7¾% Gtd. Notes due 1984	$US 80–90	97¼ (7/10/77)	5	15/4/80
150000	150000	15 Mar.	17 Mar.	$9\frac{3}{8}$	897–473	6	Total Oil Marine Ld. $9\frac{3}{8}$% Gtd. French Francs Notes due 1987	FF79–89		2	15/3/81
15000	12000	15 Jan.	15 Jan.	8	899–929	6	Town & City Nederland N.V. 8% Ln. 1988..............	$US66–76	86 (18/7/79)	8	15/1/81
40000	40000	A. F.	21 Feb.	$11\frac{7}{8}$	900–757	6	Trade Development Financial Services N.V. Gtd. Floating Rate Notes due 1986	$US91–101		2	21/8/80
15000	15000	1 Dec.	3 Dec.	10½	900–564	6	Trans Union Finance (Canada) Ld. 10½% Gtd. Notes due 1980	$C91–101	With Cpn.	due	1/12/80

MINES — SOUTH AFRICAN

When Last xd	Dividends/Interest Date Pay	Rate % actual	Total for year %	CLASS GROUP	CODE NO. ††	NAME	Unit of Quotation	Quotations Apr. 2	BUSINESS DONE
28.12	7.2	35	47	95	953—803	Western Areas Gold Mining Co. Ld. Stk. ★★(R	1	290p – 340p	318 Φ 15
28.1	6.3	112.5	160	95	954—323	Western Deep Levels Ld. ★★(R	2	£14 – 15	$US29%Φ p1470Φ $US31%
5.11	6.12	750	1290	95	954—602	Western Holdings Ld. ★★(R	0.50	£25⅛ – 26⅝	$US52% (1/4/80)

COMMERCIAL, INDUSTRIAL, &c.—Continued

GES—HAG

When Last xd	Dividends/Interest Date Pay	Rate % actual	Total for year %	CLASS GROUP	CODE NO. ††	NAME	Unit of Quotation	Quotations Apr. 2	BUSINESS DONE
25.2	1.4	28.67 ✻	37	97	T 371—546	Glass, Glover Group Ld. Ord.	5p	45p – 55p	49 (6/3/80)
11.2	1.4	3⅜	—	6	T 371—621	Glaxo Group Ld. 6¾% Uns. Ln. Stk. 85—95.	50p	22p – 27p	24% (28/2/80)
24.3	1.5	3⅞	—	6	T 371—580	Do. 7¾% Uns. Ln. Stk. 85—95.	50p	25p – 30p xd	27% (28/3/80)
5.11	4.1	22 ✻	32	67	T 371—706	Glaxo Holdings Ld. Ord. ⁞⁞⁞	50p	238p – 258p	240 Φ 50 Φ 46 ½ 5 7
10.12	31.12	3%	—	8	T 371—728	Do. 7½% Cnv. Uns. Ln Stk. 1985.	100	95 – 110	100 Φ 1
10.12	30.1	15 ✻	23.2625	18	T 372—107	Gleeson (M. J.) (Contractors) Ld. Ord.	10p	28p – 38p	32 (1/4/80)
22.10	30.11	6.304 ✻	—	18	T 373—401	Glossop (W. & J.) Ld. Ord.	25p	33p – 43p	39

Φ BARGAINS DONE ON THE PREVIOUS DAY EITHER AFTER 2.15 P.M. OR INADVERTENTLY OMITTED

✻ Net.

★★ This security is not subject to the new transfer system. Transfer arrangements for South African and certain other overseas securities; refer to Council Notice (Permanent Notice No. C—45).

1k The amount payable by the purchaser is the bargain price *plus* an amount equal to the gross interest accrued to the date for which the bargain was done, or in the case of transaction done "ex interest" *minus* an amount equal to the gross interest accruing from the date for which the bargain was done to the interest payment date.

⁞⁞⁞ Double Taxation Relief: Company is prepared to operate the revised arrangement for differential rates of tax. See Council Notice No. 52 of 4/4/73.

Figure 25

STAMP DUTIES
There are two types of stamp duty charged on Stock Exchange transactions:

1. *Contract stamps*

Consideration	Duty
Exceeds £100 but does not exceed £500	£0.10
" £500 " " " " £1500	£0.30
" £1500	£0.60

2. *Transfer stamps* (not required on transfers of gilts or other fixed interest stock)
This works out at approximately 2 per cent of the consideration money and is paid by the buyer.

Consideration	Duty
Not exceeding £5	£0.10
Exceeding £5 but not exceeding £100	£0.20 for every £10 or part of £10 consideration
" £100 " " " £300	£0.40 for every £20 or part of £20 consideration
" £300	£1.00 for every £50 or part of £50 consideration

There is also a Nominal Stamp of 50p for use when shares are transferred when no consideration passes, and for Jobbers when they take up stock for short periods.

BROKER'S COMMISSION
In addition to the stamp duties there is the commission payable to the broker. There is a standard scale of commission laid down by the Stock Exchange. The scales for the smaller transactions are shown below. The rate in brackets is for transactions where the commission is shared, for example, with a bank which has introduced the client. On each of the scales shown there are continuing reductions in the rates of commission for larger transactions.
   The consideration forms the basis for the calculation in these transactions.

On gilts having no final redemption within 10 years:
Brokers may make a minimum charge for the smaller transactions.
   The consideration forms the basis for the calculation in these transactions.

On first £2,000	.625%	(.7812%)
On next £12,000	.25%	(.3125%)
On next £986,000	.125%	(.1563%)

On other gilts except those having 5 years or less to redemption

On first £2,000	.625%	(.7812%)
On next £2,000	.125%	(.1562%)
On next £996,000	.0625%	(.0782%)

Note: Securities having 5 years or less to run - at discretion.

Debentures, bonds and other securities representing loans (other than gilts):

On first £5,000	.75%	(.75%)
On next £45,000	.375%	(.5%)
On next £50,000	.325%	(.45%)

Company stocks and shares registered or bearer, fully or partly paid:
```
On first  £7,000   1.5%   (1.5%)
On next   £93,000    .5%   (1.25%)
On next  £150,000    .4%   (1.00%)
```

American and Canadian shares (unless deliverable by transfer deed)
whether dollar or sterling basis
```
On first  £5,000    .9%   (.9%)
On next   £5,000    .4%   (.8%)
On excess           .3%   (.375%)
```

MODERN TRENDS

In 1960 there were 100 jobbing firms (with 545 partners) operating
on the London Stock Exchange, but by 1977 the number of jobbing firms
had fallen to 14 (with 203 partners). One explanation is that
business is increasingly centred on institutional investors which
buy and sell large blocks of securities. In turn the jobber is
required to hold large blocks of stocks and this not only increases
the risks involved through price changes but also ties up an enormous
amount of capital.

An article by Nicholas Colchester, 'Old Systems under Siege at the
Stock Exchange' in the *Financial Times*, 28 February 1978, includes
the following passages:

> There is an almost fatalistic belief that the days of stockjobbing
> and fixed commissions are numbered. . . . A growing proportion of
> stock exchange business is being transacted by 'put throughs',
> where brokers bring together institutional buyers and sellers
> themselves. In specialised sectors of the market - investment
> trusts for instance - the put through probably accounts for two-
> thirds of trading volume. . . . Brokers often act as principals
> by committing themselves to buy stock before they have found a
> buyer. . . . In short, brokers are already approaching 'dual
> capacity' in such trading. They are making profit through a
> combination of broker's commission and dealer's 'turn'. . . .

Dual capacity is already a feature on the New York Stock Exchange
where the specialist acts both as principal and agent. He buys and
sells stock on his own account and also acts on the instructions of
his client.

Assignment

Your first task is to answer the following multiple-choice questions

1. A broker is selling some ICI Ordinaries for a client. He
   approaches three different jobbers who quote the prices shown
   below. With which jobber does he deal?
   ```
   334-340p   A
   332-338p   B
   336-342p   C
   ```
2. A broker has been asked to buy some Cadbury Schweppes Ordinaries
   for a client. The jobbers quote the following prices. With
   which jobber does he deal?
   ```
   60-64p   A
   61-65p   B
   59-63p   C
   ```

3. A speculator on the Stock Exchange buys some British Petroleum Ordinaries. Which of the following items of news would be most welcome to him?

The government decides to increase the petrol tax	A
The government places restriction on the import of foreign cars	B
The Chancellor of the Exchequer reduces income tax by 1p in the £	C

4. A Bear speculator has sold some Allied Brewery Ordinaries which he proposes to buy back before Settlement Day. Which of the following events is he most likely to be anticipating?

An announcement of record profits by the company	A
New legislation imposing harsh penalties on drivers who drink	B
The introduction of a new non-alcoholic drink by the company	C

5. When the jobber's turn is wide for a particular security it is an indication that

The market is inactive	A
Most of the interest is being shown by buyers	B
The price of the security is rising	C

6. A serious international crisis is developing. Which of the following actions are jobbers most likely to take in anticipation of the market's reaction?

Refuse to give quotations	A
Lower both buying and selling prices	B
Raise selling prices	C

Your second task is to complete the details on the contract notes in Figure 26 and 27

Bought	Bargain No. 3174	Bargain date and tax point 20 March 198X
A. N. BROKER & CO.		IN ACCOUNT WITH Miss Jane Crombie

Daily Mail *A* Ordinary Shares of 50p each		
Amount	**Price**	**Consideration**
100	503p	
	TRANSFER STAMP CONTRACT STAMP COMMISSION VAT AT 15%	
For settlement 27 March 198X		

Figure 26

Sold	Bargain No. 372	Bargain date and tax point 20 March 198X
A. N. BROKER & CO.		IN ACCOUNT WITH Miss Jane Crombie

$3\frac{1}{2}\%$ WAR LOAN		
Amount	**Price**	**Consideration**
£1000	$35\frac{1}{4}$	
	TRANSFER STAMP CONTRACT STAMP COMMISSION VAT AT 15%	
For settlement Cash		

Figure 27

Commission is not divisible in either of these transactions.

15 Yields and Prices

A Stock Exchange investment has two basic dimensions. The first of these is the return or annual yield from the funds invested. This may not be the same as the nominal rate of interest (or *coupon rate*) on the stockholding. For example, a stock which pays a nominal dividend of 5 per cent per annum will give a yield of 10 per cent per annum if £200 of stock is purchased for £100. The simplest formula for determining the yield is

$$\frac{\text{income received}}{\text{cost of investment}} \times 100$$

The second dimension of a Stock Exchange investment is the price, which fluctuates over a period of time. An investor will look for an appreciation of capital which will be the effect when the price of a security rises.

However, probably the policy most likely to be successful is to buy a share when it is felt that an upward trend is established and to carry out a sale if a downward trend has set in. It may thus be possible to save heavy losses and protect profits. Although it may not seem to be the case judging by the way the media give market reports, it is very rare to find all types of securities to be moving in the same direction at the same time.

While the majority of investors will be concerned with both dimensions, some investors will be primarily concerned to obtain a high yield, while others virtually disregard present income and concentrate their efforts on achieving a maximum appreciation of capital.

Of course prices and yields are interrelated. For example, if the purchase price of a gilt rises, the yield obtainable by a new purchaser will be lowered. Consider the case where 5 per cent stock rises from 50 to 80 in price. In that case the yield will fall from 10 per cent to $6\frac{1}{4}$ per cent per annum, calculated thus:

$$\frac{5}{50} \times 100 = 10\% \qquad\qquad \frac{5}{80} \times 100 = 6\frac{1}{4}\%$$

Similarly, if a company increase the dividend paid to their equity holders, this will raise the price of the stock on the market.

The contra movements for prices and yields of both industrial fixed-interest stocks and ordinary shares are confirmed in Figure 28, which compares prices as evidenced by *Financial Times* indices with dividend yields. The implication is that when prices of securities rise, other things being equal, the new investor will be obliged to accept a lower yield on the investment.

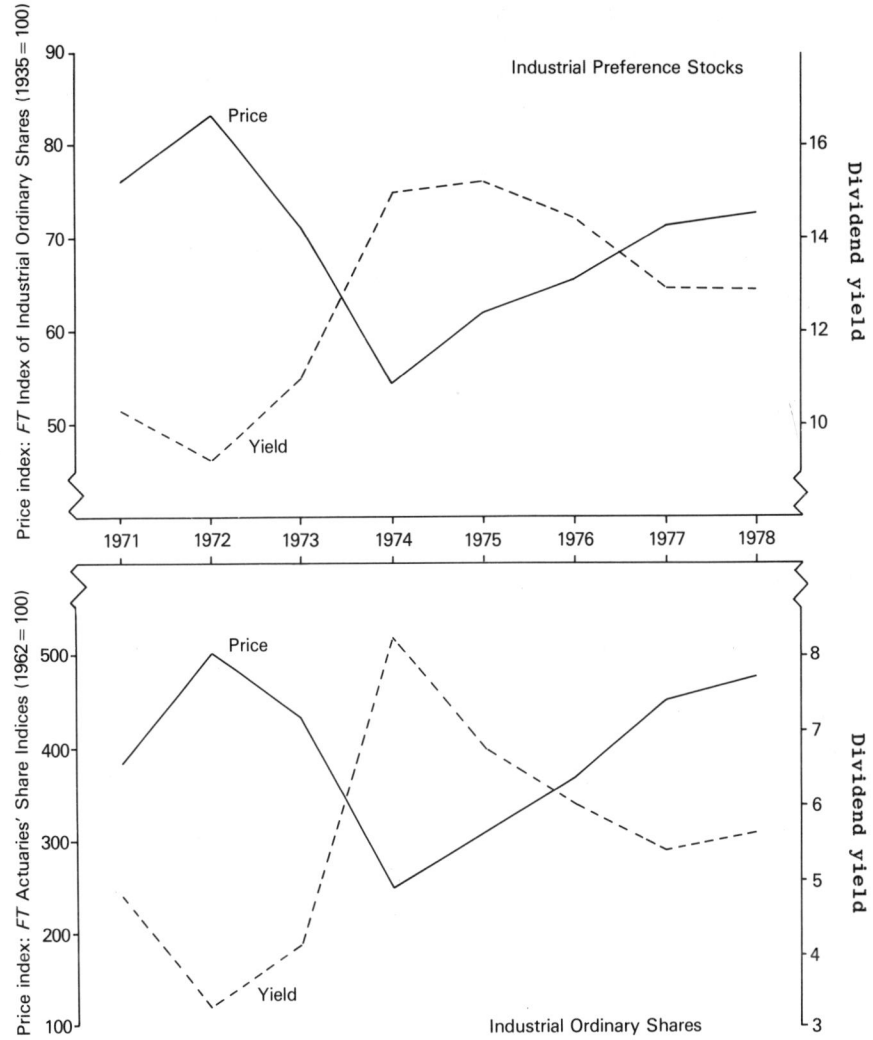

Figure 28 *Graphs demonstrating interrelationships between yields and prices*
Sources: Central Statistical Office, *Financial Statistics* (Dec 1979); *Financial Times*; *The Times*; Institute of Actuaries; Faculty of Actuaries.

YIELDS

The yield based on the price of the stock and the rate of interest is called the Flat Yield. Bearing in mind that the price of any stock includes payment for interest accrued to date, a more precise calculation can be made by 'cleaning the price', which means making an allowance for the interest element in the purchase price.

123

Interest and dividends will usually be received by the investor net of tax. To gross up a dividend it is necessary to multiply by

$$\frac{100}{100p - \text{standard rate in the £}}$$

When a stock has a redemption date it becomes necessary to calculate the yield to redemption as well as the flat yield. Consider for example a 5 per cent gilt which is purchased at a price of 80 and is redeemable in 5 years' time. The calculations would be as follows:

$$\text{Flat yield (gross)} = \frac{5}{80} \times 100 = 6.25\%$$

$$\text{Flat yield (net)} = \frac{5}{80} \times 100 \times \frac{70}{100} \text{ (assuming a standard rate of } 30p \text{ in the £)}$$

$$= 4.375\%$$

But the price of the stock would move to parity (100) in 5 years' time and so there would be a redemption gain of 20 points (from 80 to 100). The Redemption Yield can be gauged by the use of the formula:

$$\frac{\text{Gain to redemption}}{\text{Purchase price}} \times \frac{100}{\text{Years to redemption}} + \text{Flat yield (net)}$$

In the example given

$$\text{Redemption yield} = \frac{20}{80} \times \frac{100}{5} + 4.375\% = 9.375\%$$

The calculation is an approximation in the sense that the gain of 20 points is only obtained after a wait of five years and, as we shall see in Chapter 21, £20 payable in five years' time does not have the same value as £20 payable now. However, with this limitation in mind, the formula gives us a useful approximation and explains the purpose of the calculation.

There is another practical problem to cope with when a stock offers the borrower a choice of redemption dates. Take the case of 5 per cent Treasury Stock 1986-9. Will the government choose to redeem this stock in 1986, 1989, or at some time between these dates? In this case there is little doubt about when the government will redeem this particular stock. When redemption is made the government will have to make a further issue, otherwise they will be denuding themselves of funds. The crucial question for the government concerns the rate of interest they will have to offer on any new stock. If the interest rates are above 5 per cent they will leave redemption to the latest possible date. In other words, the redemption yield can be calculated on the basis that the government will redeem this stock in 1989.

Now let us suppose we are trustees who have an infant beneficiary who becomes entitled to the residuary estate absolutely at the age of eighteen, which he reaches in 1991. We have made a decision to invest part of the trust funds in a dated gilt which matures at about the time he comes of age. In the columns of the *Financial Times* we find two stocks which appear to be appropriate. The information given is as follows:

Dated stocks	*Price*	*Yield* Int.	Red.
Treasury $11\frac{3}{4}$% 1991	$85\frac{7}{8}$	13.70	14.36
Exchequer 11% 1991	$83\frac{7}{8}$	13.51	14.28

On this evidence which stock would be preferred? The Treasury stock gives a slightly higher yield both intermediately and to redemption. Assuming the prices quoted reflect the current prices obtainable by the brokers we would prefer to invest in this stock.

In another trust we might be attempting to maximise income for an elderly life-tenant. We decide to invest part of the fund in undated gilts. Again let us compare two of the stocks on offer:

Undated stocks	*Price*	*Yield* Int.	Red.
Consols $2\frac{1}{2}$%	$21\frac{7}{8}$	11.46	-
Treasury 3%	24	12.94	-

On this evidence the Treasury 3 per cent would be preferred.

Note that in both the examples given here the prices alone do not give us the information required to enable a decision to be made. We must know the yield that would be obtained before a choice can be made. Market forces will operate to ensure that yields on similar stocks do not get far out of line with each other, but this does not mean that investors should not take advantage of any variations which occur.

Yields on equities

If you look at the lists of equities in the *Financial Times* or any of the broker's booklets you will find a considerable variation in the yields obtainable. The first point to note is that past dividends are no guarantee for future dividends. But there is generally a positive correlation between risk and yield. Predictably, high risk is associated with high yield, and low risk can be expected to produce low yields.

Equity stocks in the very best companies are known as *Blue Chips*, but because the risks attaching to them can be regarded as minimal the yield obtainable is very low. The hope for an investor in such stocks is that there will be a growth in dividends over a period of time, with a commensurate appreciation in value and price.

The reverse yield gap

Since the yield is usually related to the degree of risk attached to a security, one would expect to find that the yield on gilts was

always lower than the yield on equities. But where there is high
inflation the situation may be reversed. Growth stocks at least
provide a partial hedge against inflation, while fixed-interest
securities lose a great deal of their attraction for investors. The
Reverse Yield Gap, as it is called, can be measured by comparing the
yield on 2½ per cent Consols with the average yield on equities as
indicated in the *Financial Times* All-Share Index.

PRICES
A maxim which should be followed by all investors is 'buy at the
bottom and sell at the top'. Prices of all stocks fluctuate from
time to time and the art of speculation is to buy your securities at
the most propitious moment. However, this is not as easy as it
sounds, for two reasons. First, it is as difficult to know when
share prices have finished falling as it is to know when they have
reached the peak. And second, the maxim assumes that the investor
or speculator is in a position to take the necessary action. For
example, funds may not be available for a purchase at the vital
moment. Or an upward movement in prices might be market-wide, in
which case there is a danger of liquidating one highly priced stock
only to be forced into buying another highly priced stock.
  The Stock Exchange is a highly sensitive market and stock prices
fluctuate in response to a wide variety of pressures. Investors
should always be looking to the future and attempting to anticipate
events. A number of the factors which are likely to affect prices
of securities on the Stock Exchange are listed below, under broad
classifications.

1. *Economic factors*
All businesses are affected by the general economic climate. If
there is economic growth it will be the result of business activity
of one sort or another. And businesses are interdependent to a large
extent. Orders for ships lead to orders for steel which in turn
leads to money in the pockets of shipbuilders and steelworkers to
buy television sets and carpets. By the same token, a high level of
unemployment will lead to a fall in the sales of beer which will lead
to a further increase in unemployment, this time among the brewers.
  To some extent the movement in business activity is cyclical.
Historically it has been possible to trace a distinct pattern of
boom, recession, depression and recovery. The pattern has become
confused since the Second World War, but some traces of the business
cycle remain.
  To a large extent the national economy is linked to the world
economy. The Great Depression of the early thirties started in the
United States, but the repercussions were world-wide. The effects
would be similar today. If there were an economic recession in the
United States, Americans would buy less Scotch whisky and fewer
British pop records. The recession would spread to Britain and any
other country which exports to the United States. There would be a
chain reaction. This is why we would expect to find prices on Wall
Street and the London Stock Exchange moving in the same direction
though there may be a time lag.

2. *Government intervention*
Businessmen will obviously pay attention when the Chancellor of the

Exchequer introduces a Budget. This is the time when tax rates and excise duties are subject to change. Future government spending patterns are declared to the nation and investors on the Stock Exchange anticipate the effect of the changes on their securities.

The government also gives effect to its policies through the Bank of England. Various devices are available for changing the structure of interest rates generally which in turn react on the level of business activity. The government broker is used to conducting open-market operations. This entails selling stocks when the government wants to reduce the supply of money in the market, and buying stocks when the supply of money is to be increased. The Bank of England is able to exert pressure on the commercial banks to restrict the volume of loans and overdrafts and this has a depressing effect on business.

Governmental policies on wages and inflation, expenditure on defence and social welfare, and aid to ailing industries and depressed areas will all influence prices on the Stock Exchange in one way or another. Since some political parties are likely to be more sympathetic than others to business interests, the Stock Exchange will respond to the results of general elections or even by-elections. Securities in any firm or industry threatened with nationalisation will be sensitive to changes in the fortunes of governments.

The prosperity of any company with overseas interests will be swayed by changes in exchange rates and tariffs, and the political complexities of governments in regions where they trade.

3. *Market factors*

The prices of Stock Exchange securities will also be affected by what one might describe as more parochial influences. When an individual company announces a reduction in its profits the price of its equity shares will decline, and if it is a major company the expectation of similar results in other companies operating in the same industry might have a generally depressing effect. The demand for securities will wax and wane much like any other commodity and this will produce changes in price levels of the various securities. Consider, for example, the effect of two large companies issuing a new loan stock within a short space of time. Or a government stock becoming due for redemption.

In many ways the various securities available on the Stock Exchange are competing against each other for the funds of the investor. If the institutional investors such as charitable trusts and pension funds choose to invest in equities rather than gilts, equity prices will rise while gilts will fall. And an upward movement in the prices of equities may raise expectations that the prices will continue to rise.

The operations of the jobbers will tend to reduce price fluctua-tions. By anticipating price changes they will discourage specu-lators. Thus, if investors are disturbed by some adverse political or economic developments they may wish to sell securities, but when their brokers go on to the floor of the Exchange they will find that the jobbers have anticipated a spate of sales and have lowered prices accordingly. Many of the investors who would otherwise sell their securities are discouraged from doing so by the low prices that can be obtained.

Assignment
For group work
Felicity Jones has a portfolio of securities as indicated below.
In small groups you are asked to consider the likely effect of
certain events (1-10 below) on the prices of the Stock Exchange
investments in the portfolio. Tick the appropriate column to
indicate the most likely response on the evidence available.

The portfolio

Equities   *Expected price changes*
                                             Fall - Rise - No change

A. A toy manufacturing company which
   sells 30 per cent of its output
   overseas.
B. A commercial bank with overseas
   subsidiaries.
C. An insurance company offers a
   full range of policies but
   concentrates its operations in
   the United Kingdom.
D. A South African gold mining
   company
E. A company which manufactures
   components for the UK motor
   industry.
F. An international oil company.
G. A company which runs a chain of
   food supermarkets in the United
   Kingdom.
H. A company which manufactures
   pharmaceutical products.

Gilts
I. 2½ per cent Consolidated Stock.
J. 14 per cent Treasury Stock 1998-2001

The events

1. Commercial banks' lending rates are reduced by 1 per cent.
2. Income tax is increased by 3p in the £
3. The exchange rate of sterling falls as against all other major
   currencies.
4. An extensive period of drought is experienced in Western Europe.
5. A national wages plan is approved by the CBI, the TUC, and the
   government.
6. There is a rise in the birthrate.
7. The government raise the tax on petrol by 25p per gallon in an
   attempt to conserve energy.
8. The government make major cuts in Health Service expenditure.
9. A simple and inexpensive cure is discovered for cancer.
10. There is a marked increase in the volume of world trade.

Your final task
Come together in the main group and compare results.

16 Tax Considerations

When companies make profits and individuals receive incomes above
a certain level, they are obliged to pay tax to the government.
Companies pay corporation tax. Individuals pay income tax. The
government use the taxes to finance projects related to education,
social services and defence etc. The taxes are of concern to
investors in so far as they reduce the returns from their investments.

Over a period of years both the rates of tax and the tax structure
itself changes. The principal architect of these changes is the
Chancellor of the Exchequer. A Finance Act is passed each year to
give legal force to his Budget. Investors will watch anxiously to
see the changes proposed, bearing in mind that the prices of their
Stock Exchange securities and future net yields are likely to change
as a result of the Chancellor's deliberations.

CORPORATION TAX
Since the Finance Act of 1972 a company pays corporation tax on the
full amount of its profits, while shareholders receive their dividends net with a tax credit equal to the amount of tax which has
been deducted. This tax credit allows them to claim a refund from
the Inland Revenue where they are due to pay income tax at less than
the basic rate. The tax credit is otherwise set off against their
liability for income tax. A simple example will help to explain the
principles involved.

Company X

	£
Profit for the year*	200,000
Corporation Tax	
(assume this to be 50%)	100,000
Available for dividend	100,000
Transfer to Reserves (as	
determined by Board of Directors)	40,000
Gross dividend	60,000
Income tax (assume the basic rate	
to be 30%)	18,000
Net dividend	42,000

*The profits assessed to corporation tax may differ from the
profits shown in the published accounts. The explanation is
that some deductions in the accounts will be unacceptable for
the purpose of tax assessment.

Suppose Company X has one million ordinary shares of £1 each. In this case it will pay a (net) dividend of 4.2 per cent so that a shareholder with 1000 shares would receive a dividend warrant for £42 together with a tax credit of £18. If he is liable to tax at the basic rate then his income tax liability is covered by his tax credit and he pays no more tax. If he suffers tax at an additional rate, say 40 per cent, then there will be further tax to pay.

	£
Dividend	42
Advance Corporation Tax (paid by company)	18
Grossed-up dividend	60
Income tax at 40% on £60	24
less Tax credit	18
Tax outstanding	6

When a company pays interest on debentures and loans the payment is a charge against the profits and not a distribution of such profits. The payment is made out of the company's receipts before corporation tax is levied on the profits. This explains the dearth of new preference stocks on the Stock Exchange. It pays companies to issue debentures and loan stocks instead.

When a company receives interest net this has to be grossed up in order to determine profit. The income tax already suffered is then set off against the corporation tax. By contrast, dividends received from the company's investment in other companies (known as franked income) do not form part of the profits for assessment since they have already been subject to corporation tax.

PERSONAL TAXATION

The pattern of personal taxation in the United Kingdom has been established with the following basic features:

1. A distinction is made between income earned from employment and income received from investment. There is an additional 15 per cent charge on investment income in excess of £5500 for 1980/1.*
2. An individual is granted certain allowances which are deducted from income before tax is charged on the remainder. The allowances for 1980/1 include:*

	£
Personal allowances: Single person	1375
Married	2145
Wife's earned income relief (maximum)	1375
Age allowance: Single person	1820
Married	2895

(when income is over £5900 the allowance is reduced by £2 for every £3 of income)

Life assurance relief   deducted from
                                         premiums (15%)

Additional personal allowance for
  children (essentially for single
  parents)   770

3. The rates of tax charged are progressive. For 1980/1 the tax
   bands are:*

£	%
0-11,250	30
11,251-13,250	40
13,251-16,750	45
16,751-22,250	50
22,251-27,750	55
over 27,750	60

4. When there is a high level of inflation, the various tax thresholds will need to be revised each year in order to avoid a
   situation where higher proportions of income are being taxed.
   In the words of the Chancellor of the Exchequer, Sir Geoffrey
   Howe, in his Budget Speech to Parliament (26 March 1980):   'Our
   progressive income tax system operates in such a way that those
   who pay tax at higher rates experience sharply increasing tax
   burdens in times of inflation.'

   The method of assessment will be apparent from a study of two
   simple examples:

                                                    £
Alan Foy   Income from employment   10,000
Aged 30   Investment income   4,000
Married   _____
               Total income   14,000

   Reliefs: Personal Allowance   2,145
               Mortgage Interest   795   2,940
                                      _____   _____
               Taxable income   11,060
                                               _____

   Tax on £11,060 at 30% = £3,318.00 tax to be paid (less any
   previously deducted under PAYE - Pay as You Earn).

David Carr   Income from employment   20,000
Aged 50   Investment income   9,500
Single   _____
               Total income   29,500
   Reliefs: Personal allowance   1,375
                                               _____
                                              28,125
                                               _____

---

* The thresholds for 1981/2 remain unchanged.

```
                    £                          £
Tax on first  11,250 at 30%  =    3,375.00
 "     "  next  2,000 at 40%  =      800.00
 "     "    "   3,500 at 45%  =    1,575.00
 "     "    "   5,500 at 50%  =    2,750.00
 "     "    "   5,500 at 55%  =    3,025.00
   remaining      375 at 60%  =      225.00
              _____                _____
                28,125             11,750.00
              _____                _____

Investment income surcharge
 (15% on £4,000)              =      600.00
                                   _____
Total tax to be paid         =  £12,350.00
                                   _____
```

Building Society interest

With regard to the interest paid to their depositors, most building societies have an arrangement with the Inland Revenue to pay a lump sum in lieu of income tax. This is based on a composite rate which is a notional average rate of tax for all their depositors. Thus the interest on a building society account will not be subject to further income tax unless the investor's income takes him into a band above the basic rate. If this happens additional tax will be payable equal to the difference between the tax at the basic rate and tax at the higher rate. Consider the following assessment:

```
                                                      £
Income from employment                           10,000
Building Society interest                           700
                                                 _____
Total income                                     10,700
Grossing up of Building Society interest            300
                                                 _____
                                                 11,000
Reliefs: Personal Allowance         1,820
         Dependent Relative
            Allowance                 100         1,920
                                    _____       _____
            Taxable income                        9,080
                                                 _____

Tax on £9,080 at 30%                            £2,724.00
less Credit on Building Society interest           300.00
                                                _____
Total tax to be paid                            £2,424.00
                                                _____
```

(less any previously
deducted under PAYE)

Interest on government securities

This is taxed at source by the Bank of England at the basic rate in most cases, but a person who is not normally resident in the United Kingdom can apply to the Inland Revenue to have the interest paid without deduction of tax. And when certain government securities are held on the National Savings Stock Register or Trustee Savings

Bank Register, the interest is paid gross to the stockholder.
    If there has been an overpayment of tax because the recipient is
not taxable at the basic rate, the tax (or an appropriate part of
it) can be reclaimed from the Inland Revenue.

Overseas residence income
A resident of the United Kingdom is liable to tax on the whole of
his income no matter where it arises. But a person who is physically
present for less than six months in any tax year is not regarded as
a 'resident of the U.K.'   (Section 51, The Income and Corporation
Tax Act 1970). The stay can be continuous or for broken periods.
A person who is temporarily resident will only be taxable on the
income which is remitted to the United Kingdom.
    All income arising in the United Kingdom is liable to tax whether
or not the recipient is a resident.

Double taxation relief
If an investor who is resident in the United Kingdom receives income
from overseas, he may find himself taxed both in the foreign country
and in the United Kingdom. To reduce this burden the Inland Revenue
offer relief in one of two ways:

Method 1
The foreign tax is deducted from the gross income and the net figure
only is assessed to UK tax. For example:

John Doe receives dividends from abroad as follows:

	£
Gross dividends	600
Foreign tax	120
	480
UK tax (£600 at 30%)	180
Net amount (without DTR)	£300

But with DTR the calculation becomes

	£
Dividend net of foreign tax	480
UK tax (480 at 30%)	144
Net amount (with DTR)	£336

Method 2
The total tax is limited to the highest rate assessed under either
the foreign or domestic tax codes. This relief is only available
where there is a specific double taxation treaty or convention with
the country in which the income arises. For example:

John Doe receives dividends from abroad as in the first example, but the net amount with double taxation relief is calculated thus:

		£
Gross dividends		600
Foreign tax		120
		480
UK tax		
(30 per cent)	£180	
DTR credit	120	60
Net amount (with DTR)		£420

Either method is available to the taxpayer but Method 2 usually provides the greater relief as in this example. A third way in which relief is given is where there are reciprocal arrangements to exempt income from tax in the country of origin. In these cases the income received by a UK resident would simply be subject to the UK tax.

CAPITAL GAINS TAX
Tax is charged on capital gains, that is gains accruing to a person on the disposal of assets in accordance with the Capital Gains Tax Act 1979. Tax is chargeable to UK residents 'in respect of chargeable gains in a year of assessment ... after deducting any allowable losses'. In the case of a husband and wife living together any losses of the one which are unrelieved can be applied against the chargeable gains of the other, unless they elect to be separately assessed for capital gains tax.
    The rate of tax levied on the capital gains is 30 per cent but an exemption limit of £3000 was allowed by the 1980 Finance Act.
    Assets assessable to the tax include:

1. Stock Exchange securities with the exception of British government securities which have been held for one year or more or have passed to a beneficiary on somebody's death.
2. Land and buildings, jewellery, antiques, etc.
3. Options.
4. Any currency other than sterling.
5. Any form property created by the person disposing of it (such as copyright, goodwill and paintings).

    Disposal of part of an asset will also be included for the purpose of assessment.

Exemptions
Certain assets can be disposed of without giving rise to a liability for capital gains tax. Among the most notable of these are:

(a) Private motor vehicles.
(b) The main private residence or home.
(c) Winnings from betting including pools, lotteries and premium savings bonds.

(d) Life assurance policies and deferred annuities.
(e) Chattels sold for £2000 or less.
(f) Persons who have died are deemed to have disposed of all their assets at the date of death. This may give rise to a claim for capital transfer tax (see p. 137) but no capital gains tax is payable. Whoever inherits the estate is deemed to have acquired them at the date of death and at the date of death valuation.
(g) Roll-over relief is available when a gain accrues on the disposal of a business asset. The liability to tax can be deferred so long as the proceeds are reinvested in other assets for the continuance of the business.

Deductions
Before calculating the amount to be charged to capital gains tax incidental costs in connection with the original acquisition and disposal may be deducted. Enhancement expenditure may also be deducted where appropriate.

Tax-saving investments
The majority of investors will be paying tax at one rate or another but there are a number of investments which are not subject to tax. For example:

1. Interest on *ordinary deposits* (not investment deposits) with the National Savings Bank are exempt from income tax on the first £70 of interest. A wife is also entitled to a similar exemption.
2. Interest and terminal bonuses under the contractual savings scheme run by the Department of National Savings and the Trustee Savings Banks are not taxable. The Save-As-You-Earn Index-linked scheme is particularly advantageous while inflation is high, the appreciation being calculated according to changes in the Retail Prices Index. The government compares the average prices of such things as are included in a typical household budget (such as food, clothing, electricity and tobacco) with the average prices pertaining to the previous month. Bonuses are paid at the end of the fifth and seventh years. The maximum contribution at the present time is £50 per month.
3. Prizes on Premium Savings Bonds are not taxable. The monthly prize fund is formed by calculating one month's interest, at the rate of 7 per cent per annum, on each bond eligible for the draw. A bond will be eligible for the draw three months after purchase. The winning numbers are selected by ERNIE (Electronic Random Number Indicator Equipment). The main prize draw is held every month and the top prize is £250,000.
4. The accumulated interest on National Savings Certificates is not taxable. The tax-free feature is attractive to investors but in order for the highest yields to be obtained it is necessary to retain the certificates for the full term.
The return on the 23rd issue is equivalent to a compound annual interest rate of 10.51 per cent over the full five years.

Maximum permitted holdings are prescribed by statutory regulations, but a person who holds the maximum for one issue is not precluded from purchasing further units in subsequent issues.

A favourable investment for many investors may prove to be the Index-linked National Savings Certificates (previously known as

Value and yield of the Twenty-third Issue of N.S.C.s year by year

Years after purchase	Value at end of year (£25 units)	Tax-free yield for the year %
1	£27.25	9
2	£29.86	9.58
3	£32.92	10.25
4	£36.61	11.21
5	£41.20	12.54

Granny bonds). The Second Issue is available without age restriction but subject to a maximum of 300 units (£3000). If the certificates are encashed in the first year repayment is at face value. Otherwise the percentage change in the repayment value between the date of purchase and the date of encashment will be linked to the percentage change in the Retail Prices Index during that period. The index-linking for N.S.C.s is particularly attractive because the increases are compounded. Thus, if the RPI increases by 10 per cent in the first year, a £100 unit would then have a repayment value of £110. An increase of, say, 9 per cent in the second year would raise the repayment value to £119.90 (£110 + 9 per cent of £110). A bonus of 4 per cent will be paid on the fifth anniversary of the purchase.

Such index-linking is likely to remain attractive so long as the rate of inflation is higher than the rate of interest which can be earned on alternative investments.

5. For the more affluent investor another way of minimising the burden of tax is to invest in what are described as Offshore Funds. There is an endless variety of such Funds, but the principle for the investor is unchanging. Sums are invested in companies operating in islands such as the Channel Islands and the Isle of Man. The profits of such companies are subject to local taxation which is at a much lower level than that suffered in the United Kingdom. A UK resident will be subject to tax on distributions by the Fund, and it is the non-UK resident who is likely to find investment in Offshore Funds most beneficial.

6. A considerable number of British Government securities (such as $3\frac{1}{2}$ per cent War Loan and 9 per cent Treasury Stock 1994) are exempt from all British taxes including death duties so long as the owner is neither domiciled nor ordinarily resident in the United Kingdom and makes the necessary application.

ANALYSIS OF UK TAXES

Figure 29 serves to indicate the relative importance of the various UK taxes to the Treasury. We have concentrated on those which have a direct effect on the returns to investors, but as we saw in Chapter 1 all taxes have the effect of siphoning funds away from the private sector. Furthermore, changes in the various rates of tax can reflect in the prices of particular stocks and shares. We can understand the reasons for this if we consider the purpose of taxation:

The original purpose of tax was to raise revenue to finance expenditure by the Government: this remains an important function. However, since the 1940s, it has been accepted that taxation may be used as a means of managing the economy. Consequently the structure and level of taxation, together with monetary policy, may be altered to promote certain desired objectives, the most important of which are full employment, a satisfactory balance of payments position, economic growth and prosperity. (Central Office of Information Reference Pamphlet 112, *The British System of Taxation* (HMSO, 3rd edn, 1977.)

Thus the effect of raising *value added tax* (VAT), which is a tax on sales with the burden falling on the final consumer, is to dampen business activity generally and the stock market will respond accordingly.

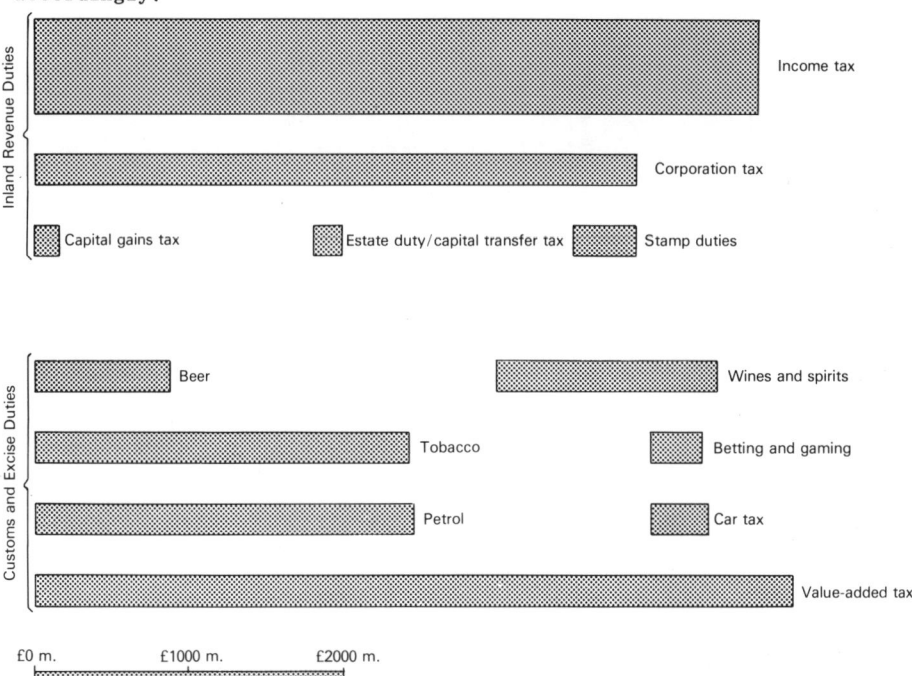

Figure 29 *Major taxes raised by UK Government, 1978-9*
Sources: Central Statistical Office, *Financial Statistics* (Dec 1979); Board of Inland Revenue and HM Customs and Excise.

By contrast, *capital transfer tax* is a death duty based on the value of the estate added to the gifts and settlements made by the deceased during his lifetime. It represents an attempt to avoid a concentration of wealth in the hands of a limited few.

The effect of changes in the so-called excise duties such as taxes on tobacco and alcoholic drink are likely to be limited to the prices of shares in companies dealing with the commodities in question though an increase in petrol tax would have wider repercussions.

Assignment
Working in twos or threes where possible study the graphs in Figures
30 and 31. The Y axis in each case shows the general level of stock
prices. The X axis indicates a period of time during which an
investor switches an investment in his portfolio for another. The
broken line shows what happens to the general level of stock prices
after the sale/switch has been made.

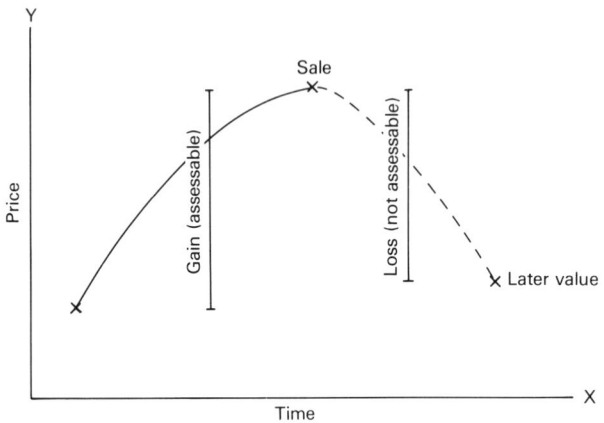

Figure 30

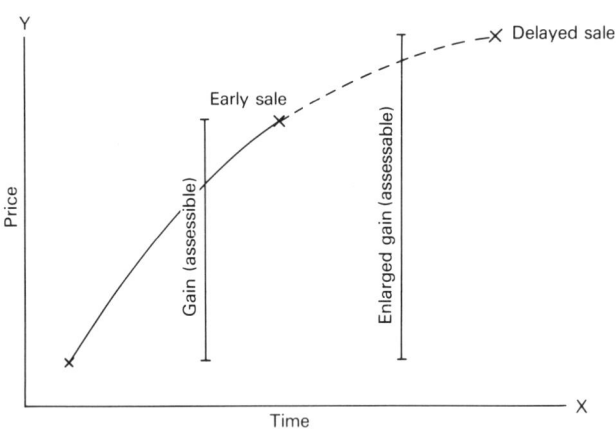

Figure 31

Your task
Explain in not more than 100 words what the graphs demonstrate.

138

17 Portfolio Planning and Management

While the objective of all individual investors and portfolio managers will be to maximise returns, certain aspects of the situation have to be clarified before an appropriate strategy can be developed. We have already seen how tax considerations can influence investment decisions, but there are a number of other angles to study before specific plans can be formulated.

THE TIME-SCALE/COMMITMENTS

How far ahead are we looking? What situations do we expect to encounter during this time-span? The policy of an insurance company may be proscribed to the extent that certain endowment policies mature within a given range of time. The policy of a bank may be proscribed to the extent that it will wish to show an appropriate degree of liquidity at the end of its financial year when the accounts will be subjected to public examination. In the same way the policy of a pension fund will be tailored to meet its ever-changing commitments.

For the private investor the problems are similar in essence. Long-term growth stocks are not likely to appeal to elderly investors - unless they have the interests of their heirs at heart. Those approaching retirement may prefer to forgo present returns in the expectation of benefiting at a later date when other sources of income dry up. For young people there will be times when the cost of education or the setting up of a home becomes a primary concern.

INCOME v. CAPITAL GROWTH

Ideally an investor would like his securities to provide him with the highest possible income (or yield) while at the same time appreciating in value at the highest possible rate both in the short run and the long run. Unfortunately it is normally necessary to choose one or other of these objectives though a compromise is also possible. Capital growth can best be achieved by holding equities in companies whose operations and profits are continually expanding. The problem is that there tends to be a shortage of suitable equities in this category. Part of the explanation lies in the fact that the more successful companies show a preference for raising funds through issues of loan stock rather than equities. And the shortage is compounded by the ever-increasing demands of the institutional investors, particularly the pension funds which not only seek out the promising companies but hold on to the stocks once they have been acquired. The result is that investment in first-class equities can be expected to produce very low yields - at least in the early years of the investment.

By contrast, fixed-interest securities can be expected to provide higher yields - at least initially - but apart from the possibilities of capital appreciation on redemption or profits taken as prices fluctuate mainly in response to changes in interest rates, long-term growth is virtually excluded.

However, a compromise can be achieved by either selecting the higher yielding equities (which inevitably carry higher risks) or by achieving some sort of balance between the *fixed-interest content* and the *equity content* in a particular portfolio.

During the course of time the objectives of a portfolio might change. For example, a reduction in the rate of capital gains tax would make growth relatively more attractive than income. Or the death of an aged beneficiary in a trust might mean that the emphasis switches from high income to capital growth in the interests of a young residuary legatee.

ATTITUDES

What is the attitude towards risk? And what is the attitude to investment in particular types of business?

Bearing in mind that high dividends are often associated with high risk how would the investor looking for high dividends view the possibility of a capital loss? Would he be prepared to take a chance? Or would he prefer to play safe? What is his attitude towards inflation, which is so effective in eroding the real value of an investment? What risks is he prepared to take to try to counter these losses?

Does the investor have any antipathies? Some people would object to investing funds in brewery shares. Others would not want to buy stocks in companies making armaments. And many Arabs would presumably not invest in companies which they considered to be under Jewish control.

DIVERSIFICATION

Risk has a different dimension for the large-scale investor. Large numbers of risks tend to cancel each other out. The principle is the same for the insurance business where risks become predictable because of the large numbers involved.

If the small investor buys US securities he stands to lose if the sterling/dollar exchange rate moves against the dollar. But if an investor has securities on both sides of the Atlantic the devaluation of the dollar securities will be offset by the increased value of the sterling securities. Or again, suppose a portfolio contains both tobacco and food shares. A fall in tobacco shares following more damning evidence of the connections between cigarette smoking and cancer would be countered by a rise in food shares as cigarette smokers ate more food.

Diversification reduces risk so long as the different shares are not affected in a similar way by the same events.

R. J. Briston explains the sort of balance one aims to achieve:

Diversification implies not only the choice of shares in different companies, but also the selection of different classes of securities. Thus a balanced portfolio would contain both equities and fixed-interest stocks, both gilt-edged and industrial securities. At the same time there should be diversification by industry and geographical area. Obviously complete diversification is impossible in a portfolio of average size, nor is it necessary or desirable, for it would by definition result in only average performance, for the greater the diversification the more difficult it is to vary the performance of the portfolio from the average level. (*The Stock Exchange and Investment Analysis* (George Allen & Unwin, 3rd edn, 1975).)

A central task for the institutional portfolio manager is to achieve an appropriate degree of diversification giving the portfolio a measure of safety, while at the same time acquiring in sufficient volume those securities which promise to provide the greatest growth. The problem is compounded by the fact that investment managers' performances will be compared and the measure of their excellence will be related to the distance between their performance and (a) the average performance and (b) the performance of their competitors.

In Michael Firth's opinion: 'In practice a carefully selected portfolio of around twenty stocks can provide virtually as much risk aversion as buying the "market". Such portfolios may be cheaper to administer and may offer greater returns.'

He also suggests:

'Not more than, say, 1 per cent of a company's equity should be acquired as any excess may be difficult to liquidate conveniently. In the U.S. there exists a fairly efficient market in the placing of large blocks of stock: this is not the case in the U.K. however, and so large holdings are undesirable for portfolios which have to be very marketable.' (*Investment Analysis: Techniques of Appraising the British Stock Market* (Harper & Row, 1975).)

FOREIGN SECURITIES

Since 1979 exchange controls have been suspended and this has opened up a new vista of markets for the UK investor, providing a wealth of opportunities and no doubt a mass of pitfalls. From the point of view of portfolio management it means that there is now greater scope for introducing foreign securities. Probably in part because of the common language UK investors have always shown interest in American and Canadian stocks. Until the freeing of exchange controls, a UK investor wishing to buy these stocks could not obtain foreign currency at the official exchange rate. Instead he was obliged to acquire investment dollars from the so-called 'investment dollar pool', this being done by a broker on his behalf. The source of the dollars in this pool arose from previous sales of US and Canadian securities. The demand for investment dollars usually exceeded the supply and so a premium was normal.

It is possible to buy various foreign stocks and bonds on the Stock Exchange with coupons payable in London. A selection of the equities of larger and better-known corporations, such as Bell Telephone and Du Pont, are also available in London, but the relaxation of exchange controls now means that UK investors are entitled to purchase securities on overseas stock exchanges. However, against the merits of including overseas securities in a portfolio have to be set an increased range of risks. For example, where there is investment in dollar securities, a strengthening of the pound against the dollar produces in itself a fall in capital values and yields for the UK investor. The exchange rates can and do move in either direction and this adds to the uncertainties. A second risk which has to be faced - particularly in certain parts of the world - is political instability. While the British Government has never defaulted on its debt payments this cannot be said of all governments. A revolutionary government may repudiate its predecessor's debts or nationalise its industries or specific firms without compensation. And even in the most politically stable country things like tax laws and currency regulations can be imposed to the detriment of overseas investors. For the private investor the main problem however is likely to be a lack of meaningful data and to overcome this certain well-tried expedients might be employed such as:

1. Investing in foreign securities which are already traded on the London Stock Exchange. Procedures for the collection of dividends etc. will be well established as will a system of market intelligence.
2. Purchasing equities in UK companies which have subsidiaries operating in appropriate overseas regions, or which are heavily involved in the export trade. Companies of this nature often offer an analysis of revenues according to geographical areas when they present their annual reports and accounts.
3. Investing in a unit trust or investment trust which is known to hold substantial blocks of shares in a particular overseas territory/industry. One of the advantages of this from the investor's point of view is that the specialist knowledge of the managers might allow a stake to be acquired in some of the less well known but nevertheless highly successful foreign enterprises. Barclays, for example, offer the following choice of Unicorn unit trusts specialising in overseas securities and aiming at capital growth:

    (i) America Trust
   (ii) Australia Trust, and
  (iii) Worldwide Trust.

LIQUIDITY
It will normally be wise to hold a proportion of a portfolio in a form which can, if necessary, be converted into cash with a minimum delay. The small investor is particularly vulnerable and should always have a reasonable sum available in the bank, building society or Trustee Savings Bank. Funds may be needed to cope with an unexpected financial problem, to pay for rights issues, or to take advantage of unforeseen investment opportunities which appear.

The great advantage of any security quoted on the Stock Exchange is that it can be fairly easily converted into cash. Having said that, it is necessary to add a rider. An investor suffers a handicap if, and when, the prices of equities and undated fixed-interest stocks are at a low point just when cash is required. This is not unlikely bearing in mind that prices are likely to fall in times of recession and when money is in short supply.

The situation can be remedied by holding securities which do not fluctuate in value or, like shorter-dated gilts, fluctuate only within narrow limits. Thus it can be seen that shorter-dated gilts have a triple value in that they may offer a stable and compara-

tively high yield, a degree of capital appreciation, and , by no means
least, a comparatively stable price coupled with 'immediate'
convertibility.

GILT-EDGED SWITCHING

Although the yields on similar stocks will tend to be the same over
a period of time, heavy buying and selling by institutional
investors will bring yields temporarily out of line. Advantage can
be taken of even small differences in price. The relatively high-
priced stock will be sold and the relatively cheap stock will be
purchased. These so-called 'anomaly' switches will be facilitated
because of the exemption from stamp duty and the fine rates of
commission which can be obtained for large transactions in gilts.
Institutional investors will be on the constant look-out for
profitable switching operations of this nature.

Policy switching would take place if the portfolio manager
anticipates a change in interest rates. If he forecasts a rise in
interest rates, he will switch into shorter-dated securities. This
is because when interest rates rise the price of gilts will fall.
The portfolio manager will cushion the fall by switching into
shorter-dated stocks which will fall less as the maturity date
approaches. The price will move to parity regardless of interest
rates. Conversely the portfolio manager will switch to longer-
dated stocks if he envisages a fall in the interest rates since the
upswing in the price of longer-dated stocks will be more pronounced.

SCALE OF PURCHASES

The large-scale or institutional investor has to be wary of a
situation where purchases of a particular security at the one time
or over a short period of time have the effect of forcing up the
price to the detriment of the purchaser.

At the other end of the scale, small holdings may prove comparatively expensive to administer and should therefore be avoided or
eliminated at an appropriate moment.

DIVIDEND DATES

Interest on gilts is normally paid twice a year. The interest rates
vary as between the different stocks. Thus 6 per cent Funding 1993
pays interest on 15 March and 15 September, while 9 per cent Treasury
1994 pays interest on 17 May and 17 November.

While the timing of interest inflows might be of little concern
to the institutional investor concerned with taking profits from
switching operations, the smaller investor may well wish to avoid a
situation where his interest and dividends are bunched around
certain dates. The effect would be the same if one's salary was
paid twice yearly instead of on a monthly basis.

PRIVATE INVESTORS

A wealthy individual will prefer capital gains as opposed to higher
taxed dividends where the latter are subject to higher rates of tax.
He will go for long-term growth rather than high income in the
shorter term, particularly if there is a possibility of favourable
changes in capital gains tax. The profits from gilts held for
longer than a year are particularly valuable to someone who can take
advantage of the exemption from capital gains tax.

Certain investments are designed to encourage the small saver but
they are not exclusive to the poorer elements. Every portfolio for
a private investor should take advantage of the beneficial terms on
offer. Particularly valuable are the Index-linked National Savings
Certificates and the Save-As-You-Earn Index-linked Scheme mentioned
in the previous chapter.

INSTITUTIONAL INVESTORS
The extent to which the financial institutions have become the
dominant influence in the stock market is evidenced by Nicholas
Goodwin, the Chairman of the Stock Exchange:

> The share of British industry owned by individuals has declined
> from around two-thirds in 1957 to under 30 per cent today, while
> the share of the major investing institutions has risen from one-
> sixth to over one-half. (*Investor's Chronicle*, 12 December 1980.)

The explanation is that individuals are tending to invest
increasingly through the media of insurance companies, pension funds
and unit trusts. These institutions are able to employ specialist
personnel practising rigorous investment analysis and applying the
various quantitative techniques to share selection and portfolio
management. One of the effects of this domination by the institutional investors is that the size of the average bargain is
surprisingly large. This is particularly true in the case of government securities (see page 109).

Unit trusts were discussed in Chapter 6 but the investment
policies of some of the other major institutions are considered
briefly here.

1. *Life assurance companies*
The cash available for investment by the life offices is the product
of the inflow of premiums and investment income, plus the proceeds
from maturing securities (such as dated gilts), less the outflow of
payments to policyholders (or their legal personal representatives).
The prime concern of the portfolio managers will be to ensure that
funds are available to meet their commitments. Their business is
founded on the faith of their policyholders that claims will be met
without delay. The companies' cash requirements are increased
through:

(a) A concession granted to many policyholders to relinquish their
    policies in return for a surrender, albeit one which tends to
    favour the company.
(b) An offer of loan facilities to some policyholders up to the
    limits of the surrender value.

The cash flows of the life office thus include the following basic
constituents:

Cash inflow	*Cash outflow*
Premiums	Claims
Interest and dividends	Administrative expenses
Maturing securities	Surrenders
Rents	Loans
Investments sold	Dividends and cash bonuses
	Taxation
	Investments purchased

The companies face four major risks. First, there is the danger
that mortality rates may be higher than contemplated (consider the
effect of serious influenza epidemics etc.). Second, the expenses
may be greater than anticpated, particularly at a time of rampant
inflation. Third, the returns from investments may be less than
expected. And fourth, the scale of new business may decline so that
there is a fall in the flow of premiums.

However, the insurance companies' actuaries are able to predict
commitments to a high degree, and the portfolios can be structured
accordingly. A typical life office portfolio would include:

(i) British Government securities (particularly medium-dated
    stock: see Figure 6, page 22).
(ii) Industrial equities including unquoted stocks (with a view to
     long-term growth).
(iii) Industrial fixed-interest stocks (to a lesser degree).
(iv) Property including industrial and commercial premises and
     ground rents.

George Clayton and W. T. Osborn summarised the investment policy
of insurance companies in the following terms and there is no reason
to suppose these objectives have changed:

The needs of life assurance companies is such that . . . they
follow a policy of keeping fully invested at all times. They are
income-conscious investors who purchase assets to hold for income
and do not normally behave as traders in securities. Subject to
the constraints imposed upon them by their liability to taxation
and currency risks, they choose their investments with the aim of
maximizing expected yields, although this objective is modified in
practice by the desire for some portfolio diversification within

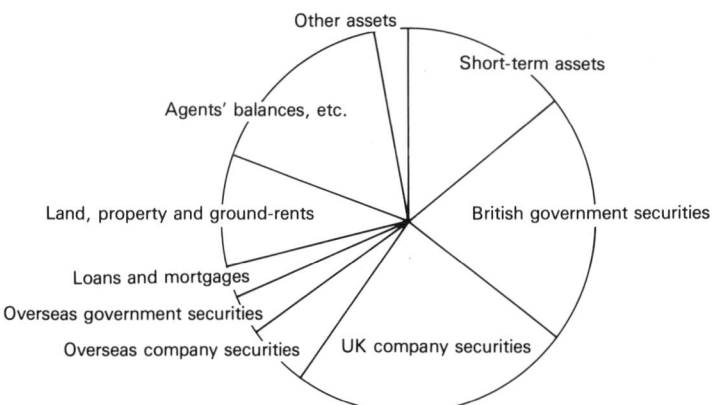

Total market value of holdings
£8458 m.

Figure 32 *Insurance companies : contents of general funds investment
portfolios as at end of 1978*
Sources: Central Statistical Office, *Financial Statistics*
(Dec 1979); British Insurance Association;
Department of Trade.

their equity holdings. (*Insurance Company Investment — Principles and Policy* (George Allen & Unwin, 1965).)

Figure 32 shows the national break-down of investments in insurance company portfolios.

2. *Pension funds*
Approved pension funds are wholly exempt from UK tax. The trustees' powers are conferred through the investment clause in the trust deed or by the terms of the Trustee Investments Act 1961:

> A young person joining a pension fund today may reasonably expect 40 to 45 years in employment and a further 15 to 20 years as a pensioner. Thus, even if he or she is the last person ever recruited by the parent company of the pension fund, some part of its investment policy will relate to a period 60 years or so away. In a continuing situation there will always be the need to consider the pension of the latest recruit, and in a normal growing fund the time horizon for policy-making will be 40 to 60 years. (Tom Heyes, *The Times*, 16 May 1980.)

In many of these funds the inflow of contributions exceed the outflow of pension payments and this results in a steady stream of funds available for investment. Commitments are known or calculable to a large extent and this means that the portfolio managers are looking for securities which mature at appropriate times. They will avoid holding too much stock which matures at around the same time, however, in case interest rates prove unfavourable when reinvestment becomes necessary. As far as equities are concerned, the larger the fund the greater the extent of diversification possible, and managers will try to avoid acquiring too large a holding in one particular company in case things go wrong.

According to the 1980 edition of *Pension Funds and Their Advisers*, the total assets held by pension funds are now in the region of £40 billion, which puts them at the same level as those held by building societies and life assurance companies. Among the largest pension schemes are the following:

	£ bn
The Post Office	2.6
The National Coal Board	2.1
British Rail	1.5
Electricity Supply	1.5
British Steel	1.1
ICI	0.9

There is at present no legal requirement for pension schemes to account to the public, nor indeed does a pension fund member in an occupational scheme have any clear right to detailed or regular information regarding the fund. But occupational pension funds are subject to detailed scrutiny by the Superannuation Funds Office of the Inland Revenue, which has power to withdraw tax exemption from any fund which does not conform to the rules. All contracted-out schemes, which cover four-fifths of the members of occupational

pension schemes, are also subject to the scrutiny of the Occupational
Pensions Board.

The types of security favoured by the pension funds generally can
be gleaned from Figure 33.

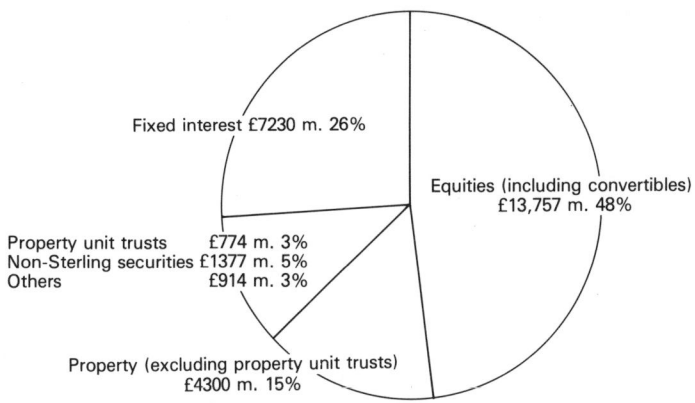

Fixed interest £7230 m. 26%

Equities (including convertibles)
£13,757 m. 48%

Property unit trusts   £774 m. 3%
Non-Sterling securities £1377 m. 5%
Others   £914 m. 3%

Property (excluding property unit trusts)
£4300 m. 15%

Figure 33 *Analysis of occupational pension fund portfolios,
           December 1979*
           Source: NAPF, *Annual Survey of Occupational Pension Funds,*
           1980.

Many institutional investors would like to invest a higher
proportion of their funds in property but prime properties are
proving hard to find:

> The problem is that as inflation takes wages to even higher levels,
> the additional income pouring into pension funds will mean that in
> order to stand still at current levels of investment funds will
> have to buy many more properties. This tightness in the United
> Kingdom property investment market has sent fund managers overseas
> scouring the United States for potential investments. (Bruce
> Kinloch, *The Daily Telegraph*, 6 May 1980.)

The fact that approved pension funds and charities (discussed next)
are tax-exempt bodies affects their investment policies. For example,
as we saw in Chapter 4 , they tend to find company fixed-interest
stocks more attractive than dated gilts since the tax-free redemption
gains have no special virtue for them.

3. *Charities*
Charities include a variety of organisations formed to pursue a
wealth of good causes and some such as Oxfam and the Nuffield
Foundation have earned world-wide respect. There is often a large
through-flow of funds and the investment of surplus funds becomes a
major consideration.

Charitable funds are also administered by trustees. As with
pension funds they are exempt from all UK tax. It is usual to find
that the portfolios of the charities tend to aim at high income
rather than long-term growth. This is because their 'self-imposed'

commitments are inclined to stretch their financial resources to the limits.

Charities are normally limited to the range of investments encompassed by the Trustee Investments Act 1961, though some of the larger of them have secured extensions to their powers through applications to the courts. Others have transferred their funds to the Charities Organization Investment Fund (set up in 1963) which has power to invest the whole of its portfolio in equities. However, bearing in mind that charities are perpetuities - that is, they continue indefinitely - the constraints have adversely affected the value of their portfolios. The inability to invest in land and property - which tend to be the best defence against rampant inflation - has proved a particularly big handicap.

William G. Nursaw estimates that there are some 150,000 charities in existence, a substantial minority of which are unregistered. He also points out a possible danger when lay committees become responsible for investing funds:

> The investment of charitable funds is often bedevilled by aged, inaccessible trustees who, when they are brought together, not infrequently disagree on investment policy. . . . Charities are very much in need of daily expert advice and should not have to rely upon a financial committee which considers that it meets frequently if it meets once a quarter. (*The Art and Practice of Investment* (Hutchinson, 3rd edn, 1974).)

4. *Banks*

The investment policies of the large commercial banks are constrained by the need for liquidity at all times. Liquidity is even more vital for banks than insurance companies since they are required to meet the requirements of their cheque-account customers on demand. Though their customers needs can be substantially predicted the overriding concern with liquidity becomes apparent from a study of a bank balance-sheet. The investments are ranked in order of liquidity:

(a) Very short loans to the discount houses (money at call and short notice)
(b) UK Treasury bills (very short-dated)
(c) Other short-dated bills
(d) Deposits with the Bank of England
(e) Government securities (tending to be short-dated: see Figure 6, page 22)
(f) Advances to customers (of varying terms and carrying greater risk and higher returns)

It is the overall need for liquidity in the banking system which gives the Bank of England the power to exercise a degree of control over money supplies. For example, by calling for Special Deposits from the commercial banks, the Bank of England is forcing them to restructure their investments. Pressure is exerted on them to reduce the volume of loans to customers. Loans and advances to customers are in every respect an investment so far as bankers are concerned.

Unlike some of their Continental counterparts the British banks have avoided acquiring equities in the companies which they finance. However, there may be new policies in the offing:

> Barclays, the largest British clearing bank, intends to put up

risk capital to back oil exploration in the North Sea . . . the move . . . represents the first serious shift by a British clearing bank towards using investors' money as equity investment behind speculative industrial projects . . . Mr. Peter Leslie, a general manager of Barclays Bank International, said: 'We have decided, following approaches from a number of oil companies active in the North Sea, to undertake equity investment in oil exploration through participation in certain of the consortiums preparing to apply for licences'. . . . The provision of risk capital, and the element of chance such decisions entail, has traditionally been the preserve of merchant banks whose investors have been prepared to accept the risk element involved in return for potentially higher rewards. (David Hewson, *The Times* Business News, 23 May 1980.)

The clearing banks have also begun to take an interest in long-term lending to house purchasers in direct competition with the building societies. The extent to which they take over this market from the building societies in future years remains to be seen.

TRUST FUNDS
When a person dies they may bequeath their estate to minors, in which case the funds will have to be invested by the trustees until the minors come of age. Or the testator (the person who makes the will) may give a life interest in the estate to one person (called the life tenant), while the estate then passes to another person (called the remainderman) on the death of the life tenant. Again this will make it necessary for trustees to invest the funds and carry out the terms of the will. The interests of all parties will have to be balanced fairly against each other.

Trustees will also be involved where a person dies intestate (i.e. without having made a will) and funds have to be held in trust for the surviving spouse and children.

Trustees are not only involved with the affairs of deceased persons. Anyone may execute a trust deed thereby setting up a trust fund which then has to be administered by the trustees in accordance with the terms of the trust. The purpose may be generally charitable or it may be to ensure that certain members of a family are financially secured. We have also seen how trust deeds are used in connection with unit trusts and debenture stocks.

Many wills and trust deeds include investment clauses which give the trustees wide discretionary powers. However, if a trust fund is established with no guidelines as to how it is to be invested, the Trustee Investments Act 1961 will apply. This empowers a trustee to obtain a valuation of the trust fund whereupon he can divide the portfolio into two equal parts, (a) Narrower-range investments and (b) Wider-range investments. The division once made is final and the value of the funds will soon diverge.

Narrower-range investments
These include:

1. National Savings Certificates.
2. National Savings Bank and Trustee Savings Bank accounts.
3. Fixed-interest securities issued by the British Government (including the Northern Ireland and Isle of Man governments unless priced at over 115).

4. Securities guaranteed by the UK Government.
5. Fixed-interest securities issued by public authorities or nationalised undertakings.
6. Fixed-interest securities issued and registered in the United Kingdom by any Commonwealth government or local authority, or by the International Bank.
7. Fixed-interest loans of local authorities and water companies in the United Kingdom.
8. Bank of Ireland stock.
9. Building Society deposit accounts.
10. Debentures issued by UK companies.
11. Mortgages on freehold properties (or leaseholds with more than 60 years to run).
12. Perpetual rent charges (ground rents) on land in the United Kingdom.

Wider-range investments
1. Fully paid-up share capital of UK companies. Such securities must be quoted on a recognised stock exchange. They must be fully paid except for new issues to be paid up within nine months. The company must have a total paid-up capital of at least £1 million and must have paid dividends on all its share capital in each of the preceding five years.
2. Building society shares.
3. Holdings in unit trusts authorised by the Department of Trade.

Advice
Apart from investing in National Savings Certificates or ordinary deposits with the National Savings Bank or the Trustee Savings Bank, the trustees are required to take expert advice before committing the trust funds. The expert will normally be a broker, but trust corporations (such as the bank trust companies) with their own investment departments would be able to dispense with broker's advice if they so wished.

Additions to the trust fund
These must be divided equally between the narrower-range and wider-range funds.

Withdrawals from the trust fund
These may be from either the narrower range fund or the wider-range fund at the trustee's discretion.

Special Range Fund
Where trustees are given specific power to hold certain categories of securities such as shares in a family company or certain categories of quoted securities, land or buildings, these will be excluded from the trust fund when the division is made between narrower-range and wider-range securities. If any securities are realised in the special-range fund and not reinvested in it, the proceeds have to be invested in narrower- and wider-range securities in equal parts.

When executors or administrators receive a grant (of probate or letters of administration respectively), they may decide to retain stocks standing in the name of the deceased. In this case they will send a Letter of Request (see Figure 34) together with the grant so that the securities can be put into their own names without reference to their fiduciary capacity.

LETTER OF REQUEST	
	(Above this line for Registrar's use only).

REQUEST BY EXECUTORS OR ADMINISTRATORS OF A DECEASED HOLDER TO BE PLACED ON THE REGISTER IN THEIR OWN RIGHT.

Full name of Undertaking.	*To the Registrar of*	
Full description of Security. (See note below)		
Number or amount of Shares, Stock or other Security and, in figures column only, number and denomination of units if any.—	WORDS	FIGURES (units of)
Full name of Deceased.	.... *Deceased*	

I/We, the undersigned, being the personal representative(s) of the above-named deceased, hereby request you to register me/us as the holder(s) of the above-mentioned Stock/Shares now registered in the name of the said deceased.

DATED this ....day of...19.........

Signature(s) of Personal Representative(s)

....

....

....

Full names and full postal addresses (including County or, if applicable, Postal District number) of the Personal Representative(s) (PLEASE COMPLETE IN TYPEWRITING OR IN BLOCK CAPITALS IN THE ORDER IN WHICH THEY ARE TO BE REGISTERED).	....

IF AN ACCOUNT ALREADY EXISTS IN THE ABOVE NAME(S) THE ABOVE-MENTIONED HOLDING WILL BE ADDED TO THAT ACCOUNT, <u>UNLESS INSTRUCTIONS ARE RECEIVED TO THE CONTRARY.</u>

The Certificate(s) in the name of the deceased, if not already with the Registrar, must accompany this form. No registration fee is payable. * A separate Letter of Request must be used for each class of Security.	Stamp or name and address of person lodging this form.

Figure 34 *A Letter of Request*

151

Assignment

Working together in small groups discuss the following portfolios
and consider whether any changes are necessary. Be specific with
your proposals. Use the Daily Official List, brokers lists and
financial papers where possible. When you have reached your
conclusions compare your proposals with those of the other groups.

Current portfolio of Mrs Amelia Jones

Aged 74, a widow with no surviving children. Estate bequeathed to
Oxfam. Lives in own house in New Forest. Only other income is
pension from late husband's company (£1000 per annum) and old-age
pension.

        1000 Bank of Ireland Ordinary Stock (£1 units)
        3200 Eagle Star Insurance Ordinary Stock (25p units)
        2500 Imperial Chemical Industries Ordinary Stock (£1 units)
        1500 British Petroleum Ordinary Stock (£1 units)
        2600 Unigate Ltd Ordinary Stock (£1 units)
          50 Distillers Ordinary Stock (50p units)
     £10,000 2$\frac{1}{2}$ per cent Consolidated Stock
      £4,500 3 per cent British Gas 1990-95
        £150 Wessex Trustee Savings Bank
             Bank Current Account varies between £200 and £300.

Current portfolio of Kenneth Crombie

Aged 55. A marketing executive. Presently earning £15,000 per
annum but in poor health. Plans to retire at 60. Pension would be
about one-third of salary. Lives in company flat in central London
with wife. They plan to join their only daughter and her family in
Somerset when they retire.

     £5000 Britannia Building Society Share Account
      3000 Tate and Lyle Ordinary Stock (£1 units)
      5000 Allied Breweries Ordinary Stock (£1 units)
     £5000 Allied Breweries 7$\frac{3}{4}$ per cent Unsecured Loan Stock 1993-98

Kenneth Crombie has an endowment policy (with profits) which is
maturing within a few weeks and wants to know how he should invest
the £15,000 proceeds.

Thomas Kershaw deceased

Tom Kershaw died last December with the following Stock Exchange
securities among his assets. His trustees have retained them intact
and have not yet split them up between narrower- and wider-range
funds, but they are about to do so. They have a further £15,000
which they intend to invest. The estate is to be held for the
benefit of Tom's widow, Margaret, during her lifetime. On her death
the funds will pass to the two grandchildren who are living with
Margaret. Their parents were killed in a car crash a year ago.
The children are aged 10 and 12 respectively. The widow is aged 72
and has an absolute title to the house (valued for probate at
£50,000). Her income consists of:

(a) A fixed pension of £1500 per annum from her late husband's firm.
    He was an advertising consultant in the textile industry.

(b) The old-age pension.
(c) The income from this trust.

The portfolio:

£10,000 4 per cent Consolidated Stock
£3,600 3 per cent British Transport 1978/88
£8,000 12 per cent Exchequer 1998
£3,000 12 per cent Exchequer 2013/17
 6,000 Courtaulds Ltd Ordinary Stock units of 25p each
£3,000 " 7 per cent Debentures 1982/7
10,000 Coats Patons Ltd Ordinary Stock units of 25p each
 5,000 " " 6 per cent Cum. Pref. Stock (£1 units)
 4,000 Tootal Ltd Ordinary Stock units of 25p each

18 Technical Analysis

Fundamental or traditional analysis is concerned with assessing the
intrinsic value of a share. What is the underlying value of the
assets? What is the 'true worth' of a share? These are the types
of questions we were posing in Chapter 10. An alternative technique
for investors is to study price movements over a period of time. By
plotting prices and projecting trends an attempt is made to discover
predictable patterns in share price behaviour. The rationale is
that this behaviour repeats itself over a period of time and that
accurate predictions become possible. This sort of treatment is
known as Technical Analysis.

For example, by means of moving averages, a share price showing
wide fluctuations can be converted to a graph showing a steady
upward or downward trend. This trend line can be projected and
investment decisions made as a result. Consider, for example, the
following figures showing share prices for Hypothetico Ltd 25p
ordinary shares.

	Price as at end of month (i)	Cumulative six-monthly total (ii)	Six-monthly moving average (iii)
January	106p		
February	105		
March	102	637p	106p
April	98	639	107
May	120	646	108
June	106	652	109
July	108	662	110
August	112	666	111
September	108	673	112
October	108		
November	124		
December	113		

Column (i) shows the price of Hypothetico ordinary shares over a
twelve-month period. It is difficult to get any sort of picture
from these untreated statistics. So in column (ii) we aggregate
the prices of six months' prices, placing the resultant total against
the centre months. In column (iii) the cumulative total is divided
by six and this then provides us with a six-monthly moving average.
A distinguishable upward trend has emerged and this is plotted in
Figure 35. If one preferred a twelve-monthly moving average the same
technique is used but twelve months are aggregated instead of six.

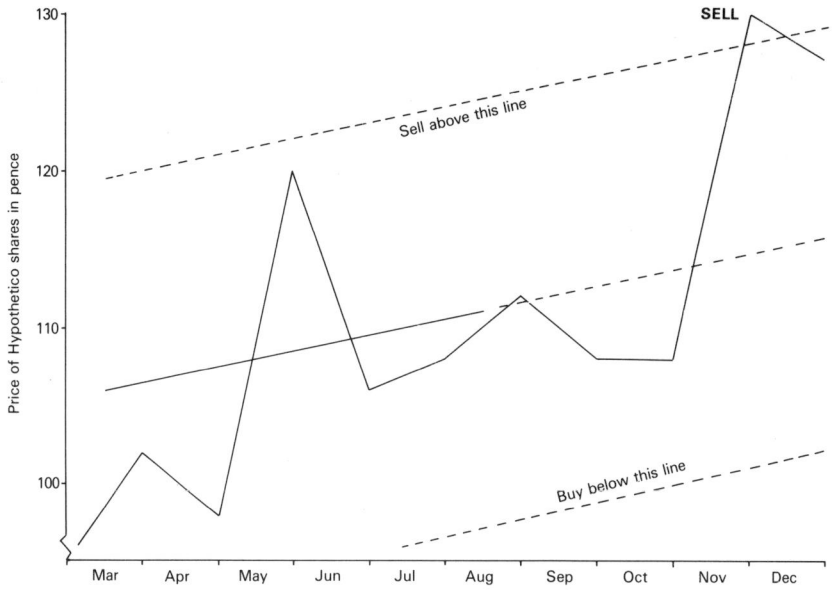

Figure 35 *Hypothetico shares*

Using this analysis as a basis for transactions in these shares a policy might be formulated whereby a specific number of shares would be purchased whenever prices fell to $12\frac{1}{2}$ per cent or more below the trend line. Conversely, whenever prices rose to $12\frac{1}{2}$ per cent or more above the trend a certain number of shares would be disposed of. In this way a series of favourable bargains would hopefully be executed.

The trends are possible to classify in terms of the time period to which they relate. The *primary trend* indicates the direction in which prices are moving over a period of a year or more. There are likely to be a number of deviations from the primary trend. Thus, over a shorter period of weeks or months a series of *secondary trends* can be expected to develop in either an upward or downward direction from the main or primary trend. These fluctuations can be explained as a result of bouts of profit-taking in a generally bullish market or spates of buying as investors decide to buy shares at 'bargain' prices in a bear market. In addition to these deviations there are likely to be even shorter-term vacillations in prices. The *tertiary trends* describe the changes in share prices over the course of a few days or weeks.

Resistance levels appear when buyers begin to buy shares as the price falls to a particular point or when holders begin to sell shares as the price rises to a particular point. The indication is that investors generally have some measure of the underlying value of the shares. When the share price rises to the resistance level twice in quick succession the pattern is known as a 'double top' – three times and the pattern is a 'triple top'. Conversely, when the price falls to the lower resistance levels twice or three times in quick succession, they are known as 'double' or 'triple bottom' respectively. Figure 36 shows such a situation in chart form. Note that if the price of Hypothetico Ordinaries had been rising generally over the past twelve months (an upward primary trend), what appears in July is a secondary downward trend. The shorter period vacillations are the tertiary trends. Thus, between x and y there is an upward tertiary trend.

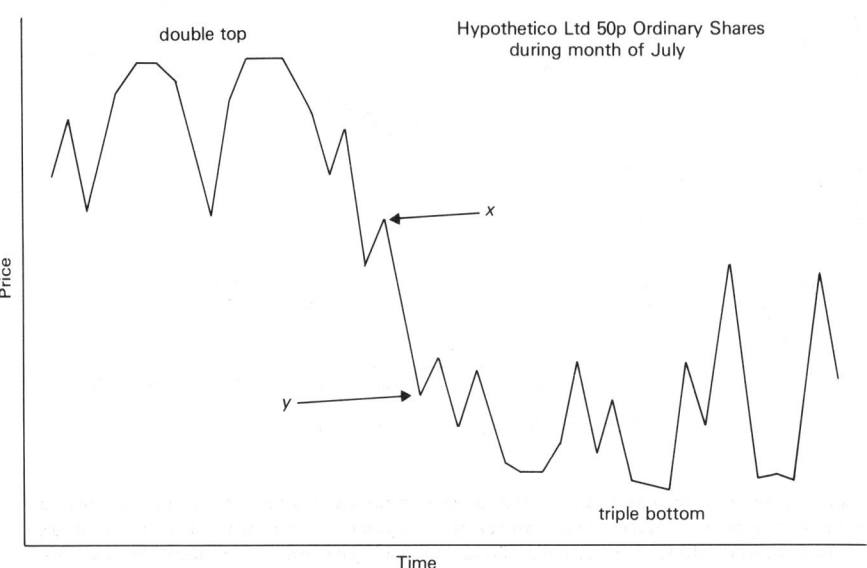

Figure 36 *Example of resistance levels*

In the words of R. J. Briston again:

As charts are used by so many investors, they have become a material market influence. Signals given by charts, like purchases suggested by financial editors, tend to be self-realising, for if they are sufficiently positive and enough investors act upon them the share price will automatically move in the suggested direction. (*The Stock Exchange and Investment Analysis* (George Allen & Unwin, 3rd edn, 1975).)

The data on which analysts base their calculations will be the same so it is likely that their conclusions will be the same. When the price falls to a certain point there will be a spate of buying which will make the price rise again - as predicted. When the price rises to a certain point there will be a burst of selling which will make the price fall again - as predicted. This will ensure that the trend is perpetuated in the prescribed direction.

The Random Walk Theory is a counter-argument to technical analysis. The suggestion is that prices fluctuate (or wander) randomly, within fairly narrow limits, around the intrinsic (or fundamental) value. This theory accommodates the views of the fundamental analysts who are concerned with finding a 'true worth' for any particular

security. The price of such a security will fluctuate in response
to external pressures, be they international tensions or gloomy
economic forecasts, bad trade figures or whatever, but the 'true
worth' will act as a magnet constantly drawing market price back
towards it.

Denis Weaver has referred to the theory in the following terms:

> A number of investigators . . . have argued that the changes in a
> representative market index such as the Dow Jones Index or the
> Financial Times Industrial Share Index are random . . . the level
> of the index at any moment discounts all known factors and . . .
> changes are due to unknown factors which emerge randomly. If this
> argument, the strongest form of the Random Walk hypothesis, can be
> substantiated, much of what has been regarded as the skill and
> judgement of the investment manager is little more than luck. . . .
> On the other hand, the majority of random walkers will concede that
> it is possible to forecast the movement in the price of an indivi-
> dual share over a limited period. (*Investment Analysis* (Longman,
> 1971).)

The Efficient Markets Theory is another strong counter-argument
to technical analysis. It is based on the implication that prices
on the stock market are determined by a host of investors who are
between them capable of interpreting and assessing the data available. If the price of a security falls then this should be accepted
as the combined best judgement of investors in the market. When
events occur which affect the prospects of individual companies,
investors will anticipate the effects through adjustments in prices.
Such a theory cannot live with the completely different notion that
prices fluctuate in predictable patterns.

Computers are likely to be the tools of the trade for the market
analyst. They can be used to build charts from data banks of share
prices. The computer can be programmed to construct trend lines,
measure deviations, and highlight various patterns in the share price
fluctuations. By no means least, the program can be devised to put
on notice the portfolio manager and analyst when prices of particular
shares reach levels at which decisions are required.

The common feature in all market analysis is the attempt to
benefit from the fluctuations in prices, essentially buying at a low
price and selling at a high price. Among the mechanical rules which
can be employed is what is termed Pound Averaging. This entails the
investor first choosing an appropriate stock to invest in. He then
allocates regular sums to be used for the purchase of the shares.
The fixed sum is used for purchasing the shares regardless of the
price level. If the price is low, more shares will be purchased.
If the price is high, fewer shares will be purchased. The effect
can be seen in the following example:

X invests £4000 in Apex equities when they are standing at 50p
each at the start of period 1.
Y uses the pound averaging technique and buys £1000 of shares at
the commencement of each of 4 periods, thus:

Period	Market price of equities	Number of shares purchased	Cumulative total of shares held
1	50p	2000	2000
2	25p	4000	6000
3	75p	1333	7333
4	50p	2000	9333

Comparing the results of X's buy and hold policy with Y's pound averaging we find that at the end of period 4 X has 8000 shares valued at £4000, while Y has ended up with 9333 shares valued at £4666.50. Averaging has gained £666.50 for Y.

The more voltatile the share prices, the greater the profit shown. One can see this from a rework of the example with smaller fluctuations in the prices. The purchasing schedule for Y becomes:

Period	Market price of equities	Number of shares purchased	Cumulative total of shares held
1	50p	2000	2000
2	40p	2500	4500
3	60p	1666	6166
4	50p	2000	8166

The averaging has still proved beneficial for Y but he has 8166 shares worth £4083. The technique has gained him just £83 this time.

Technical analysis is concerned to a considerable extent with the analysis of charts and in the United Kingdom attention tends to be focused on the *Financial Times* indices. The principle on which an index is compiled is as follows. Suppose you want to create an index which shows what is happening to equity prices of companies in the leisure industry.

Equity index for the leisure industry

Company	Market price 1 Jan 31 Jan (i) (ii)	Price relative 31 Jan (iii)	Weighting factor (iv)	Weighted price relatives (v)
A	11½p 23p	200	2	400
B	60p 60p	100	5	500
C	20p 22p	110	8	880
D	40p 36p	90	3	270
E	52p 39p	75	12	900
F	15p 12p	80	10	800
			40	£3750

Index number at 31 Jan = 93.75

The equities in six companies have been selected for this index. In column (i) the prices of these shares are shown as they were on 1 January. These prices will serve as a base for the index. A month later the prices have changed for five of the six companies as indicated in column (ii). The price relatives are now calculated

and the results appear in column (iii). The calculation for share
A is

$$\frac{\text{new price}}{\text{old price}} \times 100 = \frac{23p}{11\frac{1}{2}p} \times 100 = 200$$

For share D the calculation is

$$\frac{36p}{40p} \times 100 = 90$$

Similar calculations are required for the other shares.
   The weighting factors are shown in column (iv). These indicate
the comparative importance of each equity in the list. In our
example there are, say, 2 million A Ordinaries, and so the weighting
factor is shown as 2. It follows that there are 5 million B
Ordinaries, 8 million C Ordinaries, and so on.
   In column (v) is shown the result of multiplying the price
relative for each share by its weighting factor.
   The final stage entails aggregating these weighted price relatives
and dividing the total by the total of the weighting factors. This
provides us with an index number which indicates the extent to which
equity shares in the leisure industry have fallen during the month
of January.
   The *Financial Times* Actuaries Share Indices are constructed
according to the same basic principles. An example is given in
Figure 37. These indices enable a number of important questions to
be answered for the portfolio manager, such as:

1. Are shares in one sector faring better than those in another?
Is this a continuing trend? If shares in a particular sector are
showing bigger price rises than elsewhere, should we be purchasing
shares in this sector and selling our shares in the depressed
sectors? Are our shares in the depressed sectors going to follow
the trend even if they are doing comparatively well at the moment?
2. Are prices at the present time significantly above a generally
downward trend? Is this then a propitious moment for selling stocks?
Which stocks? Should we switch sectors at the same time as we
switch securities?
3. Are prices at the present time significantly below a generally
upward trend? Is this a propitious moment to buy? Are prices
likely to fall even further? Which sectors are the most promising?
Which have the best 'track record'?
4. How are the shares in our portfolio performing in comparison
with the index? Are we able to demonstrate our special skills and
knowledge by producing above average results? How much above
average?
   Another index of note is the *Financial Times* Ordinary Share Index,
which was created in 1935. It is based on the prices of 30 wide-
ranging industrial equities. Some of the original thirty companies
(such as GKN, London Brick and Dunlop) continue to feature in the
index. Each of the constituents is a leader in its field and
together they represent a relatively large slice of the equity

159

FT-ACTUARIES SHARE INDICES

These indices are the joint compilation of the Financial Times, the Institute of Actuaries
and the Faculty of Actuaries

EQUITY GROUPS & SUB-SECTIONS						Wed., Jan. 23, 1980		Tues., Jan. 22	Mon., Jan. 21	Fri., Jan. 18	Thurs., Jan. 17	Year ago (approx.)
Figures in parentheses show number of stocks per section		Index No.	Day's Change %	Est. Earnings Yield % (Max.)	Gross Div. Yield % (ACT at 30%)	Est. P/E Ratio (Net)		Index No.	Index No.	Index No.	Index No.	Index No.
1	CAPITAL GOODS (172)	229.71	—	18.95	6.79	6.66		229.74	232.48	231.45	226.67	228.60
2	Building Materials (27)	220.67	+ 0.7	17.83	7.10	7.20		219.07	224.22	221.16	214.03	203.25
3	Contracting, Construction (29)	344.74	−0.5	26.77	7.02	4.62		346.34	350.58	346.70	340.86	346.80
4	Electricals (15)	582.62	−0.1	13.90	4.26	9.59		583.35	586.26	587.55	578.21	533.44
5	Engineering Contractors (11)	293.47	−0.3	26.43	8.72	4.84		294.31	296.78	296.72	291.71	355.63
6	Mechanical Engineering (74)	160.86	+ 0.1	21.36	8.06	5.78		160.74	162.32	161.71	158.92	178.10
8	Metals and Metal Forming (16)	158.69	−0.7	21.01	9.57	5.72		159.85	162.47	161.10	157.69	159.23
11	CONSUMER GOODS (DURABLE)(50)	210.01	+ 0.4	16.99	5.81	7.27		209.23	209.78	209.07	206.35	203.69
12	Lt. Electronics, Radio, TV (15)	287.18	+ 0.2	13.35	4.48	9.62		286.50	286.25	285.33	281.61	259.19
13	Household Goods (14)	113.68	−0.6	26.62	9.53	4.54		114.39	114.23	114.64	113.63	164.18
14	Motors and Distributors (21)	113.03	+ 0.9	23.78	8.24	4.96		111.99	113.35	112.74	111.18	116.12
21	CONSUMER GOODS (NON-DURABLE) (173)	222.23	—	18.17	6.81	6.78		222.35	226.99	226.65	221.79	205.50
22	Breweries (14)	263.62	−0.6	16.81	6.64	6.96		265.29	273.68	273.08	266.35	224.87
23	Wines and Spirits (5)	315.91	−0.7	17.18	5.87	7.18		318.00	322.79	322.01	317.60	289.82
24	Entertainment, Catering (17)	298.51	+ 0.3	18.70	7.01	6.73		297.75	307.55	310.41	302.04	269.29
25	Food Manufacturing (19)	201.42	−0.4	20.12	7.23	6.14		202.30	205.38	205.21	201.90	194.74
26	Food Retailing (15)	317.45	−0.6	12.98	4.47	9.21		319.37	325.52	321.59	316.76	226.26
32	Newspapers, Publishing (13)	425.56	−0.1	23.43	7.06	5.87		426.06	432.54	427.83	422.39	381.01
33	Packaging and Paper (15)	124.72	−0.1	23.88	9.11	5.39		124.83	126.72	125.89	123.56	131.76
34	Stores (43)	219.07	+ 0.6	14.05	5.20	9.19		217.87	222.12	221.87	215.04	189.83
35	Textiles (23)	130.17	+ 0.2	28.29	12.46	4.47		129.95	132.33	132.61	132.38	174.01
36	Tobaccos (3)	216.71	—	26.30	10.29	4.29		216.68	221.33	221.71	213.46	236.05
37	Toys and Games (6)	43.54	−0.3	37.59	16.45	3.36		43.66	43.85	43.62	43.48	88.91
41	OTHER GROUPS (97)	199.72	+ 0.2	15.75	6.76	7.73		199.39	203.03	202.29	198.98	193.01
42	Chemicals (17)	295.70	+ 0.6	16.58	6.82	6.97		293.96	299.39	299.75	296.59	272.66
43	Pharmaceutical Products (7)	208.97	+ 1.0	12.19	6.11	10.01		206.89	210.69	209.91	201.34	236.79
44	Office Equipment (6)	108.03	−1.3	18.14	7.91	6.81		109.40	110.66	109.15	105.87	128.91
45	Shipping (10)	427.63	−0.7	12.38	7.55	10.31		430.80	439.36	432.44	420.56	422.55
46	Miscellaneous (57)	236.24	−0.2	16.85	6.67	7.52		236.77	241.25	240.19	235.48	209.67
49	INDUSTRIAL GROUP (492)	224.77	—	17.70	6.72	6.99		224.68	228.44	227.78	223.35	214.70
51	Oils (8)	697.18	−0.5	16.12	6.84	6.71		700.97	710.74	714.28	715.29	497.67
59	500 SHARE INDEX	262.31	−0.1	17.38	6.75	6.93		262.51	266.76	266.41	262.35	238.22
61	FINANCIAL GROUP (117)	191.19	−0.4	—	5.78	—		192.03	195.28	193.55	189.86	367.35
62	Banks (6)	221.72	−1.4	37.51	5.86	3.40		224.92	229.61	226.46	223.68	201.78
63	Discount Houses (10)	243.01	+ 1.1	—	8.16	—		240.49	240.14	239.59	241.11	211.85
64	Hire Purchase (5)	181.88	−0.5	19.47	5.23	6.50		182.86	184.58	182.52	183.14	160.30
65	Insurance (Life) (10)	159.67	−0.1	—	6.59	—		159.89	162.32	159.91	156.67	130.49
66	Insurance (Composite) (9)	127.49	−0.2	—	7.62	—		127.77	130.56	128.66	126.68	118.01
67	Insurance Brokers (10)	294.20	−0.2	16.95	6.67	8.44		294.88	299.96	299.52	287.39	293.74
68	Merchant Banks (14)	97.88	−0.4	—	6.08	—		98.31	98.05	98.26	95.67	79.68
69	Property (44)	342.84	+ 0.4	3.85	3.13	37.26		341.48	347.07	346.93	336.70	269.44
70	Miscellaneous (9)	127.50	−1.2	16.29	7.15	8.06		129.06	129.82	128.82	128.83	114.07
71	Investment Trusts (109)	210.42	−0.4	—	5.86	—		211.36	212.96	210.35	207.65	209.70
81	Mining Finance (4)	184.54	−0.8	12.49	4.79	9.72		185.99	199.51	195.62	186.67	113.77
91	Overseas Traders (20)	376.35	−0.3	13.09	6.87	9.32		377.61	383.11	377.02	369.95	317.03
99	ALL-SHARE INDEX (750)	245.18	−0.2	—	6.48	—		245.64	249.91	248.89	244.72	220.12

FIXED INTEREST PRICE INDICES						FIXED INTEREST YIELDS British Govt. Av. Gross Red.			Wed., Jan. 23	Tues., Jan. 22	Year ago (approx.)
British Government		Wed., Jan. 23	Day's Change %	xd adj. today	xd adj. 1980 to date	1	Low	5 years	11.85	11.89	10.23
						2	Coupons	15 years	11.85	11.89	11.98
						3		25 years	11.85	11.89	12.78
1	Under 5 years	101.69	+ 0.16	—	0.45	4	Medium	5 years	13.96	14.03	13.42
2	5-15 years	107.83	+ 0.28	—	1.55	5	Coupons	15 years	13.39	13.43	13.42
						6		25 years	13.27	13.31	13.42
3	Over 15 years	114.90	+ 0.30	—	0.24	7	High	5 years	14.42	14.47	13.54
4	Irredeemables	134.74	+ 0.31	—	0.00	8	Coupons	15 years	13.85	13.89	13.92
5	All stocks	107.95	+ 0.25	—	0.63	9		25 years	13.56	13.60	13.94
						10	Irredeemables		10.93	10.06	12.47

		Wed., Jan. 23		Tues., Jan. 28	Mon., Jan. 21	Friday, Jan. 18	Thurs., Jan. 17	Wed., Jan. 16	Tues., Jan. 15	Mon., Jan. 14	Year ago (approx.)
		Index No	Yield %								
15	20-yr. Red. Deb. & Loans (15)	50.88	14.53	50.87	50.87	50.63	50.31	49.92	49.83	49.75	54.14
16	Investment Trust Prefs. (15)	47.96	14.06	47.81	47.83	47.78	46.92	47.00	47.00	46.90	50.76
17	Coml. and Indl. Prefs. (20)	62.01	14.45	61.86	61.86	61.81	61.68	62.14	61.89	61.64	72.14

Figure 37

160

market. It differs from the Actuaries Shares Indices in that it is a geometric mean. It is calculated by multiplying together the prices of the 30 shares and taking the 30th root of the product after bringing in a constant to relate the index to the base date. The problem of weighting is eliminated.

The changes, monitored on an hour-to-hour basis, depend only on price movements from one index to the next. The result is that the index is particularly sensitive to the changing moods in the market. On the other hand the index can be brought down rather sharply if one price falls very sharply out of line with the other constituents. The collapses of Rolls-Royce and British Leyland brought the index down with them far more severely than would have been the case with an arithmetic index.

Assignment

Working in pairs (where possible) study the problems posed below. Then devise precise responses and finally compare your findings in the main group.

1. Figure 38 shows a so-called triangle or flag pattern. Describe what has been happening to share X. Give possible explanations.

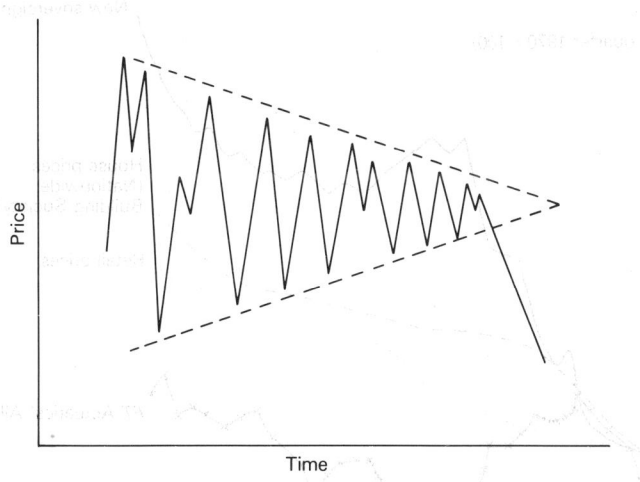

Figure 38

2. Figure 39 shows what is called a head and shoulders effect.
Describe what has been happening to share Y. Can you offer any
explanations?

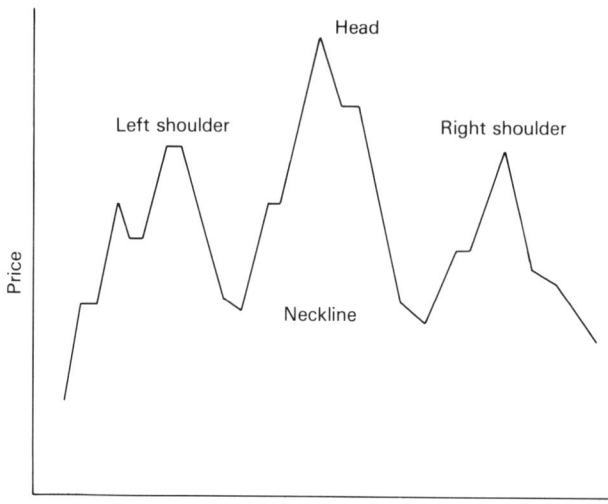

Figure 39

3. Figure 40 is based on one which appeared in the *Financial Times*
on 29 December 1979 in an article written by the Financial Editor,
Richard Lambert. Interpret the information and draft a brief
report of about 200 words on your findings and their implications.

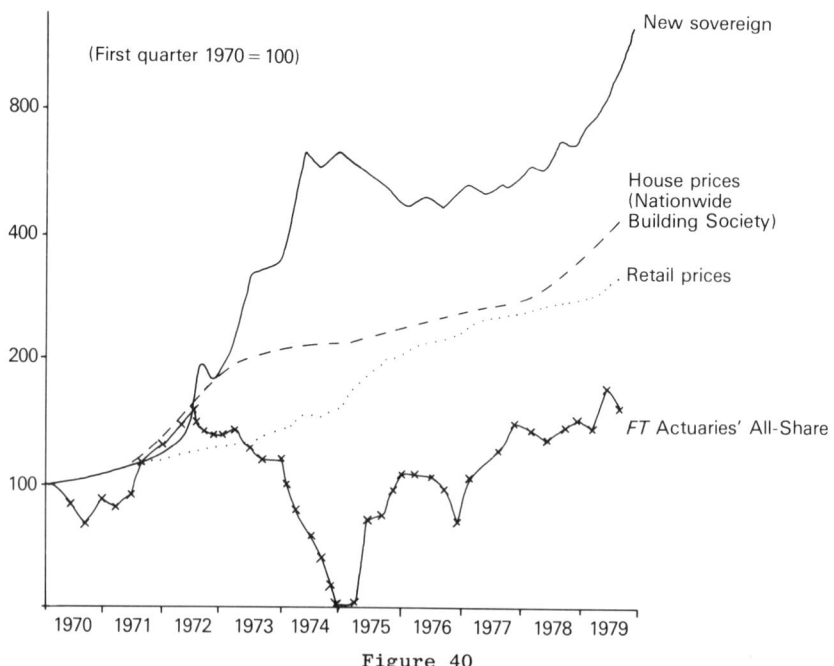

Figure 40

4. Figure 41 shows a plot of the *Financial Times* Index of Industrial
   Ordinary Shares Index for eleven months in 1979. From this can
   be seen the wide fluctuations which occur in the equity market.
   Draw up a list of the six most likely explanations for major
   upswings and downswings in the index, without necessarily
   referring to the period covered here. Be as specific as possible.

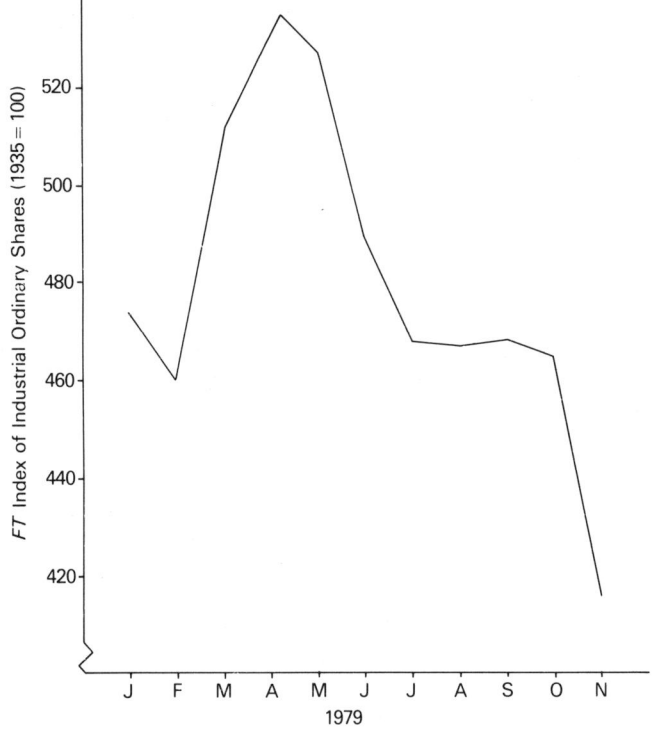

Figure 41

19 Alternative Investment Media

During a period of high inflation it is understandable that private
investors particularly should seek alternative forms of investment
in an attempt to stop the slide in the real value of their personal
savings and wealth. A number of opportunities present themselves
and will be considered here.

COMMODITY FUTURES
An article by Jonathan Ward in the *Daily Telegraph*, 8 December 1979,
indicates one of the options available:

> A decade of watching the stockmarket successively cough, splutter
> and move sideways, has prompted many hard-headed American investors
> to turn their backs on the 'big board' and put their money into
> the boom or bust world of the commodity markets.
>
> Because of the attitude of the United Kingdom authorities, the
> British commodity markets have remained a closed world to most
> United Kingdom investors. Not so in Chicago where it is as normal
> to gamble on a rise in the price of grain, coffee or even frozen
> orange juice, as it is to punt on the future prosperity of General
> Motors.
>
> The commodity markets are definitely not for widows and orphans
> but the fact remains that the opportunity exists and for those
> with money to risk, it can be a profitable business.
>
> Perhaps the best way for the uninitiated is to join a syndicate
> or fund which operates like a unit trust, where professionals
> handle the investments.
>
> There are many funds and syndicates in the United States - all
> since the abolition of exchange controls open to the British
> investor.

How does the commodity market differ from the Stock Exchange?
The first difference to be noted is that the Stock Exchange deals
with securities, while in the commodity market the trade is in raw
materials. Prices on the commodity markets are reached through
formal auctions without the intervention of jobbers such as we find
on the London Stock Exchange. Another fundamental difference between
the two markets is that the vast majority of investors on the Stock
Exchange are looking for price rises whereas on the commodity
markets there is a more even spread between those looking for a price
rise and those hoping for stable or lower prices. Producers will be
hoping for high prices. Manufacturers will benefit from lower
prices. Some will hedge against prices rising. Others will hedge
against prices falling.
Finally, there is the degree of leverage which exists in
commodities. The investor is only required to put down about 10

per cent of the purchase price. This means that if the price of the commodity increases by 10 per cent the investor will make 100 per cent profit. Against this, however, the dealing costs are higher in commodities and they are calculated on the total value of the contract (as opposed to the 10 per cent deposit). And there are no interest payments or dividends for the investor in commodities.

If there were only the markets in existing commodities (the so-called 'spot' market) they would be of little interest to the majority of investors. But a contract known as a futures contract has evolved which gives a merchant, or a speculator, the right to buy or sell a given quantity of a particular commodity at a future date and at a pre-agreed price. Thus a food manufacturer might require large quantities of cocoa for his product. He needs to know the cost of cocoa for the future as well as the present in order that he can quote the prices for his own product with reasonable accuracy. If the price were to rise unexpectedly during the course of a contract to supply his product he might well be forced into insolvency. However, he can guard against this by entering into a futures contract to buy an appropriate amount of cocoa, say, six months ahead. If the price of cocoa rises between now and then, the manufacturer takes a profit on the futures contract which will offset the extra cost of the cocoa when it is purchased on the 'spot' market.

Suppose on 10 January a speculator thinks the price of sugar will fall. He therefore agrees to sell sugar on 30 September at the ruling price for September-sell futures. He will then counteract this contract in, say, June by buying on the futures market, the contract being for the same quantity and for the same terminal date. If the price of sugar falls between January and June as anticipated the speculator will make a profit.

On 10 January the speculator would be described as holding a 'short position'. If by contrast he had expected a rise in the price of sugar and had reversed his buy and sell futures, he would be said to be holding a 'long position'.

Commodities traded on the London futures market include:

Soft commodities	Metals
Cocoa	Copper (wirebars and cathodes)
Sugar	Lead
Coffee (graded as Robusta	Zinc
or Arabica)	Tin
Grains (wheat and barley)	Silver
Wool	
Soyabean oil	
Palm-oil	
Rubber	

Physical trading in commodities is unlikely to be warranted so far as the typical speculator is concerned for the following reasons:

1. When taking delivery of the commodity the full purchase price is required (as opposed to the 10 per cent deposit).
2. The cost of storage has to be paid and this will reduce any profit made.

165

3. In some cases freight charges will be necessary. The speculator should be aware of the importance of the situation of the commodity since it will affect his selling price. Thus cocoa located in Liverpool is more valuable to Rowntrees than cocoa located in Marseilles.

OPTIONS
Options are traded on both the commodity future markets and the Stock Exchange. The principle is the same in each case. A speculator acquires the right to buy or sell shares or a commodity at a given price during the next, say, three months. Call options entitle the party to buy the shares or commodities in question, while the right to sell is acquired through a put option. For the privilege of an option the taker pays a premium but this represents the maximum amount which can be lost.

A double option, or a 'put and call option' as it is sometimes called, is more expensive but allows the investor to make money whichever way the market moves. A profit will be made out of the contract so long as there is the required degree of instability in the market.

Suppose a speculator thinks Apex ordinary shares will rise in value. They are currently priced at 100p. The cost of the option might be 5p per share and it might convey the right to purchase 60,000 shares at 105p. The speculator takes an option on 60,000 shares. The cost is £3000 (60,000 × 5p). Consider now two possibilities:

(i) The price rises as predicted - to 125p in fact. The speculator now takes a profit of £12,000 (60,000 × 20p) less £3000 = £9000.

(ii) The price rises to 102p. The speculator will not exercise his option since he could buy the shares on the Stock Exchange for less than the option price.

Any profits made on option dealings are subject to capital gains tax, while offset relief will be given where a loss is incurred, but the cost of the option is only allowed for tax-loss savings if dealings take place.

In a limited number of shares it is possible to buy options which can be (a) exercised, (b) abandoned, or (c) transferred to a purchaser. To enable this to happen the Stock Exchange pre-sets the exercise prices and the durations for the options, which are known as traded options.

The London Traded Options Market was set up in April 1978. The dealings are in units called 'contracts'. Each contract gives the holder the right to buy or sell 1000 shares in the selected company within a given period. When first created the traded option has a life-span of nine months. The expiry date - in April, July or October - falls on the second Wednesday of the last Stock Exchange Account within the nine months. The time factor is relevant. Thus the right to buy shares within the next three months will not be as valuable as the right to buy shares during the next six months. If the hope is that the share will rise in price, the longer the period available for it to do so, the more attractive the bet.

Each contract also specifies the price at which the shares can be
bought (or sold). The right to buy a share may be fixed at, say,
100 p, in which case you would expect to pay more than if the so-
called 'exercise' or 'striking' price were 110 p or 120 p.

The quoted price for the contract (called the 'premium') will fall
gradually over time - until it becomes valueless on expiry. In the
meantime, when the share price is above the exercise price a traded
call option is described as 'in the money' because it has intrinsic
value. When the share price is below the exercise price, the traded
call option is described as 'out of the money'. It has no intrinsic
value - only time value. When the share price and exercise price
are identical, the traded call option is said to be 'at the money'.

The traded options market can be used for highly geared gambles
or for minimising risks. Quentin Lumsden in the *Investor's
Chronicle*, 4 April 1980 - describes one of the strategies possible -
the '90-10' strategy:

> 90 per cent of the funds available to an investor are placed in
> gilt-edged stocks or money market instruments, with the rest in
> traded options. The income on the gilts or cash, at present rates
> of interest will exceed 10 per cent. Assuming the gilts prices
> stay reasonably stable, the investor suffers no capital loss, at
> least in money terms, yet because of the gearing effect he can
> benefit as much from a rise in share prices as if he had invested
> all his money in ordinary shares.

CURRENCY DEALINGS

In much the same way as a speculator can become involved with the
commodities markets it is possible to use foreign currencies as
investment media. Again, the dealings can be to hedge against
adverse fluctuations in a particular currency, or to speculate on
likely movements in the rate.

Let us suppose that a speculator thinks that the sterling-dollar
rate is going to move against sterling over the next three months.
The spot rate is $2.20 and the three months forward rate on the
market is $2.30 for a purchase. The speculator contracts to buy
$10,000 three months hence. Ignoring commission the deal will cost
the speculator £4348 ($10,000 ÷ 2.30). If the rate moves as expec-
ted to, say, $2.10, the speculator will be able to sell the dollars
he has contracted to buy for £4762 ($10,000 ÷ 2.10), thus making a
profit of £414.

As in the commodities market considerable leverage is possible
where a proportion of the cost is required as a deposit to cover the
forward contract. Options in currencies function similarly to those
in the commodity markets.

Delivery dates for sterling are March, June, September and
December. Among the currencies traded are Canadian dollars, German
deutschmarks, Swiss and French francs, Dutch guilders and Mexican
pesos. One of the distinctions between currencies and commodities
is that taking delivery of commodities is impracticable while actual
delivery of currencies is much more feasible for the private
investor.

GOLD

Gold is prized because of its scarcity rather than because of its usefulness, though no doubt the acceptability of the metal world-wide is also part of the explanation for its value. How scarce is gold? According to Robin Duthy in *Alternative Investments* (Michael Joseph, 1978): 'The entire world stock of gold above ground amounts to 163 billion ounces, while the world's known reserves that could be profitably mined at a price of $200 an ounce total the same amount. The entire world stocks of gold above and below ground with a current value of $400 billion could be comfortably fitted into a single giant tanker yet its value is roughly equivalent to the value of all the shares of all the companies quoted on all the stock markets of Europe.'

How can one invest in gold? There seem to be four possible options:

1. The physical acquisition of gold bars, usually described as bar hoarding. Two factors make this sort of investment impracticable for the normal investor. First is the cost and second is the security aspect.
2. Carat gold jewellery has the advantage of being ornamental, giving pleasure in its display. The problem for the investor is that the intrinsic value of the gold content is normally much less than the cost of the jewellery.
3. The purchase of equities in a gold-mining company gives an opportunity for the investor to benefit from any appreciation in the value of gold though the yield from such an investment may be comparatively low and every gold-mine must be a wasting asset - in the long run.
4. An investor may purchase gold coins such as sovereigns or krugerrands. Krugerrands were originally imported from South Africa where they are the official gold coin. They contain one ounce of pure gold as compared to the quarter-ounce of the British gold sovereign. In many countries there are restrictions on the purchase of gold bullion but gold coins can still be purchased.

COLLECTIONS
Many people who have invested in Stock Exchange securities will have found it difficult to keep pace with the eroding influence of inflation. They will perhaps be galled to learn of a few individuals who have made fortunes from investment in what might be called art objects. But there are many pitfalls. As Robin Duthy points out (*Alternative Investments*): 'Without knowledge people are not merely less likely to make money, it is rather that without knowledge they are very likely to lose it.'

If one wishes to invest in some of the media mentioned briefly below certain general warnings can be sounded:

1. Investors will depend on the integrity of dealers and their expertise to a high degree.
2. Dealing costs are likely to be as high as 25 per cent of the price fetched in many auctions.
3. There is no continuous method of valuing the investment as there is with Stock Exchange securities. The value of an art object is what it fetches (net) at an auction. Uniqueness makes an item valuable. It also makes the price it will fetch uncertain.

4. A worthwhile investment is normally preceded by a great deal of expenditure in terms of time and energy. And the investments are sterile, producing neither dividends nor rents.

On the other hand it is not difficult to see the bonuses which can emerge from the investment, apart from a possible marked increase in value with the passage of time. The owner of even a small collection will no doubt enjoy what behaviouralists would describe as psychic income, based on the aesthetic qualities of their possessions even when beauty is only in the eye of the beholder. The items can usually be displayed in one way or another and can generate discussion either with fellow enthusiasts or uninformed laymen.

The list which follows indicates some of the many items which might be used as investment media, together with some suggestions as to what might be their major merits and demerits.

Media	Merits	Demerits
Diamonds	Highly portable Very small in proportion to value Ornamental	Easily lost or stolen Substitutes available Special insurance required
Chinese ceramics	Can be displayed in the home Ornamental	Requires expertise which is scarce Possible breakages
Coins	No storage difficulties Can be acquired singly Easily transportable	Danger of forgeries A need to specialise in a particular country or period
Stamps	Can be acquired singly Easily stored	Intrinsically valueless Danger of forgeries
Books	Easily stored and displayed	Can be damaged unless carefully handled Danger of forgeries Language may limit the market Experts often have differing views on what is happening in the market
Antique furniture	Can be used and displayed in the home Large number of retail outlets	Not so easily transported Possible problem of preservation

Assignment
Your first task
Working in twos or threes study the following information which appeared in the *Financial Times* dated 13 November 1981, then after

exchanging ideas draft individual reports explaining what the extract shows.

London Traded Options

Option	Exercise price	Jan. Closing offer	Vol.	April Closing offer	Vol.	July Closing offer	Vol.	Equity close
BP(c)	300	22	–	36	2	46	–	310p
BP(c)	320	14	1	–	–	–	–	"
BP(c)	350	7	5	–	–	–	–	"
BP(c)	360	–	–	11	4	–	–	"
BP(p)	280	8	1	13	–	–	–	"
BP(p)	300	14	15	28	48	34	–	"
BP(p)	320	22	3	–	–	–	–	"
ICI(c)	260	32	4	40	–	50	–	286p
ICI(c)	280	18	19	28	2	38	–	"
ICI(c)	300	9	1	16	3	–	–	"
ICI(p)	260	10	25	17	–	22	–	"
ICI(p)	280	17	6	24	–	28	–	"
ICI(p)	300	24	7	32	–	–	–	"

c = call   p = put

Your second task
Still working in the small groups where possible, consider the following problem.

A client has approached your manager for some investment advice. He has just been left a legacy of £30,000 in his father's will. He wants to know how he might invest his bequest in a way which will ensure that the capital retains its value in spite of the present rate of inflation. He is 35 and a senior executive in an engineering firm. He has recently married and lives in a house provided by the firm. Your manager has asked what you think would be appropriate advice. Draft him a brief report.

20 The Human Factors

When a bank manager is vetting an application for a loan he does not simply study facts and figures, vital though these may be. What may be regarded as an acceptable risk when proposed by someone with un-doubted integrity, acumen and diligence may be unacceptable when the applicant lacks some or all of these qualities. Similarly when the Stock Exchange Council study an application for a quotation they will be as concerned with the identity of the directors as they are with any of the financial records to be investigated. At a different level of the organisation but equally vital, one would be unwise to consider investing in the shares of a company which was in the throes of an industrial dispute - or, even worse, suffering from endemic industrial relations problems. In essence, people matter.

If we break down a business into its constituent parts we find two basic elements. The first of these is the capital equipment and property provided by the stockholders. These are inanimate objects, however, and they are ineffective until the second element is added - the workforce - which energises a business and gives it life and direction. Both elements are vital to a business and need to be nurtured if a business is to survive in a highly competitive world. Yet we find an interesting phenomenon when we study the accounting function in a business. The role of an accountant might be described in the following terms. He has to:

(1) Ensure that adequate records of physical and financial assets are kept.
(2) Assess profits and losses over a period of time, and
(3) Provide data for the board of directors (or other governing body) so that decisions can be made which will maintain and improve the effectiveness and dynamism of the firm/organisation.

You will note that attention is focused on physical and financial assets. If a new typewriter is purchased, entries are made in the books to record the acquisition. But when a new member of staff joins the organisation, no matter how much has been spent previously on his training and education, no accounting entries are required. Football League clubs are prime examples of businesses whose financial accounts only tell half - or even less than half - of the story. Study the clubs' accounts and you will find valuations of the ground, the equipment, the vehicles - but nowhere in the accounts will the value of the players be mentioned.

What should worry the investor is that a company may appear to be doing well, according to the last accounts, but if morale is falling among the workforce, future profits are bound to suffer. Of course it can be argued that the conventional accounting system will eventually register the deterioration in morale as it shows up in

171

the form of sagging sales, increasing returns of goods sold etc., but the real danger is that managers who are orientated towards the achievement of physical and financial targets may neglect the people in the organisation - with disastrous results. At the very least they will not treat their human assets with the same care and attention they lavish on their physical and financial assets. What adds to the predicament is that motivation and morale can be eroded during the course of a single management-worker confrontation, whereas a fightback to recover lost harmony could last a very long time indeed.

Consider the case of two companies operating in the same industry, producing similar goods, on a similar scale.

Company A: Net assets £10 million   Average annual profits £1 million
Company B: Net assets £10 million   Average annual profits £2 million

A number of explanations could be offered for this situation. For example, Company B might have any or all of the following:

(a) a more enlightened or better balanced board of directors
(b) a more effective team of senior executives
(c) a more skilled team of workers
(d) a more highly motivated workforce
(e) a more efficient organisation structure.

The last point needs elaboration, albeit briefly here. Large organisations will tend to have long lines of communication and the resultant managerial diseconomies will sometimes outweigh the benefits arising through economies of scale. The problem might be alleviated where decision-making in the organisational hierarchy is diffused - or decentralised.

The important point to be made is that these factors ought to be brought into account when an investment is being considered in a particular company.

Let us use three brief case studies to illustrate different aspects of the people theme in relation to investment problems.

Case 1
Five years ago Karl was looking for a suitable hotel in which to invest his life savings. He was advised that he could expect a return of about 10 per cent per annum in this particular trade. He found a hotel on the south coast which was making average annual profits of around £20,000 per annum. The price of £200,000 seemed about right. He was impressed by the general standard of cuisine and service. He bought the hotel.

In the years which followed he had a number of personality clashes with various members of his staff. Chefs came and went. Managers proved unreliable. Other members of staff were prone to absenteeism and unpunctuality. Largely as a result of staff problems Karl became disenchanted with the hotel and put it on the market.

Over the past two years profits have fallen to an average of £15,000 per annum. Karl is advised by the agent that a return of about 10 per cent per annum is still expected by investors in the trade.

What price can Karl expect for his hotel - on the evidence available here? What advice do you think might have been useful at the outset? And what advice would you give him at this stage?

Case 2

March 1. On this day Andrew bought some ordinary stock in Kaytel Electronics Ltd. He had studied newspaper reports. He had plotted prices over a period of time. He had worked out various ratios. All the indications were that this company was in the van of the microprocessor revolution. At 150p for a 25p unit the ordinary stock seemed a bargain. Last year's dividend was 60 per cent.

March 2. On this day news was received of a transatlantic plane crash. A team of Kaytel's top executives were *en route* to the United States to finalise details of a contract to provide a major American company with vital components for one of their new products. The plane has crashed. There were no survivors.

Do you thinks the events of 2 March will affect Andrew's investment?

To what extent is it possible for a company like Kaytel to minimise the adverse effects of such a catastrophe?

Case 3

P. Benedict & Sons Ltd have been making luxury armchairs for over half a century. Their main line has always been the Royal Velvet range which has acquired a deserved reputation for quality in both material and craftmanship. Faced with rising costs and falling profits in the mid-seventies the Board of Directors brought in a new Managing Director, Nigel Peters, with the task of reversing these trends. Nigel cut costs by using cheaper woods for the chair-frames and changing production methods so that fewer craftsmen were required.

In the early years this policy seemed to be paying off. Unit costs were reduced. Profits began to climb again. The ordinary share prices on the Stock Exchange rose to their previous levels. Apparently Nigel Peters had worked a miracle and Benedict's had staged a recovery. But the recent results have been disastrous. Profits have plunged. And the order books have virtually dried up.

The explanation is that Peters has been trading on the company's past reputation. Customers have continued to buy Royal Velvet chairs in the mistaken impression that the standards have remained unchanged. Only after a few years of wear has it become obvious that Royal Velvet chairs are not what they used to be. Retailers have started receiving complaints. The word has got round. People do not want to buy Royal Velvet chairs any more.

Would you be concerned about this situation if you were holding (a) ordinary shares or (b) debentures in the company? Why? How would you justify Nigel Peters' policies if you were in his shoes?

GOODWILL

The need to develop some method of accounting for human as well as financial resources is generally appreciated among businessmen, but the practical difficulties are enormous. Yet we can find something

akin to human resource accounting in the traditional methods of
accountants. Consider the concept of 'Goodwill'. Here are two
common definitions:

'Goodwill is an evaluation of the benefits arising from connections
and reputation.'
'Goodwill is the financial benefit arising from the fact that old
customers will continue to resort to the same place.'

Do the words 'connection' and 'reputation' have any meaning unless
they are related to human beings? Will customers 'continue to resort
to the same place' if they are not attended by capable and willing
staff?

Following on from the conventional accounting concept of goodwill,
we might ascribe any 'excess value' or earning power to 'collective
know-how' or 'collective skill at interacting effectively to produce
favourable results for the organisation'. The idea of a human
assets account on the same lines as a goodwill account may seem far-
fetched, but every firm has its human assets whether or not they are
formally acknowledged in the balance sheet.

DEPRECIATION
Physical assets depreciate over time unless they are properly maintained. The same applies to a firm's human assets. Human assets
need to be nurtured. In the words of Amitai Etzioni in *Modern
Organisations* (Prentice-Hall, 1964):

the organisation solves certain problems other than those directly
involved in the achievement of the goal and excessive concern with
the latter may result in insufficient attention to other necessary
organisational activities, and to a lack of co-ordination between
the inflated goal activities and the de-emphasized non-goal
activities. . . . Thus, a bank may pay all its attention to making
money and completely ignore the morale of its employees. This lack
of attention to non-goal activities may result in staff dissatis-
faction which may express itself in poor work by the clerks which
in turn results in decreased efficiency, or even in a wave of
embezzlements which ultimately reduces the bank's effectiveness.

Conclusion
Whenever an investment decision is being made the human factors may
be difficult to evaluate, but they remain a vital part of the data.
An investor who ignores them does so at his peril.

The Stock Exchange is sensitive to labour troubles as evidenced
by a headline in the *Financial Times* of 9 February 1980: 'Steel
talks breakdown send equities into reverse and dampens demand for
Gilts.'

EMPLOYEE SHARE SCHEMES
Many of the larger companies have long since offered their employees
some form of co-ownership in the form of profit-sharing or staff
shares. Such schemes are a healthy sign of recognition of the need
to involve and motivate the workforce. It is at least an attempt
to break down the barriers between 'them' and 'us' which are in
danger of destroying our national prosperity.

On 28 April 1978 Guest, Keen and Nettlefolds Ltd, the engineering group, sent out to their shareholders details of a scheme which could well be a blueprint for long-term improvements in industrial relations. The circular read:

Your directors consider that it is in the interests of the Company to encourage employees to acquire shares in the Company and thus to have both a stake in the success of the Group and a greater community of interest with the shareholders. Accordingly your directors propose, and seek authority for, the introduction of share option schemes for Group employees.

Under the first scheme proposed (the SAYE Scheme), all full-time employees aged 25 years and over who have at least 5 years' continuous service and who are not within 3 years of normal retirement may be invited to apply for options to subscribe for shares in the Company at a 10% discount on the market value ruling on the business day prior to the date of invitation, if they commit themselves to regular savings through a Save-As-You-Earn (SAYE) contract. The options will not normally be exercisable before 5 years from the date of grant and in no case after 7 years.

Under the second scheme proposed (the Executive Scheme), senior employees (including full-time executive directors) may be invited to apply for options to subscribe for shares in the Company at the full market value at the date of the grant. The options will not normally be exercisable before 3 years from the date of the grant or after 10 years.

At the same time authority is sought for the future introduction of similar schemes for the Company's major overseas subsidiary companies as and when local regulations and conditions permit. . . .

The notion of an Executive Share Option is an import from the United States. The executives and key staff of a firm are offered the opportunity to buy shares in the future at the present market price. Guest, Keen and Nettlefold's scheme is typical in that it gives the directors an absolute discretion to determine the number of shares to be offered to each of the selected employees. The scheme is also typical in allowing the exercise of the options only while the employee is working for the company, though certain exceptions are made where the employee becomes, for example, sick or disabled.

This is how a typical share option scheme would work in principle. John Doe is offered by his employer the right to buy 2000 ordinary stock units of £1 each in the company. There must be some consideration for a legally enforceable contract to be executed, so the company are usually paid a notional sum for each £100 covered by the option. The GKN scheme, however, does not require any payment from the employee. Reverting to a typical case, by the terms of his contract, John Doe is entitled to exercise his option to buy £2000 ordinary stock or a proportion of this holding, at any time after three years from the date of the option. The price of the stock is fixed at the middle price ruling on the Stock Exchange on the day of the contract. If this is 218p but the purchase price rises to 318p by the end of the three-year period, the executive is able to buy ordinary stock units in his company for 218p though they are worth 318p in the market. If John Doe does not wish to hold the stock he can sell it and make a profit of £2000, i.e. (318p - 218p) × 2000. The profit is subject to capital gains tax but this could work out less than income tax on normal earnings. In John Doe's case the options are non-transferable, expire on his death, upon his leaving the company, or on, say, the tenth anniversary of his contract for the options.

Merits from the executive's point of view
1. It gives the executive job satisfaction in that he knows his efforts are appreciated.
2. There is a good chance of making a considerable profit over a period of time.

Merits from the company's point of view
1. It should lead to a lower turnover of key staff.
2. It should act as a stimulus to motivation, with a resultant increase in productivity.

Demerits from the executives point of view
1. The contract is non-transferable and ties him in with the company.
2. The benefits are uncertain and at a comparatively distant future date.

Demerits from company's point of view
1. Some executives will be demoralised because they are either not offered any or they are offered what they regard as insufficient stock options.
2. Staff may stay on simply to get the benefit of the option without being committed to the support of their company.

Companies Act 1980
Benefits in kind are usually taxed as if they were part of an individual's earnings. However, Section 47 of the Act allows that benefits received by a director or employee under any new *approved* savings-related share-option scheme will be free of capital gains and other taxes. Unfortunately the provision does not apply to existing schemes.

Tax concessions are also extended to profit-sharing schemes generally by Section 46. Distributions of shares will be free of tax provided no individual receives shares exceeding £1000 in value in a particular tax year.

Assignment
A final set of multiple-choice questions for you to answer
1. You own some ordinary stock in a company which produces accessories for the motor industry. Which of the following events is likely to make the shares more valuable?

A. The trade unions in the motor industry enter into negotiations with the employers for a reduction in the standard hours for the working week.
B. The company have failed to obtain a renewal of the contract to supply one of the major manufacturers with switchgear equipment.
C. The company have just concluded a productivity agreement with the trade unions representing the workers at their main plant.

2. You own equities in a company which produces aero-engines. There is a great deal of publicity in the newspapers about a deal for the sale of £400 million of engines to the US Army. However, you have it on excellent authority that the engines have been under-costed and the company will eventually face serious cash-flow problems. On this evidence, and bearing in mind that the shares have risen in price following the news of the deal, which of the following options would you choose?

A. Sell your shares while the price is inflated.
B. Retain the shares for the time being, but sell them before the public generally become aware of the problem.
C. Retain the shares.

3. One of the companies represented in your portfolio of securities has sent you notice of a general meeting at which it is proposed to elect three new directors to the board. Which of the following is the least logical reason for staying away from the meeting?

A. The company have sent you a proxy which will allow you to vote without attending the meeting.
B. The stake in the shares is too small to warrant the expense of the journey.
C. The new directors would have no effect on your stake in the company.

4. You are the Managing Director and principal shareholder of X Ltd. The Personnel Manager has been carrying out some research on the workforce. He has now produced evidence that the average I.Q. of employees has been falling dramatically over the past five years though the nature of the work is unchanged. How do you think this information should be viewed?

A. Interesting but irrelevant.
B. An indication that the human assets of the company have been depleted during this period.
C. There is a fault with the recruitment policy, which is a problem for the Personnel Manager, but it has nothing to do with the company's performance.

21 The Time Factor

In appraising any investment proposal one compares the costs of the investment with the returns expected. What complicates this process of evaluation is the fact that there is a time-lag between the cash outflows and inflows. Time is of the essence in any investment problem and thus a scientific appraisal would require the introduction of compensations for any delays in the flows of cash.

The problem can be personalised. You have been left a legacy of £1000. Would you prefer to have the legacy paid to you today - or in one year's time? Conversely, if you were making a substantial purchase, would you prefer to pay the bill today - or in one year's time? The time factor is important and it is this simple truth upon which the Discounted Cash Flow technique of investment appraisal is based.

With personal investments the cash flow will generally be uncomplicated. Typically, there will be an outflow of cash and an anticipated inflow of dividends or interest, and proceeds of sale or realisation in due course. With business decisions the range of options may be greater in which case there is a need for a systematic approach if the time factor is to be accommodated.

BASIC PRINCIPLE

£1 earned now is worth more than £1 received next year, because we can invest the money if we have it now. It will earn us interest. For the same reason £1 paid out now is a bigger burden than £1 paid out next year. We can introduce the necessary compensations by using the compound interest formula:

$$\frac{1}{(1 + i)^n}$$

where

i = interest rate e.g. 12 per cent = .12

and

n = time (in years).

EXAMPLE 1

A firm is faced with the problem of providing a service. There are two options which would provide the service with equal merit apart from cost.

Option A
This involves a cost of £1000 at the outset
                        and £1000 at the end of each of 5 years.
            Total cost £6000

Option B
This involves a cost of £1000 at the end of year 3
                        £2000 at the end of year 4
                        £4000 at the end of year 5
            Total cost £7000

Without making any allowance for the time factor Option A is clearly
preferable since it produces the service required at a lower cost
than the alternative option.
    But what happens if the expenditures are discounted at an appro-
priate rate? The rate will vary according to prevailing interest
rates generally, let us take 12 per cent as appropriate and consider
the effect of this on our deliberations.

Option A
By referring to the Tables for finding Discount Values, at the end
of the chapter, the following calculations can be made:

		£
Immediate cost		1000
Discounted value of £1000 at end of year 1		893
" " " £1000 " " " " 2		797
" " " £1000 " " " " 3		712
" " " £1000 " " " " 4		636
" " " £1000 " " " " 5		567
	Discounted cost	£4605

Option B

		£
Discounted value of £1000 at end of year 3		712
" " " £2000 " " " " 4 (.636 × 2000)		1272
" " " £4000 at end of year 5 (.567 × 4000)		2268
	Discounted cost	£4252

Decision
If a discount rate of 12 per cent is applied, Option B is preferable
- not Option A as would have appeared evident.
    The discounted cash-flow (DCF) technique can be applied to answer
two fundamental questions:

1. Is the project justifiable?
2. Which is the best alternative among those available?

Justification
What sort of return is required on the investment? A rate of return

has to be determined as a prerequisite. Let us say the decision-makers are looking for a return of 8 per cent per annum. Is the following project justifiable?

EXAMPLE 2
Cost (in instalments)

At start of 1st year	£10,000
At end of 1st year	£9,000
" " " 2nd year	£8,000
" " " 3rd year	£7,000

Returns
These are expected randomly over 6 years. The anticipated total returns would be £40,000 over this time. If we take a centre-point at the end of the 3rd year an equal volume of receipts might be anticipated either side of the centre-point. Figure 42 shows the reasoning behind the proposition.

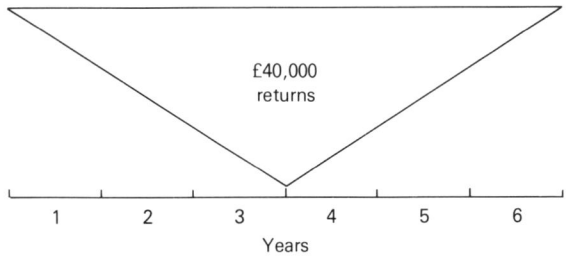

Figure 42

Therefore we can make our calculation based on the notion that the £40,000 is going to be received at the end of the 3rd year.

Calculation

Returns £40,000 × .794 (3 years)   £31,760

Cost

	£	
At commencement	10,000	
1st year £9,000 × .926	8,334	
2nd year £8,000 × .857	6,856	
3rd year £7,000 × .794	5,558	£30,748
Discounted profit		£1,012

Decision
As there is a discounted profit the investment is justifiable. If there had been a 'negative' profit, i.e. if the discounted costs had exceeded the discounted returns, the project would not have been justified.

Comparison
Which of the available options is best to choose? Here is another
simple example.

EXAMPLE 3
Option A
This would involve an initial outlay of £20,000 and there would be
no other expense. The project would yield additional revenue as
follows:

At end of	1st year	£10,000
"	"	"	2nd year	5,000
"	"	"	3rd year	5,000
"	"	"	4th year	˙4,000

Option B
An initial outlay of £20,000 would yield annual savings as follows:

At end of	1st year	£7,000
"	"	"	2nd year	6,000
"	"	"	3rd year	5,000
"	"	"	4th year	4,000

The machinery purchased would have an estimated scrap value of
£3600 at the end of the 5th year.
Note: There is a parameter to either of these projects in that they
would be expected to achieve a minimum return of 10 per cent per
annum if they were to be acceptable.

Calculations
Option A

		£
1st year	£10,000 × .909	9,090
2nd year	£5,000 × .826	4,130
3rd year	£5,000 × .751	3,755
4th year	£4,000 × .683	2,732
Discounted revenue		19,707
Cost		20,000
Discounted loss		£293

Option B

		£
1st year	£7,000 × .909	6,363
2nd year	£6,000 × .826	4,956
3rd year	£5,000 × .751	3,755
4th year	£4,000 × .683	2,732
Discounted savings		17,806
Scrap value £3,600 × .621		2,236
Total savings		20,042
Cost		20,000
Discounted profit		£42

Decision
Option B is preferable - and just satisfies the requirement that a
project should earn a minimum return of 10 per cent per annum.

RISK AND UNCERTAINTY
One of the trickier problems in the area of investment appraisal is
when the returns are uncertain - as they often are - and when
projects carry varying degrees of risk. A useful method of coping
with uncertainties is to produce three basic forecasts of the outcome. Varying weights are given to these forecasts according to the
likelihood of them occurring. Groups of executives have been used
in the United States to reach a consensus as to the likely outcome
and the weighting to be allocated.
   The possible outcomes can be assigned to the following headings:

1. The possible worst (What is the least favourable outcome
   envisaged?)
2. The most probable (What is most likely to happen?)
3. The possible best (What is the most optimistic outcome?)

A simple example may help to explain the principles involved.
Consider the following options:

Option A
The cost is £100,000 and the discounted profit - arrived at by the
method shown previously - is estimated at £4500.

Option B
The cost is £100,000 and the discounted profit is estimated at £4000.

Initial decision
Option A is obviously preferred - on this evidence. But this may
be a riskier option. How can we quantify risk? Here is the
technique.

Outcomes *(Discounted profits)*	*Weighting for probability*	*Weighted total* £
Option A		
Possible worst - £3500 - considered very likely	.4	1400
Most probable - £4500	.5	2250
Possible best - £5500 - considered very unlikely	.1	550
Expected outcome after revision		£4200

182

Option B

Possible worst - £3000 - considered very unlikely	.1	300
Most probable - £4000	.6	2400
Possible best - £6000 - considered quite likely	.3	1800
Expected outcome after revision		£4500

Revised decision

After bringing the risk factor into account, Option B becomes preferable. Summing up briefly, while Option A was preferable originally, once it is agreed that there are likely to be more favourable results than originally credited to Option B, the pendulum swings in favour of the latter option.

The pros and cons of the discounted cash-flow

There is a danger, perhaps, that the technique will be cloaked in a false aura of accuracy. The mathematical precision called for should not blind us to the fact that our calculations can be no more accurate than the data on which they are based.

On the other hand, this technique focuses attention on important factors which might otherwise be disregarded. The problem is looked at from different angles. The technique may be criticised, but what are the alternatives? Should we disregard the time factor? At least the attempt is made to apply scientific thought to the decision-making process. And if we are able to improve the quality of business investment decisions, a large number of people will benefit. Specifically:

1. National Income will grow and with it the pool from which welfare payments are drawn.
2. Unemployment will be reduced.
3. The fund available for wage increases will be enlarged.
4. Investors will benefit from higher dividends and/or enhanced security.

Of course, all policies and plans have to be implemented by *people*. A 'correct' decision can still be bungled by incompetent administrators or a poorly motivated workforce, while a good team will be able to transform a 'bad' decision into a 'good' one.

Assignment
Case study (for group work)

Elite Inc. are a firm of international financial consultants and they are acquiring a new computer for their London headquarters. The Computer Manager has selected the appropriate model but the accountants are now considering which is the best method of paying for the new item. The manufacturers have offered Elite three alternatives, viz.

Option One
The cash price is £100,000 payable within three months of instal-

lation. It has been accepted that the computer will become obsolete and need replacement after six years. The manufacturers have guaranteed to buy it back in six years for a sum of £6000, which they estimate will be the value of the components at that time.

Option Two
Elite will have to pay £20,000 per annum for a 3-year lease - with a further option to renew the contract for another 3 years at £22,000 per annum. If this option is chosen, there will be no maintenance costs incurred because the manufacturers offer a full servicing contract.

Option Three
This involves the payment of an immediate deposit of £40,000 together with instalments of £24,000 payable at the end of each of the first three years. These instalments include the charge for interest.

Note
If Options One or Three are selected, the maintenance costs - estimated by the manufacturers and confirmed by Elite's own experts are likely to be

    £4000 at the end of the 4th year and
    £2000 at the end of the 5th year

Your first task
Working as a group, decide on an appropriate DCF rate to apply.

Your second task
Break up into small groups and work through the necessary calculations together. When you have completed your calculations report the results to your tutor. The group as a whole can then make their final decision as to which is the least costly of the alternatives offered by the manufacturers.

Table 2   Table for finding discounted values (of £1)

Year	1%	2%	3%	4%	5%	6%	7%	8%	9%	10%	11%	12%	13%	14%
1	.990	.980	.971	.962	.952	.943	.935	.926	.917	.909	.901	.893	.885	.877
2	.980	.961	.943	.925	.907	.890	.873	.857	.842	.826	.812	.797	.785	.769
3	.971	.942	.915	.889	.864	.840	.816	.794	.772	.751	.731	.712	.693	.675
4	.961	.924	.888	.855	.823	.792	.763	.735	.708	.683	.659	.636	.613	.592
5	.951	.906	.863	.822	.784	.747	.713	.681	.650	.621	.593	.567	.543	.519
6	.942	.888	.837	.790	.746	.705	.666	.630	.596	.564	.535	.507	.480	.456
7	.933	.871	.813	.760	.711	.665	.623	.583	.547	.513	.482	.452	.425	.400
8	.923	.853	.789	.731	.677	.627	.582	.540	.502	.467	.434	.404	.376	.351
9	.914	.837	.766	.703	.645	.592	.544	.500	.460	.424	.391	.361	.333	.308
10	.905	.820	.744	.676	.614	.558	.508	.463	.422	.386	.352	.322	.295	.270
11	.896	.804	.722	.650	.585	.527	.475	.429	.388	.350	.317	.287	.261	.237
12	.887	.788	.701	.625	.557	.497	.444	.397	.356	.319	.286	.257	.231	.208
13	.879	.773	.681	.601	.530	.469	.415	.368	.326	.290	.258	.229	.204	.182
14	.870	.758	.661	.577	.505	.442	.388	.340	.299	.263	.232	.205	.181	.160
15	.861	.743	.642	.555	.481	.417	.362	.315	.275	.239	.209	.183	.160	.140

22 Compendium

Data are included here which, though important, would impinge on the flow of the learning process if included in the main text.

Application money
The sum due from a would-be purchaser when applying for shares in the event of a new issue or an offer for sale. It may be the whole amount or the first of a series of instalments.

Arbitrage
Prices sometimes vary in different places and arbitrage transactions take advantage of these differences. Thus if a security or a currency is marginally dearer in Tokyo than in New York it may become profitable to buy in New York for sale in Tokyo, until the prices come into line. It is through arbitrage transactions that prices throughout the world are brought into line with each other.

Ariel
This is a computer-based system which by-passes the Stock Exchange and allows institutional investors to deal with each other directly. The effect is to reduce the costs of such deals.

At best
This is probably the most common instruction given to brokers. It is a request to deal 'at the lowest possible price' in the case of a buying order, or 'at the highest possible price' in the case of a selling order.

Authorised capital
The amount of capital which a company has authority to issue. This may be more than the issued capital which has been acquired by the stockholders.

Backwardation
The amount paid by a Bear to compensate the buyer for deferring the delivery of the shares until the next Account. Also when one jobber is offering shares at a price lower than another jobber's bid price.

Bear market
A market in which prices are generally falling.

Bearer securities
In some cases a register of stockholders is not kept and ownership passes with the possession of the certificate. There is no way in which the company can know the identity or address of the stock-holder and so coupons have to be forwarded to the company when distributions are due.

Best terms
This term is used to describe the rates of commission charged by brokers when the commission does not have to be shared with an agent.

Blank transfer
When shares are used as collateral for a bank overdraft or loan, it is common practice to take a form of transfer signed by the borrower. The section to be completed by the transferee is left blank so that if the bank needs to sell the shares the purchaser is able to complete the details and effect a valid transfer.

Blue chips
This term describes equities of the highest calibre. They will tend to be low-yielding, long-term growth stocks.

Bond washing
This is the practice of selling stocks cum accrued interest coupled with an agreement to buy them back ex interest. Since this is aimed at avoiding tax the Inland Revenue has now made the practice illegal.

Broken amount
A seller of a small or odd number of shares may find he has to take a less favourable price. He may also have to pay transfer stamp duty. The jobber would quote a price for the 'broken amount'.

Bull market
A market in which prices are generally rising.

Buyers only
This is a warning from the jobber that he can buy, but not sell, stock.

Buying-in
If a purchasing broker does not receive delivery of the securities on the due date he may require the Buying-in and Selling-out Department of the Stock Exchange to purchase the securities on his behalf. The selling broker will be charged with any difference between the buying-in price and the original contract price.

Calls
Where a share is only partly paid the company can make a call for all or part of the outstanding capital.

Cash and New
This is the term used when shares bought during an account are sold at the end of the account and are immediately repurchased for the new account.

Cash settlement
Transactions are normally settled within the Stock Exchange Account. When settlement is for cash, as for gilt-edged securities, payment is due the following day.

Cheap money
Money is described as cheap (to the borrower) when interest rates are low. Conversely, money is dear when interest rates are high.

Common stock
A term used to describe North American equities, usually of 'no par value'.

Consortia
Some investment projects require such enormous funds that even the largest banks would be unable or unwilling to provide all the funds required. One thinks of the research and development that went into North Sea Oil as a prime example. Instead of one bank financing a project, a number of banks join together in a consortium or partnership. Funds are provided jointly. Profits from the venture are shared. And the risk is reduced for any individual bank.

Contango
A bull or bear may wish to carry over his position in a security from one account to another without paying for or delivering the stock. Interest (or contango) is payable or receivable for this privilege.

Coupon
When interest or dividends are claimed by the holder of bearer securities, they send the appropriate coupons to the issuing authority. There will normally be a sheet of coupons attached to the bearer certificate. When a fresh supply of coupons is required a special voucher called a 'talon' is sent to the issuing authority. Coupon is also a term used to indicate the interest rate on a fixed-interest stock.

Cum dividend
This is the opposite of ex-dividend. The price includes the right to receive the dividend or interest which is shortly due. 'Cum capitalisation' and 'cum rights' have similar implications for bonus issues and rights issues respectively.

Day-to-day stocks
When government stocks are within five years of their redemption, dealings are automatically on a day-to-day basis. The gross interest accrued since the last dividend day is added to the purchase cost, or in the case of an ex-dividend purchase, interest to the next dividend date is subtracted from the proceeds.

Dealing within the Account
Purchases and sales of the same security completed within the Account during which the bargains take place. In this case no stamp duty is payable and only one commission is charged - on the opening transaction.

Discount houses
The institutions which concentrate their business on buying acceptances from their owners are called discount houses. They make their profit out of the difference between the face value of the acceptance and the sum they pay for the acceptance. This is determined by the discount rate. Discount houses borrow 'at call' from banks and other financial institutions.

Dow Theory
This theory is based on two of the principal Wall Street indices,

the Dow Jones Transportation Average and the Dow Jones Industrial
Average. The argument runs that if both indices are rising (or
falling) the trend is significant, but if only one is changing
direction the reversal should not be relied upon.

Drawings
Some stocks which are issued are redeemable by drawings annually.
The usual arrangement is for the numbers of all unapid bonds to be
listed and the appropriate number of bonds to be repaid are
selected randomly.

Floating rate
On certain stocks the rate of interest is not fixed at the date of
issue but is tied to the level of another interest rate such as that
for Treasury bills. The coupon (or interest rate) on such stocks
fluctuates with interest rates generally and their prices should
therefore tend to be more stable than the prices of fixed-interest
stocks.

Franked income
When dividends received by an institution are paid out of profits
which have already suffered corporation tax, they are exempt (or
franked) from further corporation tax when distributed by the
institution.

Fringe benefits
One of the most cost-effective ways of reducing the tax burden for
both employer and employee is through the company car, the company
pension and life assurance scheme, staff housing loans, etc. These
are described as fringe benefits. An executive who is suffering
high rates of tax and looking for maximum tax reliefs should make
sure he is paying the maximum contributions to the company pension
scheme and taking full advantage of other 'perks' provided by the
employer. The yield on such 'investments' is likely to be favourable compared to most other options open to him. This assumes that
the schemes in question have been approved by the Inland Revenue.

Front loading
An insurance term used to denote that the benefits offered in a
particular contract tend to fall in the early years. This would be
the case where the policy covered an outstanding mortgage on the
death of the house-owner. The premiums would be the same every year
but the insurer's liability would be reduced each year.

Hammered
This is a term applied to a member of the Stock Exchange who is
unable to meet his commitments. An announcement is made on the
floor of the house.

Imputation
A company pays corporation tax which is imputed to the shareholder.
This is used to discharge the tax which the shareholder would other-
wise have to pay on the dividends received.

Indemnity, letter of
A stock certificate may be lost or destroyed. In this case the
registrar will probably be prepared to issue a duplicate certificate.
However, the stockholder will need to produce a letter undertaking
to indemnify the company against any loss arising from the issue of
the new certificate.

Index-linked gilts

In his March 1981 budget speech the Chancellor announced the issue
of an index-linked Treasury Stock which would be available to
insurance companies in connection with pension business. The first
of such stocks to be issued was 2 per cent Treasury Stock 1996. The
redemption payment will be related to the Retail Prices Index during
the life of the stock.

Inscribed securities

The evidence of ownership in the case of these securities is the
entry in the stockholders' register. There is no certificate of
ownership. If the stockholder wishes to transfer all or part of his
holding he (or his representative) will have to attend and sign the
stockholders' register.

The Insurance Companies Act 1974

One of the special features of life assurance is the length of time
between payment of the first premium and the eventual claim against
the insurance company. Policy-holders are 'at risk' for a long
period of time, which is why they should choose a reputable company
in the first place. In other classes of insurance the policyholder
is always dependent on the company meeting its commitment when the
claim is made. In an effort to protect the public as far as it is
possible to do so, Parliament has passed a series of acts, culmi-
nating in the Insurance Companies Act 1974.

In essence, this consolidating act designates persons who are
permitted to carry on insurance business, viz.

    (i) a member of Lloyd's,
   (ii) a registered friendly society,
  (iii) a trade union or trade association so long as the business
        is restricted to its members, or
   (iv) an authorised company, being one which was in the insurance
        business before 1966 or one which has been approved by the
        Secretary of State.

A company engaged in insurance business is required to produce
audited annual accounts and balance-sheets for the Secretary of
State. Policyholders as well as shareholders can call for copies
and for abstracts of any reports by the company's actuary.

The Secretary of State is given power to restrain a company from
pursuing insurance business generally, or any particular class of
insurance contract. He also has power to place restrictions on an
insurance company's investments and to ensure that assets equal to
the domestic liabilities are maintained in the United Kingdom.

Misleading statements in advertisements are an offence (s.37) and
the Secretary of State may 'take such action as appears to him to be
appropriate for the purpose of protecting policyholders' (s.37).

Interim dividend

Dividends are sometimes paid more than once a year. The payments
on account are called interim dividends. The directors have power
to declare and pay interim dividends but final dividends normally
have to be sanctioned by the shareholders in general meeting.

Kerb dealing

When a market is particularly active dealing might continue after
the normal market closes.

Limit
When a client instructs a broker to buy or sell stock on his behalf, he may specify a price below which, or above which, he is not prepared to go. The broker receiving the instruction will need to know for how long the instruction is to be kept in force. One possibility is that the instruction will be 'good till cancelled'.

Market capitalisation
A term used to describe the total market value of a class of shares, usually equity. The total number of shares issued is multiplied by the market price.

Marking (a bargain)
This occurs when a member of the Stock Exchange officially records the price at which a transaction in a particular security has taken place. There is no way of telling whether the transaction was a sale or a purchase.

Marrying
This involves a broker matching a sale with a purchase of the same shares. A broker should put the deal through a jobber (*see* 'put through') in order to ensure a fair price for both buyer and seller.

Middle price
A price which is halfway between the two extremes of the double-barrelled price used on the Stock Exchange. Most financial news-papers publish their own estimate of middle prices for a range of securities, but these prices may differ from those quoted in the Official List next day.

Moodies Services Ltd
The service provided involves rearranging company accounts in a standardised form for the benefit of investors and investment analysts. Detailed information about individual companies is recorded on cards.

New time
During the last two days of an account it is possible to buy or sell shares for the new account as opposed to the present account. This gives the investor additional time to complete his arrangements.

Nominal value
This is the face value of a share or bond.

NTP
A jobber might be prepared to provide certain securities and quote a price, but only if the buyer agrees 'not to press'. This would happen where the securities are in short supply.

Paid-up shares
The shareholder has no further liability to the company. The shares are fully paid. Occasionally shares are only partly paid, in which case the stockholder remains liable for the outstanding amount.

Pari passu
This term is used to indicate that a new issue of shares is equal in
every respect to the existing shares of a class.

Passed dividends
When a company decides not to declare a dividend, normally because
of poor results, the dividend is said to be passed.

PLC
In future a company will not be able to issue its shares or debentures to the public unless it is registered as a 'public company'.
In order to qualify as a public company the memorandum must state,
in accordance with the Companies Act 1980, that:

   (i) the company is a 'public company'
  (ii) the name ends with the designation 'public limited company'
      or 'PLC' (or the Welsh equivalent) and
 (iii) the nominal value of the allotted share capital is at least
      £50,000.

Preferential form
Companies offering shares for public subscription usually give their
own shareholders and employees preferential treatment in the
application. Such forms are normally pink in colour to distinguish
them easily.

Premium
When a share is issued at a particular price but is greatly in
demand, the market price might be above the issue price in which
case the difference is described as a premium. When the market
price is lower than the issue price, the difference is called a
discount.

Prevention of Fraud (Investment) Act 1958
The aim of this act is to limit trading in securities to responsible
dealers such as

   (i) a member of a recognised stock exchange,
  (ii) the Bank of England or municipal authority, or
 (iii) any manager or trustee under a unit trust scheme authorised
      by the Department of Trade.

  Anyone else requires a licence from the Department of Trade before
they can invite persons to acquire securities.
  Under s.13, as amended by the Protection of Depositors Act 1963,
s.21, a person is liable for any misleading statement, concealment
of material fact, or reckless promise or forecast.

Protection of Depositors Act 1963
The purpose of this act is to penalise fraudulent inducements to
deposit funds, and to restrain advertisements for deposits. S.2
provides that no person shall issue any advertisement inviting the
public to deposit money with him. The exceptions are:

   (i) investments within Schedule 1 of the Trustee Investments Act
      1961;

(ii) deposits with a bank, discount company, building society, or friendly society;

(iii) any company which has an established place of business in Great Britain and has complied with Department of Trade regulations both in the contents of the advertisement and the submission of accounts;

(iv) any deposits prescribed or permitted by the Department of Trade.

Public dividend capital

When funds are provided for a nationalised industry it would be possible for the government (through the appropriate minister) to set a rate of dividend to be paid on the capital. This rate of interest would vary according to the profits earned by the industry.

Put through

When there is a deal which does not go through the normal Stock Exchange procedures it is sometimes put through a jobber in order to establish a proper market price for the transaction. The Stock Exchange have asked jobbers to keep a special watch on these transactions to prevent the creation of false markets in shares dealt in infrequently.

Scrip issue

Another name for a capitalisation issue or bonus issue. New shares are allotted to existing shareholders in proportion to their existing holdings.

Selling-out

If a buying broker omits to pass on a name ticket in respect of the shares purchased, the selling broker will request the Buying-in and Selling-out Department to identify the buying broker.

Shadow directors

Some individuals, though not formal directors, remain extremely influential in determining the company's policies. Section 63 of the Companies Act 1980 describes such individuals as 'shadow directors'. Bearing in mind the possibility of their influence being used to personal advantage at the expense of others, such individuals are to be treated as directors and must disclose their interest in any transactions.

Shorts

British Government and municipal loans with less than five years to maturity (redemption).

Sinking funds

Amounts are set aside each year and placed in a sinking fund which then becomes available for the repayment of bonds.

Stags

When a company offers new securities to the public it has to ensure that the price is favourable so that all the shares will be taken up. Some speculators (known as stags) may take advantage of the situation by applying for more shares than they are intending to purchase. They are often aided by the fact that the applicants are only required to pay a part of the total price on application. Once the shares have been allotted the stags can take their profit by selling their shares at a premium.

Stop loss
This is an instruction to a broker to sell particular shares if and when the price falls to a certain point. The object is to avoid retaining shares which are falling in value.

Talon
This is a voucher attached to bearer share warrants. It is surrendered when a fresh set of coupons are required.

Tap issues
When the government makes a new issue of securities, substantial amounts are sometimes taken up by official holders (government departments) who gradually release the stock on to the market. The market is aware of the availability of the stock at a certain price and takes up the securities over a period of time.

Time horizon
When an investment programme is being devised it is necessary to determine how far ahead one is looking to maximise returns. One type of investment may produce better returns in the short run, while another investment may be profitable in the long run. Until one has selected an appropriate time horizon it is not possible to decide which stocks to hold.

Treasury bills
These are short-term bearer securities, usually with a life of 91 days. The Treasury, which issues them, invites tenders on Friday for bills being issued in the following week. Treasury bills 'on tap' are those issued directly to government departments including the Bank of England. This allows the government to meet its weekly commitments which are eventually met from taxes.

Unlisted Securities Market
The securities of companies too small to warrant a full listing (or quotation) might nevertheless be traded - in the Unlisted Securities Market set up by the Stock Exchange in November 1980. It is relatively easy for a company to satisfy the Stock Exchange requirements and take advantage of this facility. For example, there is no need to produce a full-scale prospectus complete with an accountant's report. A five-year statistical table extracted from audited accounts will normally suffice.

The new market is aimed at encouraging private investment in the small to medium-sized companies which are otherwise likely to be deprived of equity funds. Also they can be brought to the market with a smaller proportion of the total share capital made available than is the case for a listed company.

Woods v. Martins Bank Ltd and Another 1958
This case indicates one of the dangers confronting a bank manager who gives advice to a customer. In May 1950 Woods, who was in the sheet metal business, asked the manager of his bank to act as his financial adviser. The manager encouraged Woods to invest a large

sum in some 6 per cent Preference shares in BR Ltd, a private company which banked with his branch and had a substantial overdraft. According to the judgment (by Salmon J.) the manager should have acquainted the plaintiff with the fact that BR Ltd was in a weak financial position. The advice was not given 'with ordinary skill and care'. Judgment in the sum of £15,790 plus costs was awarded against the bank.

XC
An abbreviation for ex-capitalisation which means that the price quoted excludes the recent bonus/capitalisation issue.

XD
An abbreviation for ex-dividend. This term, associated with a quoted price, indicates that the dividend will be paid to the present owner of the stock. In the case of a probate valuation the dividend will have to be added to the xd price in order to assess liability to capital transfer tax.

A share is quoted xd on a particular date (fixed by the Stock Exchange) usually about five weeks before the date on which the dividend is due. This means that for any transaction during the ex-dividend period the seller, not the buyer will receive the next dividend. This is reflected in a drop in the price of the stock equivalent to the value of the dividend.

XR
An abbreviation for ex-rights. The recent rights issue is not included in the sale.

23 Examination Technique: Questions and Answers

Good examination technique is no substitute for adequate preparation and methodical revision. However, for the marginal student the way he tackles the paper can make the difference between success and failure. Perhaps the first thing a candidate for any examination should know is how the examination is going to be assessed. In all cases a marking scheme is necessary so that the examiners can award marks (or grades for BEC) as objectively and consistently as possible. It has to be borne in mind that a number of examiners might be involved and that marking might take place over a number of days. The detailed marking scheme avoids a situation where different examiners have widely different views on the excellence of a particular piece of work. Let us consider a typical marking scheme for a question which appears on many examination papers from time to time:

'What are the differences between unit trusts and investment trusts? What are their respective merits and demerits for the investor?'

Marking scheme

	Marks
Investment Trusts	
Limited companies	1
Prior charge capital and ordinary shares	1
Rights issues	1
Profits ploughed back	1
Stock purchased on the Stock Exchange (price determined by demand and supply)	1
Unit Trusts	
Trust deeds	1
Management companies	1
Units bought from managers or Stock Exchange	1
Price determined by formula laid down by Department of Trade and Industry	1
Management charges	1
Merits – Investment Trusts	
Diversification – particularly geographical	1
Underlying assets value is discounted	1
Proven management – build up of reserves	1
Effects of gearing can be beneficial	1

Unit Trusts

Diversification - particularly for the small investor	1
Protection afforded by the professional trustees	1
Portfolio known to investors	1

Demerits – Investment Trusts

Low yielding	1

Unit Trusts

May lack flexibility	1
Specialised trusts carry some risk	1
	——
	20
	——

It is not always possible to allocate single marks in this fashion. Sometimes the marking scheme is less specific, but there is always a framework along similar lines to this.

One is entitled to ask whether this approach to assessment reduces the importance of written style. Written style remains important for two reasons. First, any examiner is going to expect a minimum standard of presentation regardless of the content of an answer. Second, the examiner is bound to find himself occasionally uncertain whether to give a mark or withhold it, and on these occasions he cannot help being influenced by the general style of the work he is studying.

Another useful tip is to show workings whenever you are asked to make calculations. It will help the examiner to assess you fairly if you are able to set out the steps you have taken to reach your answer. It may also help you to check your working if you want to do so at a later stage. If you simply put down your answer to the calculation you are giving the examiner no opportunity to credit you for using the correct method even though you made an error in the calculation.

Everyone studying a subject like Investment will already have passed a number of important examinations and they could feel they need no help in developing an examination technique. A few, however, could be grateful for any ideas which might lighten the load of an examination. They might consider these suggestions. In the first twenty minutes of an examination any student is likely to find the adrenalin flowing. This is when the mind is liveliest. Two hours later and even the toughest candidate is likely to be feeling the strain. What happens if we leave our weakest questions till last? We find ourselves facing the most difficult part of the examination when we are most exhausted. The suggested way round this problem is to use our knowledge of the marking scheme approach to assessment in conjunction with our understanding of our personal strengths and weaknesses.

Use a piece of 'rough' paper and in the first ten minutes or so of the examination jot down as many key words and phrases as you can against the questions you intend to tackle. While your mind is fresh you should be able to prepare yourself to list quite a few of the points the examiner will be looking for.

Then you start on your strongest question but as you write out
your answer you will no doubt think of points which could be added
to your list for the later questions. Whenever you think of such a
point it should be written down, however briefly.

By the time you get through to your weakest questions at the end
of the paper you will have had a couple of hours to think about
further points you want to include. You will still be tired at this
stage but at least you will hopefully have a few ideas to start your
mind working in the right direction. The result should be a better
balanced paper with a more even spread of marks. And many students
will find it helpful to have a series of key words which can be used
to plan their essays.

Finally, a word on revision. Little and often is likely to be far
more effective than eve of the examination 'marathons', noble though
these might be. The mind functions best if it is used in fairly
short spurts, say, half an hour at a time. Sitting 'looking' at a
book is not revising. Revision is only effective when concepts and
facts are being absorbed or retained. Take frequent short breaks.
Revise methodically. And make sure you get ample practice at writing
essays on Investment topics under examination conditions.

SOME SAMPLE QUESTIONS AND MODEL ANSWERS

Question 1

Discuss the merits and demerits of non-voting ordinary shares from
the point of view of (a) the investor and (b) the company which
issues the shares.

Suggested answer

Although non-voting shares are regarded with disfavour by the Stock
Exchange there is nothing to stop a company issuing them. Indeed,
there are a number of reasons why the existing equity owners would
benefit from such an issue. The directors will normally own a
substantial block of voting shares between them and they will be
concerned to ensure that control does not slip from their grasp.
From the point of view of the equity owners generally there will be
a likely financial advantage in that their voting shares will be
more sought after than the non-voting shares, particularly in the
event of a takeover bid. The voting shares become relatively more
valuable when they represent a comparatively small proportion of the
total equity stock.

Of course, the investing public will be aware of the disadvantages
of non-voting shares and the terms of issue will have to be made more
attractive to ensure they are taken up. In other words, non-voting
shares will probably have to be offered at a lower price to compensate for the lack of voting power. This will certainly be the case
where sophisticated institutional investors are expected to subscribe.
But the directors may consider the price differential acceptable
where other benefits accrue.

Non-voting ordinaries are often described as 'A' shares but this
designation does not of itself indicate a restriction of voting
power. The non-voting shares will normally rank *pari passu* for
dividends, and for the existing equity owners this will have the
effect of dissipating a proportion of any future profits the company
might make. And in the event of a winding-up the non-voting shareholders may well rank equally with the existing equity owners.

Perhaps the most important demerit from the point of view of the investor is the fact that the non-voting shareholder still takes the full risk though he has no power to control the company, and it will be difficult to dislodge a poor management which is holding a controlling interest in the voting capital. It is no doubt for reasons such as this that non-voting capital is debarred in the United States. Obviously what is beneficial to the existing shareholders will tend to be disadvantageous to the new non-voting shareholders. Thus the latter will lose out in the event of a takeover and will find their shares attracting a lower price than the voting shares on a resale.

On the other hand, it could be argued that voting powers tend to be illusory. How many small investors ever attend a meeting to vote anyway? The non-voting shares might be acquired more cheaply without any reduction of earning power. Furthermore, where the voting shares are tightly held by management the non-voting shares might even enjoy a freer market. And non-voting equities may still be comparatively attractive when compared with the alternatives of preference and loan stocks.

Question 2
State briefly the meaning of the term 'Rights Issue'.

The XYZ Co. Ltd announces that it is raising £2 million by a rights issue to ordinary shareholders on the basis of one new ordinary share at 125p for every four shares already held. A dividend of 10p was paid in respect of the past financial year. The directors are now forecasting a dividend of 15p on the increased capital, for the current financial year.

The market price of the shares immediately before the announcement of the rights issue was 150p.

(a) Calculate the value of the rights.
(b) Calculate the expected 'ex-rights' price of the shares.
(c) Calculate the estimated premium on the new shares (nil paid) before dealings commence.
(d) Calculate the yield on the shares:
    (i) historically immediately before announcement of the rights issue;
    (ii) as expected after the rights issue, other things being equal.
(The Chartered Insurance Institute Qualifying Examination, April 1979)

Suggested answer
A rights issue is an issue of securities for cash made to the existing shareholders of a company. It is a cheap method for the company to raise funds and the only expenses involved are those of notifying the shareholders of their rights and the underwriting costs. The entitlement of each shareholder is determined on a proportionate basis, say, one new share for each two existing shares. The new shares are offered at a price materially lower than the current market price.

If the shareholder receiving the offer of shares does not want to buy them it is normally possible to sell the rights or part of them. The purchaser of the rights will then acquire the right to subscribe for the new shares.

XYZ Co. Ltd
How many ordinary shares were there prior to the rights issue?

If 125p per new share produces £2m.

there must be $\dfrac{£2m}{125p}$ = 1,600,000 new shares

Since this represents a 1 for 4 issue
there must be 1.6m × 4 = 6,400,000 old shares

(a) The market's valuation of the original holding was

£6.4m × £1.50	=	£9.6m.
new cash injected	=	£2.0m.
		———
new total value	=	£11.6m.
		———

There are now 6.4m. + 1.6m. = 8.0m. shares

the new value per share = $\dfrac{£11.6m.}{£8.0m.}$ = £1.45

Since the new value is £1.45
and the cost of each new share is   1.25
                                   ———

the value of the rights are   20p per share (5p per old share)
                               ———

(b) The ex-rights price will be the amended value of the old shares,
    viz. £1.45.

(c) The premium is the difference between the value of the new
    shares and their cost, viz. 20p.

(d)   (i) Yield before rights

$$= \frac{10p}{150p} \times 100 = 6.7 \text{ per cent p.a.}$$

(ii) Yield after rights

$$= \frac{15p}{145p} \times 100 = 10.3 \text{ per cent p.a.}$$

Question 3
Explain the features of a convertible loan stock. To what extent
would such a stock be attractive to the following:

(i) the company issuing the stock,
(ii) a trustee, and
(iii) a private investor?

Suggested answer

See Chapter 4. Additionally note the value of such an investment to a trustee.

Convertible debentures are regarded as narrow-range investments for trustees who are bound by the provisions of the Trustee Investment Act 1961. This enables trustees to increase the equity content of their portfolios without exceeding their powers. If and when the option to convert is exercised, however, the stocks must be transferred into the wider-range section of the portfolio. (Can you work out what the marking scheme might be for this question?)

Question 4

An investor has a large capital gains tax liability on a shareholding he is thinking of selling. He plans to reinvest the proceeds. What factors do you think he should bear in mind when making his decision?

Suggested answer

The first point to consider would be whether it is going to be possible to set off the prospective gain against a loss made on another shareholding during the same fiscal year. Chargeable gains or allowable losses are aggregated in arriving at a computation for capital gains tax. Towards the end of a fiscal year in which profits have been realised the remaining holdings in a portfolio will have to be scrutinised to see if there are any showing an allowable loss which, if taken, would reduce the forthcoming assessment.

A second point to bear in mind is that capital gains tax can only be postponed. If the value of a stock has risen, the tax will have to be paid sooner or later. Admittedly the rates may be reduced in a future budget, but it is also possible for the rate to be increased. The best hope for the investor is that the tax might be abolished altogether. Will that happen in the next Budget? If there is a reasonable chance that this might happen, a delay in the sale might be advisable.

Before commenting on the switch one would need to consider the prospects attaching to any proposed new shareholding. What is the prospect of an appreciation in value? If one could be confident that the new share would grow in value, this could more than cover any liability for tax.

The cost of the switch would be another factor to bear in mind. Brokerage and stamp duties have to be reckoned with, and in planning the reinvestment of the proceeds it will be necessary to ensure that cash is available to meet the capital gains tax in due course.

If a general fall in share prices was expected affecting both the shares presently held and those to be acquired, there is a danger that capital gains tax will become payable even though the substituted shares will fall in price shortly after the switch has taken place. There would be no way in which the tax could be recouped. If a general fall in prices was anticipated, it might therefore pay the investor to wait until prices stabilise before making the switches.

If a general rise in prices was envisaged so that both the 'old' and the 'new' shares were affected, an early disposal would be favoured. To delay would merely increase the capital gains tax payable in the immediate future.

Suppose you are offering advice to a client who is considering
investing in equities. Which industries would you suggest were
destined to expand in the foreseeable future, and which are likely
to decline? Give reasons for your suggestions.

Suggested answer
Note: An answer to a question like this requires an up-to-date
knowledge of industrial prospects which can only be obtained from a
regular reading of the financial press. At the present time the
following industries would be appropriate to discuss:

The toy industry. The contraceptive pill has reduced the numbers
of babies being born. Initially it is pram manufacturers whose sales
decline. Eventually the smaller age group of under-fives become the
smaller group of teenagers, and a wider range of manufacturers are
affected by the lower birth rate. The effects are already being felt
in the toy industry, where shrinking markets are evident. High rates
of unemployment and the economic recession aggravate the problems
further and it is obvious that toy manufacturers face difficult times.
It would be unwise to buy equities in the toy industry, with long-
term growth in mind, on this evidence.

The motor industry. The problems of industrial relations in certain
sections of the UK motor industry are well known. But there are
many firms which produce accessories for the motor industry and they
are bound to be affected by the ailments of their principal customers.
Industrial conflicts cause damage beyond the confines of the firms
which are directly involved. Increasing encroachment in the UK
market by foreign manufacturers can be expected so long as labour
troubles plague the industry and those who supply the UK motor
manufacturers with accessories are bound to share the problems. The
fuel crisis which brings with it continually rising petrol prices can
only make things even worse in the long run.

The leisure industry. It is not easy to find growth industries
when there is general economic recession. However, there are a
number of bull factors for the leisure industry arising out of the
development of the microprocessor. Assuming that the long-term
effect of microprocessors will be to shorten the average working
week, there will be more time available for leisure pursuits. If
people are to enjoy more holidays, longer holidays, and more spare
time generally, it can be envisaged that those who provide
accommodation, transport and entertainment stand to benefit. However,
it would be wise to study a particular company's activities carefully before deciding it was one of those likely to enjoy long-term
benefits.

The manufacturing industry. Those manufacturers who are able to
take advantage of the new developments in microprocessing will
obviously benefit from the effects of lower labour costs, fewer
conflicts with their workforces (pay claims will present less
difficulties), greater precision and more continuous production.
All this must reflect in higher profits. There will be early
teething problems, but some companies in manufacturing have a bright
future thanks to the microprocessor. The problem for the investor is
to identify the favourites.

A married customer, aged 30 with three children aged 3, 5 and 8,
seeks your advice on the investment of £20,000, which he has
inherited on the death of his mother. He has a steady job with a
salary of £6000 per annum, but neither he nor his wife has other
sources of income. He is not averse to risk, but would not wish to
take more risk than is necessary to try to maintain the real value
of his capital. He would also like to supplement his income. He
owns his house subject to a mortgage, the balance of which is about
£10,000, and says he is thinking of paying this off. He has been
asked to invest some money in the private company for which he works.

(a) Detail the advice you would give this customer concerning the
    investment of the inherited sum, and suggest a suitable port-
    folio structure (you are not required to suggest individual
    holdings).
(b) State the advice you would give him in connection with the
    proposals (i) to pay off the mortgage, and (ii) to invest in the
    shares of his employer.
(c) If your customer wished to give £1000 to each of his three
    children, how would you suggest these sums were invested?
(d) Your customer says he has heard about index-linked investment.
    He asks you (i) to explain what this means; (ii) to describe
    briefly the available index-linked investments; (iii) to advise
    him on whether any of them is suitable for his circumstances,
    and (iv) to let him know whether any of them would be suitable
    for the investment of £300, which his mother has left to her
    unmarried sister aged 62. What answers would you give? (40
    marks).
    (Institute of Bankers, Banking Diploma, Stage 2, April 1979)

Suggested answer (based on the Examiners' Report)
On the evidence available one would advise the customer on the
following lines:

 (a) With a young family such as the customer has, he would need to
ensure there were adequate funds available in sufficiently liquid
form to meet a variety of conceivable commitments. He might therefore invest about £4000 in building societies, say, £2000 in a
deposit account and £2000 in a share account. As an alternative to
the building society shares, the customer might purchase National
Savings Certificates of the latest issue, assuming he does not
already hold the permitted maximum already.
 A sizeable proportion of funds, say between £6000 and £8000, might
be invested in dated gilts with up to about eight years to redemption.
These would provide the portfolio with a degree of flexibility to
take up any favourable investment opportunities which arise. The
maturity dates would also provide the customer with an opportunity
for an ongoing assessment of commitments for the education of his
children etc. An alternative investment for this section of the
portfolio would be investment in local government mortgages with
varying terms up to a maximum of ten years. If interest rates were
expected to fall over a period of time the customer would be advised
to choose slightly longer dated gilts and choose longer terms for the
local government securities.

The third and largest section of the portfolio might have long-term growth as its objective. Some £8000 to £12,000 might be invested in unit trusts and/or insurance bonds with both UK and overseas interests. The funds are not sufficient in themselves to allow diversification, but this can be achieved through the medium of a short selection of unit trusts or managed bonds. Any element of life cover in the latter could provide useful protection for his young dependants.

(b) Paying off the mortgage would be unwise for two reasons, viz.

    (i) the interest element in the repayments is subject to full tax relief, and

    (ii) monies used to repay the mortgage would deplete the funds which are aimed at capital growth. The mortgage by contrast is a fixed-sum liability.

The suggestion for the customer to invest in the shares of his employer could be criticised on the grounds that private company shares are not easily disposed of under normal circumstances. The price is left to negotiation between buyer and seller, with the buyer often aware that there are few other takers. A further drawback to this suggestion is that the customer already has a high stake in the well-being of the private company through his employment. Any failure on the part of the company would eliminate his earnings and (if he held shares in the company) and part of his capital.

(c) The choice of investment for the children would rest between

    (i) a suitably dated gilt, i.e. one which matures at about the time the customer's child comes of age. The youngest child would have the longest dated stock,

    (ii) £500 in a dated gilt and £500 in a general unit trust, or

    (iii) investment in a single-premium endowment policy giving an enhanced capital sum on maturity. This would avoid any tax problems.

National Savings Certificates are considered too short-termed in these circumstances, and other cash-type investments are similarly unsatisfactory.

(d) Index-linked investments are useful media for coping with high levels of inflation. When the rate of interest on savings is below the rate of inflation, the saver is penalised for his thrift. It was to protect the small saver from such injustice that two index-linked schemes were introduced (see Save-As-You-Earn, page 135, and Index-linked National Savings Certificates, page 136).

Question 7

The abolition of UK exchange control has given UK investors complete freedom to invest in overseas markets.

(a) What are the main advantages and disadvantages for the private investor of investing in overseas securities? (8 marks)

(b) Are there any simple ways of overcoming any of the disadvantages? (4 marks)

(c) List the principal overseas markets used by UK investors and in each case mention briefly any special characteristics of the markets. (8 marks)   (Total 20 marks)
(Institute of Bankers, Banking Diploma, Stage 2, April 1981)

Suggested answer (based on the Examiners' Report)
For main discussion see pages 141-2.

(a) A wider spread of investments is possible including investment in companies without a UK equivalent, such as gold or diamond mining companies or those in certain areas of high technology such as fibre optics. Advantage can be taken of economies with faster growth rates than the UK, and advantage can also be taken of the strength of sterling, or its weakness hedged against. But dealing in and servicing overseas investments is comparatively expensive and there are inevitable economic, political and currency risks.

(b) Investment in overseas stocks could be through the medium of a unit trust or an investment trust. Resort could also be made to overseas shares listed on the London Stock Exchange. Companies operating from the UK but with overseas subsidiaries and other interests could be utilised.

(c) Overseas securities markets used by UK investors include USA, Canada, South Africa, Australia, Japan, Hong Kong, Singapore/Malaysia and Germany/France/Holland. In the USA, for example, stockmarkets are regulated by the Securities Exchange Commission (SEC), institutional investors are influential, there is a wide range of sectors, and market capitalisation accounts for 50 per cent of the total world stock market capitalisation.

24 Assignment Guidelines and Solutions

Gazebo Electronics Ltd

		Last year	This year
24	Annual profits before loan interest	£388,945	£394,250
32	Annual loan interest	80,000	80,000
	Distributable profits	308,945	314,250
	Preference dividend	18,750	18,750
	Available for ordinary div.	250,000	275,000
	Percentage for ordinary div.	10%	11%

If all loan stockholders convert the ordinary dividend (based on this year's figures) will be calculated thus:

	£
Annual profits (distributable)	394,250
Transfer to Reserve	20,500
	373,750
Preference dividend	18,750
Available for ordinary div.	355,000

$$\text{Div. for ordinaries as a percentage} \quad \frac{355,000}{3,500,000} \times 100 = 10.1\%$$

This is a higher rate than can be obtained from the loan stock but the decision would hinge on whether the loan stock was charged on the company's assets. It may not be wise to elect to gain a few per cent extra and lose the right to a prior charge, especially as profits are static and even declining in real terms.

53 Your table may read something like this:

	Merits	*Demerits*
Unit trusts	1. Diversification	1. Possible inflexibility
	2. Skilled management	2. Charges
	3. Small stakes possible	3. Specialised trusts limit diversification
Endowment policies	1. Tax concessions	1. Capital value erodes through inflation
	2. Regular savings	2. Benefits are long term
	3. Benefits on death	3. Investor's circumstances may change
Annuities	1. Financial resources of annuitant fully utilised	1. No hedge against inflation
	2. Maximises income	2. Decision is irrevocable
	3. Elderly annuitants assured of regular payments for life	3. Capital is 'lost'

59 (1) B (2) A (3) A (4) C (5) C (6) A

66 Ordinary shares to be issued at a premium? This would give John Kendrick greater proportional voting power.

74 *Original ordinary dividend*

	Etna Ltd £	*Zeta Ltd* £
Trading profit	200,000	100,000
½ to Reserve	100,000	50,000
	100,000	50,000
Preference dividend	15,000	
	85,000	

Last year's
ordinary dividend $= \dfrac{£85,000}{£400,000} \times 100 \qquad \dfrac{£50,000}{£600,000} \times 100$

$$= \quad 21\tfrac{1}{4}\% \qquad\qquad 8\tfrac{1}{3}\%$$

Ordinary dividend after 12% fall in trading profit

Original profit	200,000	100,000
12% fall	24,000	12,000
	———	———
Reduced profit	176,000	88,000
½ to Reserve	88,000	44,000
	———	———
	88,000	44,000
Preference dividend	15,000	———
	———	
	73,000	
	———	

Reduced ordinary
dividend $= \dfrac{£73,000}{£400,000} \times 100 \qquad \dfrac{£44,000}{£600,000} \times 100$

$$= \quad 18\tfrac{1}{4}\% \qquad\qquad 7\tfrac{1}{3}\%$$

81   *Hypothetico Ltd*

Present valuation = 1m. × £2.50   = £2,500,000
New number of shares

$$= \text{1m.} + \text{1m.} + \dfrac{\text{2m.}}{8}$$

$$= £2,250,000$$

New valuation $= \dfrac{£2,500,000 + £250,000 \text{ (new cash)}}{£2,250,000}$

$$= £1.22$$

Bonus issue £1000 new stock for Miss Trelawney plus
Rights issue £250 new stock. Her options:

(i) to take up rights
(ii) to sell rights
(iii) to sell sufficient to take up remainder

(a) *Priority Percentages*

	Athena PLC	Spartacus PLC	Zeus PLC
Debentures	$£\dfrac{5,000}{50,000}$	$£\dfrac{5,000}{50,000}$	
	$= 0\text{-}10\%$	$0\text{-}10\%$	
Preference	$£\dfrac{15,000}{50,000}$	$£\dfrac{10,000}{50,000}$	$£\dfrac{5,000}{50,000}$
	$= 10\text{-}30\%$	$10\text{-}20\%$	$0\text{-}10\%$
Ordinaries	$£\dfrac{37,500}{50,000}$	$£\dfrac{40,000}{50,000}$	$£\dfrac{45,000}{50,000}$
	$= 30\text{-}75\%$	$20\text{-}80\%$	$10\text{-}100\%$
Retentions	$= 75\text{-}100\%$	$80\text{-}100\%$	nil

(b) *Earnings per Ordinary Stock Unit*

Athena PLC	Spartacus PLC	Zeus PLC
£50,000 – (£10,000 + 5,000)	£50,000 – (£5,000 + 5,000)	£50,000 – £5,000
$£\dfrac{35,000}{150,000} \times 100 = 23\frac{1}{3}\text{p}$	$£\dfrac{40,000}{200,000} \times 100 = 20\text{p}$	$£\dfrac{45,000}{300,000} \times 100$ $= 15\text{p}$

(c) *Price/Earnings Ratio*

$\dfrac{£1.10}{23\frac{1}{2}\text{p}}$	$\dfrac{£1.20}{20\text{p}}$	$\dfrac{£1.00}{15\text{p}}$
$= 4.7$	$= 6.0$	$= 6.7$

(d) (i) Zeus Preference Stock preferred because of better
cover: see priority percentages above.
(ii) Athena Ordinary Stock preferred because the EPS
and P/E Ratio is better but dangers of highly
geared structures when profits are variable.

119   (1) C (2) C (3) C (4) B (5) A (6) B

(a) £522.97 (b) £349.87 (ignoring minimum for commission)

128   For example:
A devaluation of sterling would raise the price of gold shares. A national wages plan would benefit the labour-troubled motor industry.
A reduction in interest rates would raise the price of gilts.

152   *Amelia Jones*
Portfolio lacks a sufficient cash reserve? No index-linked NSCs? If Mrs Jones is finding it difficult to meet out-goings there could be a switch to high-yielding gilts, taking advantage of present high interest rates. There might also be an argument here for switching into an annuity which would deprive the charity but benefit the client.

Kenneth Crombie
The largest future commitment here appears to be the purchase of a house within the next five years. It is probably too early to use the £15,000 towards this. Investment in short-dated gilts maturing within 5 years would probably give best returns and provide liquid cash when accommodation was needed. Can net yield on building society holding be improved upon? Should this be switched into growth stocks? Or in short-dated gilts?

Thomas Kershaw deceased
Sell fixed-interest industrials? Use proceeds to diversify equity holdings? There is too much weight given to textiles in present portfolio?
12 per cent Exchequer Stock is too long-dated bearing in mind age of life tenant? It will be necessary to insure that there is an adequate near-cash reserve in this trust. Advancement and maintenance claims for the children should be anticipated. It might be wise to invest a substantial part of the £15,000 in building society accounts? Use the remainder of this cash to diversify the equity content of the wider-range fund.

161   From a special feature on Charting in the *Investor's Chronicle*, 6 February 1981:

A signal that a trend is ending is given by the development of a reversal pattern. Typical reversal patterns are heads-and-shoulders, double tops (or bottoms) and V-reversals. These patterns look much as their names imply; to be meaningful they should come at the end of a long rise (or fall) in prices. Their significance is only confirmed by a break-out from the pattern. Sophisticated chartists look for further confirmation from appropriate volume behaviour, i.e. higher volume on the break-out.

Continuation patterns are the other main type of
pattern. They occur in mid-trend and, when confirmed
by a break-out in the right direction, imply a
substantial further move in the direction of the main
trend (some say as much again; others calculate targets
by the size of the pattern). The most important
continuation patterns are triangles, diamonds and flags.
Again they look as their names imply; they are most
reliable when preceded by a near-vertical rise or fall
in prices, known as a flagpole.

176   (1) C (2) A (3) C (4) B

Index